THE PUBLIC DEBT PROBLEM

Also by Pierre Lemieux

Somebody in Charge: A Solution to Recessions? (2011)
The Idea of America, edited with Bill Bonner (2011)
Une crise peut en cacher une autre (2010)
Comprendre l'économie. Ou comment les économistes pensent (2008)
Le droit de porter des armes (1993)
Apologie des sorcières modernes (1991)
L'anarcho-capitalisme (1988)
La souveraineté de l'individu (1987)
Du libéralisme à l'anarcho-capitalisme (1983)

THE PUBLIC DEBT PROBLEM

A COMPREHENSIVE GUIDE

By Pierre Lemieux

First published in 2013 by
PALGRAVE MACMILLAN®
in the United States—a division of St. Martin's Press LLC,
175 Fifth Avenue, New York, NY 10010.

Where this book is distributed in the UK, Europe and the rest of the world,
this is by Palgrave Macmillan, a division of Macmillan Publishers Limited,
registered in England, company number 785998, of Houndmills,
Basingstoke, Hampshire RG21 6XS.

Palgrave Macmillan is the global academic imprint of the above companies
and has companies and representatives throughout the world.

Palgrave® and Macmillan® are registered trademarks in the United States,
the United Kingdom, Europe and other countries.

ISBN: 978–1–137–29807–2 (paperback)
ISBN: 978–1–137–29806–5 (hardcover)

Library of Congress Cataloging-in-Publication Data

Lemieux, Pierre.
    The public debt problem : a comprehensive guide / Pierre Lemieux.
        p. cm.
    Includes bibliographical references and index.
    ISBN 978–1–137–29807–2 (alk. paper)—
    ISBN 978–1–137–29806–5 (alk. paper)
        1. Debts, Public. 2. Financial crises. I. Title.

HJ8015.L46 2013
336.3'4—dc23   2012028027

A catalogue record of the book is available from the British Library.

Design by Newgen Imaging Systems (P) Ltd., Chennai, India.

First edition: January 2013

10 9 8 7 6 5 4 3 2 1

CONTENTS

CHARTS

FOREWORD AND ACKNOWLEDGMENTS

This book aims to make the multifaceted problem of the public debt—or the "sovereign debt"—understandable for the intelligent layman and the student, as well as for the more seasoned journalist or academic. For the first class of reader, I go to some lengths to explain the basic financial, accounting, and economic concepts that are necessary to approach this complex issue. To the advanced reader, I try to provide new keys to open the Pandora's box.

But let not my potential reader be scared by the Pandora's box analogy. There is no risk that, after he opens this book, all the evils of the world will come out of it. For they are already out and lurking. Hopefully, though, this book will render them more understandable and, perhaps, controllable.

As usual, I have accumulated many debts (but not public debts) in writing this book. Let me just mention some.

My former colleague at San Jose State University, Professor Jeffrey R. Hummel, was nice enough to read a previous version of my manuscript, and to make many useful comments and suggestions besides pointing out a few errors. Over the past few years, I have learned much from him. I also wish to thank Professor Christian Calmès of the University of Québec in Outaouais who similarly made several very useful comments that prevented me from being too complacent with my prior beliefs. In the end, of course, I wrote what I thought was closer to the truth, and any remaining error is mine.

I am very grateful to the Earhart Foundation as well as to the Montréal Economic Institute for a grant that allowed me to take time away from bread winning activities to write this book.

ACRONYMS

AMT	Alternative Minimum Tax
BEA	Bureau of Economic Analysis
BIS	Bank of International Settlements
BLS	Bureau of Labor Statistics
BPD	Bureau of the Public Debt
CalPERS	California Public Employees' Retirement System
CBO	Congressional Budget Office
CDS	credit default swap
CEA	Council of Economic Advisers
CHIP	Children's Health Insurance Program
CPI	Consumer Price Index
DC	District of Columbia
EBA	European Banking Authority
ECB	European Central Bank
EU	European Union
FDIC	Federal Deposit Insurance Corporation
Fed	Federal Reserve System
FMS	Financial Management Service
FY	Fiscal Year
GAO	Government Accountability Office
GDP	Gross Domestic Product
GSE	government-sponsored enterprise
IMF	International Monetary Fund
IRS	Internal Revenue Service
M2	A measure of the money stock
NBER	National Bureau of Economic Research
OECD	Organization for Economic Co-operation and Development
OMB	Office of Management and Budget
PPP	purchasing power parities

SEC   Securities and Exchange Commission
SSA   Social Security Administration
TARP   Troubled Asset Relief Program
UCLA   University of California at Los Angeles
UN   United Nations

CHAPTER 1

THE GENIE OUT OF THE BOTTLE

Just as one can practice safe sex, there used to be a way to do safe finance by holding safe assets. In its most general sense, an asset is anything that allows one to obtain goods and services in the future. In normal times, cash—actual dollar bills and coins—is the safest of all assets: you put it under your mattress and retrieve it when you need to buy something. The problem is that you don't get any interest or other return on cash hoardings. It is better to put your money in the bank and earn some interest. Cash in the bank is pretty safe, especially since the federal government's deposit insurance scheme protects you against bank failures. In times of inflation, of course, cash ceases to be safe, for its value diminishes as the prices of goods and services rise, but this problem can be ignored in normal times.

Safe State

Not long ago in our countries, something else was considered as safe as cash, while bringing a return higher than bank deposits: this other form of safe asset was government securities. These securities are the different types of bonds that governments issue to finance their deficits or sometimes their investments. (Private businesses also issue bonds as well as shares of stocks, another type of security.) The purchaser of a bond receives interest and, when the bond matures, gets his principal back. Since governments, and especially higher levels of government like the federal government in the United States, do not go bankrupt nor cease payments on their debt, it was thought, government securities are as safe as cash. Indeed, when you read in the financial press that businesses or banks are holding "cash," this cash is usually government securities.

It is not that governments never default. On the contrary, they have often done so in the course of history. However, defaults of central governments among the major developed countries during the twentieth century have been exceedingly rare, and investors had become confident that, at least for those countries, the risk of holding government securities was, for all practical purposes, zero.

When a government does default, getting your money back is not easy. Ten years after the government of Argentina defaulted on $81 billion of bonds issued in dollars and sold to international investors, some creditors have still not agreed to the loss that was imposed on them. The government of Argentina had made a take-it-or-leave-it offer: accept 35 cents on the dollar, or you will get nothing. Some 93 percent of the bondholders ended up accepting the offer: better a 35 percent settlement than nothing. The remaining 7 percent rejected the offer, and have been trying since then to force the government to pay the full principal of the bonds plus accrued interest. Some of the original holders have chosen to sell their bonds, so that the current holders are not always among the original 7 percent. Many bonds were sold on the secondary market to so-called vulture funds, which have spent millions trying to get a full reimbursement from the Argentine government. Vulture funds are hedge funds (more risky investment funds) that buy distressed assets that have fallen to a fraction of their value, wait for the issuer to go bankrupt, seize its other assets, and try to make a profit by reselling them. The problem is that nobody can force sovereign states to go bankrupt and to be sold in pieces.[1]

If the Argentine government decides not to pay the money it owes you, you will not be able to persuade its domestic courts to dissolve it, and to reimburse you with bankruptcy proceeds. You cannot hope to be reimbursed with government buildings, public roads, army equipment, police stations, and so forth. You may sue the Argentine government before the courts of your own country or a third country, but you will not be able to have the judgment enforced against a foreign sovereign. As an American judge reminded plaintiffs in the Argentine case, "You have rights but may not have remedies." Hence the hurdle faced by holdouts on Argentine sovereign debt.

The vulture funds and a few other holders of defaulted Argentine debt have been fighting hard. Their strategy was to buy the bonds cheap and redeem them at a higher price. They have obtained hundreds of judgments against the Argentine government. Two vulture funds are sitting on $3-billion worth of favorable rulings. Since the Argentine government will not reimburse them, they have tried to seize money held by the Argentine central bank at the Federal Reserve Bank of New York, at the Bank of International Settlements (BIS), which is the central bankers' bank, and in private banks outside Argentina. The lawyers of one hedge fund apparently served a subpoena to the BIS's general manager just as he was about to speak at a public event.

"His Excellency" was probably not happy! But all these efforts have failed. The creditors have had only symbolic successes, such as seizing $90 million from a New York trustee who was holding shares of a privatized Argentine bank, or seizing a few million dollars that the Argentine science ministry had deposited in an American bank account in order to buy telescopes. However, this activism probably means that the Argentine government cannot return to international financial markets until it reaches an agreement with its disgruntled creditors, as proceeds from the sale of Argentine bonds issued in an international financial center would likely be seized.

The Greek government has been more prudent. In early 2012, it proposed a deal to its creditor: you accept a loss (or "haircut," as people in finance say) of three-fourths on your bonds, or else we will reimburse you nothing. A large majority of domestic bondholders accepted this offer under duress; the recalcitrants were later forced to swallow it by a retroactive law. But as in the case of Argentina, a minority of bondholders, some of them hedge funds, had bought Greek government bonds issued under foreign law, and refused to yield. The Greek government could not retroactively change the terms of foreign-law contracts. Greek finance minister Evangelos Venizelos had clearly warned the potential holdouts: "Whoever thinks that they will hold out and be paid in full, is mistaken."[2] Yet, when the first of these foreign bonds matured in May 2012, the Greek government chose to repay it in full for €435 million. The holdouts had won! Needless to say that the bondholders who had been cheated by the Greek government's bluff were not happy. It remains to be seen what the Greek government will do when a few billion euros more of the holdout-held bonds mature, but it is clearly fearful of holdout activism.

At least with foreign lenders, a sovereign borrower is not all-powerful. Yet, he is immune to many of the constraints that ordinary debtors face; he has sovereign immunity. He can walk away from his debt without being pushed into bankruptcy. That's part of being a sovereign. The sovereign debt crisis in Europe has brought these facts to the forefront of the scene. And many more facts.

What exactly is the "sovereign debt"? A narrow definition refers to it as the debt issued by a national government but denominated in a foreign currency. What's special about the sovereign debt in this sense is that foreign holders often have little legal recourse against a defaulting sovereign, as the Argentine case demonstrates. Their claims will not be recognized in the defaulting sovereign's courts; if they are recognized, typically by foreign courts, they can't be enforced anyway. Under the Foreign Sovereign Immunities Act, signed by President Gerald Ford in 1976, national governments may claim sovereign immunity from seizure of anything they own (or anything owned by one of their agencies) for noncommercial purposes. Even when a commercial purpose is involved, American courts are sometimes "deferring to Leviathan," as *The Economist* recently put it in a case involving a hedge fund and a nationalized Irish bank.[3] As we will see in this book, people often defer to Leviathan.

We will often meet Leviathan, but under different aliases. It is impossible to talk about the public debt and avoid him. Leviathan is the invincible Biblical monster to whom seventeenth-century philosopher Thomas Hobbes favorably compared the nascent modern state. One strand of contemporary economic analysis, related to the so-called Public Choice school, tries to understand the state, or the sovereign, as Leviathan.[4] We shall see why.

According to a broader definition, sovereign debt is simply a sovereign's debt, emphasizing the fact that the borrower, whether its creditors are locals or foreigners, is a sovereign with special status and special privileges. A defaulting sovereign often prevents his own nationals from enforcing their claims: after all, the sovereign is the one who, by definition, makes the law, including laws pertaining to his own obligations. The sovereign debt is not like other debts, like yours or mine. Not only can a sovereign block enforcement of claims against him, but he also can guarantee his debt with future tax receipts, that is, it can reimburse them with the future production and earnings of the taxpayers. In the broader sense, sovereign debt is synonymous with "public debt" or "government debt." It covers the debt of subordinated government entities (such as municipalities or, in a federal country, states or provinces). I will generally use the term in its broader sense, and use it interchangeably with its synonyms.

Because of the sovereign's power and immunity, government securities are not totally safe. This point has been brought home by the developing sovereign debt crisis. The Greek government, for instance, "restructured" its debt by promising to reimburse less than one-fourth of what it owed to its bondholders.[5] Safe government looks more difficult than safe sex.

Mountains, People, and Governments

Our countries are not under the yoke of kings, so who exactly is the sovereign? And can we seriously say "he" when we talk about "it"? To answer the first question, the sovereign is simply the one, or the ones, who run the state. The state, in its more general sense, is the whole apparatus of government—executive, legislative, and judiciary—at all levels. In a democracy, it is claimed that the state is run by all citizens, and that "the sovereign," "the state," and "the people" (or "the public") are more or less synonymous. A moment of thought suggests that the real sovereign is more often represented by the group of major politicians and bureaucrats who make most of the day-to-day decisions than by the electors who vote only occasionally. In any event, the state and the sovereign are closely related, and the distinction between them can often be neglected for all practical purposes.

We mean something slightly different, but related, when we say that the state is sovereign, when we talk about the "sovereign state" implying that sovereignty is an essential attribute of the state. This notion of sovereignty is external and pertains to the relation between the state and the world external to the country over which the state rules (compared to the internal power of the sovereign within a country). But the two uses of sovereign do have a common denominator: power. The sovereign state cannot be challenged by outside forces, just as the sovereign rules over his own subjects or citizens.

The answer to the second question—can we say "he" (or "she") when talking about the sovereign?—is yes, provided we heed some caveats. In saying "he" for the sovereign, I am not implying that he is a single physical person, nor suggesting that the state is a sort of super-individual endowed with humanlike cells, organs, and brain. The sovereign is generally a group of individuals, even in autocratic regimes. But he often behaves *as if* he were a single person, in the sense that he naturally pursues the welfare of the rulers, "his" own welfare, and that he acts to reach this objective. These observations also apply to the state. The Greek state acts in its own interests when it tries to get subsidies from the European Union, its interests being the interests of those who rule or influence it. Similarly, General Motors acts in its own interests, that is, the interests of its shareholders and management. Each time a group is involved, there are of course conflicting interests, and it is the individuals closer to the center of power who succeed in imposing their own.

In certain cases, standard political terminology is so confusing that making and keeping clear distinctions is imperative. Consider the words "government," "state," and "country": we use them sometimes to mean the same thing and sometimes to refer to very different entities. We say "the country has magnificent mountains," "the country is aging," and "the country [or, say, France] fights foreign imports." Country names are used to refer to the geography, the people, or their political rulers. We say, "China is keeping the yuan undervalued" when we want to say "the Chinese government" or, more precisely, "the Chinese state" at all levels. Similarly, when we say that "the United States is fighting the war on drugs," we mean in fact "the US government" or, more exactly, all the powers and levels of the US government, that is, the whole American state. We cannot mean that the Grand Canyon fights the war on drugs. We cannot either seriously mean that all Americans, "the people," are fighting the war on drugs, for there are obviously Americans on both sides of the fight. We must distinguish between a country's geography, its people, and its state.

American parlance promotes a further confusion between state and government. When, in America, we say "the government," we often mean "the state," that is, the whole apparatus of government—executive, legislative, and judiciary—at all levels—federal, State, and local. When we say, "the government is fighting the war on drugs," the subject of the sentence includes Congress, federal and local judges, the States' assemblies and administrative machines, the municipal councils and police, as well as the federal administration. Similarly, the judges and bureaucrats who enforce the tax laws in order to levy taxes and reimburse the public debt, as well as the politicians, are all part of the state. This is made more confusing by the fact that, in America, "States" refer to one level of government in the federal system. When we reserve the term "state" for this usage (describing a territorial division of government), we are left without a clear and distinctive term for the whole apparatus of government, which is rather inconvenient.

To try and clarify what we are talking about, I will often use "the state" to describe the whole apparatus of government at all levels. When, in contrast to "the state" in general, I want to refer to a particular State in the Union, or to several States, I will capitalize the term. I will speak of "the American state" in order to refer to the whole apparatus of government in America, at all levels (federal, State, and local) and with all powers combined (executive, legislative, and judicial).

I will also try, whenever it seems important, to distinguish states, countries, and peoples, by using, say, "the Greek state" instead of "Greece" when I want to talk about the state or the sovereign, as opposed to the Greek people or the islands of the territory. It is not clear that Greece has defaulted on its debt; indeed, many Greeks and many Greek businesses have not. It is the Greek state that has.

We are so accustomed to see government representatives and activities around us—in taxes, regulations, assistance, enforcement, and so on—that the state seems to be omnipresent and immortal. The state is naturally deemed to be a solid institution, the most solid of all. Everybody is supposed to trust it. This is why the sovereign debt is, or was, supposed to be totally safe. Those who continue to buy government securities still seem to think so. As *The Economist* writes with a whiff of British humor: "If governments aren't safe, after all, what is?"[6] Many people were surprised when, in 2009, the sovereign debt crisis appeared in Europe. Suddenly, the state itself looked fragile. After the first, disguised default of the Greek state, large corporations in many countries were suddenly considered safer than their countries' governments: in February 2012, the cost of insuring bonds (through financial instruments called "credit default swaps" or CDSs) was lower for ENI (an Italian multinational corporation in oil and gas), for Telefónica (a Spanish telecom multinational), for Danone (a French food product multinational), for Bayer (a German pharmaceutical multinational), for IBM (an American computer service multinational), than for their respective home governments.[7]

Thus, there is a sovereign risk, a risk that states will not reimburse their debts, as happened often historically, although we seem to have forgotten it. The world of trusted state securities is over. "Sovereign risk is out of the bottle," wrote *The Economist* in early 2010. "There is no easy way of putting it back in."[8]

Many Americans believe that the US government, although glorious and immortal, is not financially safe. A national telephone survey conducted by *Rasmussen Reports* in May 2012 asked Americans the question: "Which is more likely to occur first, that the federal budget will be balanced or that the federal government will go bankrupt and be unable to pay its debt?" Fifty-one percent of Americans (plus or minus 3 percentage points, statistically true 95% of the time) think that the second alternative will occur first—that the federal government will go bankrupt and be unable to pay its debt. Only 36 percent believe that the federal budget will be balanced first.[9] One may argue that the average respondent knows little about the issue, that he may even not clearly see the difference between the deficit and the debt. There is much truth in such skepticism, for reasons of "rational ignorance" that I will explain later. The economic concepts involved are often more complicated than they look like, and we will spend much time reviewing them. The opinion survey still suggests that a large proportion of Americans don't believe that the federal government is financially solid and safe. Finding out whether they are right or wrong is one of the goals of the discovery adventure that this book constitutes.

How did European states come to face a major debt crisis? Is a similar crisis brewing in the United States? What are the solutions? Higher taxes or lower expenditures? What would be the consequences of the federal government defaulting? In exploring these questions, we'll release other genies from the bottle.

CHAPTER 2

UNDERSTANDING THE PUBLIC DEBT

A billion here and a billion there and you are soon talking about real money.[1]

Until August 3, 2011, the federal debt ceiling was set at $14.3 trillion, meaning that the federal government was not legally allowed to increase its debt above that amount. On that day, Congress increased it to $15.2 trillion. Otherwise, an imminent shutdown of nonessential government operations and payments was looming, if not a default on the Treasury securities (bonds issued by the federal government) that were soon becoming due. It was not the first time that Congress had jacked up the debt ceiling: since the ceiling was established in 1917, it has been increased more than 100 times.

What Is a Trillion Dollars?

Before the start of the Great Recession, which hit America and most of the world in 2008 and 2009, we mostly read and talked about billions of dollars, not trillions. This changed with the trillions of dollars of mortgage loans that became suddenly at risk in 2008, the $1.5-billion bailouts and stimulus programs that George W. Bush and Barack Obama pushed through Congress, the $1.4-trillion deficit of 2009, the trillions of dollars that the Federal Reserve System (the American central bank, also called the Fed) tried to pump in the economy, and so forth. Suddenly, trillions of dollars were everywhere. We now have heard about them so often that the number has lost any surprise effect, and that mere billions now look innocuous.

One trillion, that is, one thousand billions, is a very large number. Counting to one trillion would take 31,710 years at one number per second. The number of dollars in the federal debt just before the ceiling was increased, 14.3 trillion, is even more monstrous. There have been only 5 trillion days since the Big Bang. Or consider sand. A grain of fine sand is about 200 microns (or 0.0002 of a meter) in diameter. Assuming it to be spherical, its volume is 4,188,800 microns. One cubic meter has a volume of 1 trillion microns and contains 155,175,706,646 grains of fine sand, that is, slightly more than 155 billion. This estimate is calculated as (1,000,000,000,000×0.65)/4,188,800, the 0.65 taking into account that approximately 65 percent of the space is lost when you pile spheres into a cube.[2] Now, a ten-wheel dump truck contains a sand load of about 11 cubic yards or 8.4 cubic meters, which amounts to 1,303,475,935,829 grains of sand. You would thus need more than 11 of these trucks to carry 14 trillion grains of sand. Imagine that you have to replace every grain of sand by a one-dollar bill as the 11 trucks dump their loads, and you get the federal debt—before the ceiling was increased on August 3, 2011.

Basic Concepts of the Federal Government Debt

The public debt originates from an immediate cause that is quite simple: when a government spends more than it takes in revenues, it must borrow to make up the difference. The public debt is the total of previous borrowings net of reimbursements. From this point of view, the sovereign is just like an ordinary individual or family. If, in any given year, your spending is higher than your revenues, you incur a deficit. If you have no previous savings, you must borrow (through bank loans or increasing credit card balances, for example) to finance this deficit. Your total debt is the sum of your previous deficits minus any reimbursements.

Everything gets slightly more complicated in case of a government as large and complex as the US federal government. The federal government borrows in different ways from different lenders. Some of its internal entities even borrow from other internal entities. All the information is available in several forms and in many different reports, all of which are available online. But one needs to know what to look for, and where to look. Will you check with the Office of Management and Budget (OMB), the executive agency charged with establishing the annual budget of the Administration? Or with the Congressional Budget Office (CBO), the nonpartisan agency that evaluates budget and other policies? Or with the Bureau of the Public Debt (BPD), which manages the government's borrowings and reimbursements? Or with the Financial Management Service (FMS), a bureau of the Department of the Treasury that provides government-wide accounting and related services? Or with the Government Accountability Office (GAO), a nonpartisan congressional agency that audits how the

	2010	2009
Federal deficit	-1.3	-1.4
Off-budget transactions and other financial activity	-0.2	-0.4
"Cash requirements" or "cash deficit" to be financed	**-1.5**	*-1.8*
Gross federal debt	*13.6*	*11.9*
Intragovernmental	4.6	4.4
Debt held by the public	9.0	7.5
Net new external borrowing	**1.5**	

Chart 2.1   The Federal Government's Deficit and Debt, 2009 and 2010

Source: Bureau of the Public Debt, Office of Management and Budget, Congressional Budget Office, and Government Accountability Office. Reconciliation and rounding by author.

government spends the taxpayers' money? Or somewhere else among the hundreds of federal agencies and commissions? There is no simple answer: it depends on what exactly you are looking for and from which perspective. There are several concepts of debt or liabilities. And one has to interpret one's findings, which requires knowing how to reconcile the different concepts and statistics available.

Let's try to make all this simple. Start with the 2009 gross federal debt of $11.9 trillion, on the first line of the bottom panel of Chart 2.1.[3] Note that debt is a stock, calculated at a precise moment in time, in this case on September 30, 2009, the end of the 2009 fiscal year (the fiscal year of the federal government runs from October 1 to September 30). This concept of gross federal debt is (with some small adjustments) the number we hear when the debt limit has to be increased.

Now jump to the top panel of Chart 2.1 and consider FY (fiscal year) 2010, the latest one for which all figures were available when this chapter was written. During FY 2010, the federal government incurred a deficit of $1.3 trillion dollars. In budget parlance, these expenditures and revenues are called "outlays" and "receipts," to stress the fact that they are generally on a cash basis, as opposed to an accrual basis. But we don't need this terminological distinction for our purposes, and I'll take "expenditures" and "outlays" on the one hand, and "revenues" and "receipts" on the other hand, as synonymous. The outlays and receipts are given in the annual budgets, produced by the OMB, audited by the GAO, and analyzed by the CBO. During FY 2010, outlays were $3.5 trillion and receipts $2.2 trillion, producing the $1.3-trillion deficit. (For FY 2012, CBO's January 2012 forecasts were for respectively $3.6 trillion, $2.5 trillion, and $1.1 trillion.)[4]

Revenues or receipts, expenditures or outlays, as well as surpluses or deficits, are all flow concepts, calculated over a certain period of time, as opposed to stocks like the debt. Flows during a certain period of time accumulate into stocks, which are calculated at a given point in time. Imagine the deficit as the flow coming from the faucet; the debt is the plugged sink into which the water flows. The top panel of Chart 2.1 shows flows, the bottom one stocks.

A certain number of noncash items (such as the interest accrued and to be paid later on the debt) are included in the budget deficit figure and must be deducted in order to obtain cash borrowing requirements. For the same reason, a certain number of cash items not included in the budget must be included—such as interest paid by the Treasury to debt holders. We must also consider the change in the government's cash balances, as cash can be used to finance part of the deficit (when cash decreases) or, on the contrary (when cash increases), can be a result of this financing. Netting all these off-budget cash components, we obtain a negative amount of about $200 billion ($0.2 trillion) for FY 2010. There was therefore financial hole of $1.5 trillion dollar to finance, which we may call the "cash requirements" or "cash deficit" of the federal government during FY 2010 (I put these terms in quotes because they are not official terms in government accounting). They represent the cash missing to make ends meet and the major factor in the increase of the debt.

Let's return to the bottom panel of Chart 2.1. At the end of FY 2010, the gross federal debt totaled $13.6 billon. In some government documents, the amount given is $13.7 trillion, because certain components are calculated differently, but we need not be concerned with these technical intricacies here.[5] The federal gross debt is made of two broad categories. The main category is the "debt held by the public," also called "external debt," for an amount of $9 trillion. The debt held by the public should not be confused with the broader concept of public debt, which incorporates the former. The public debt is "public" not necessarily because it is held by the public, but because it will have to be reimbursed by the taxpaying public. The debt held by the public is the sum of the federal government securities—mainly Treasury bills, notes, and bonds. (Bonds issued by the US Treasury are called "notes" when they mature between one and ten years, "bills" when their maturity is shorter, and they go by the generic terms of "bonds" if they mature in more than ten years after their issuance.) A typical Treasury security with a maturity longer than one year pays a regular interest, face value of which is reimbursed to the lender at maturity, and it can, in the meantime, be traded at prices determined on financial markets.

"The public" in "debt held by the public" is made of all federal government's lenders, that is, anybody who buys its securities: individuals, corporations, banks, State and local governments, Federal Reserve banks, foreign governments, and any other entity outside the federal government itself.

The second broad category in the gross federal debt is "intragovernmental debt," also called "debt held by Government accounts." It amounts to $4.6 trillion as of September 30, 2010.[6] As its name implies, this debt is owed by some entities of the federal government to other entities within the same government. Nearly half of it is made of federal securities held by funds administered by the Social Security Administration, which is required by law to invest any surplus in federal securities. In other words, the money the Social Security Administration (SSA) holds for future payments to its customers (senior citizens mainly) is lent to the Treasury, which uses it to finance the government's other expenditures. Another big chunk of intragovernmental debt is the civil servants' and military personnel's retirement funds, which are also invested in Treasury securities. The government borrows the money in its employees' retirement funds, just as it borrows the money in the Social Security fund and the Medicare funds (also included in intragovernmental debt).

Let's make sure we understand this. What the SSA owes you is not in the form of dollars deposited in the bank but in government securities that the government will have to reimburse before your Social Security check is cut; similarly for Medicare hospital insurance and for pension funds if you are employed by the federal government. Creepy? Remember that government securities, especially short-term securities, are widely considered as good as cash, that is, as good as actual dollar bills under the mattress or money in the bank. In that sense, the trust funds of Social Security, Medicare, and employee retirements do hold cash. But satisfying their future obligations will depend on the capacity and will of future administrations to reimburse the internal part of the public debt. On top of this, the Social Security and Medicare funds are rapidly dwindling.

Since the debt of one part of government to another is a claim of the latter to the former, intragovernmental debt cancels when the federal government's *consolidated* debt is calculated. So many analysts believe that the true debt of the federal government is better represented by its external debt, or debt held by the public. Note, however, that this will do nothing to pay for the future obligations of Social Security and Medicare. The central role that the external debt, or debt held by the public, plays in statistics and debates can thus be misleading.

Every year, the federal government reimburses the part of its external debt that becomes due, that is, the securities that mature, and issues new securities if necessary. Typically, it does not reimburse anything, but issues new securities to reimburse the old ones: we say that the debt is "rolled over." When the government borrows more than it reimburses, the total debt held by the public rises. As Chart 2.1 shows, this is what happened during FY 2010, where the net borrowing was $1.5 trillion, pushing the debt held by the public from $7.5 trillion to $9.0 trillion. That this amount corresponds exactly to the deficit to be financed is no surprise: this increase in the debt held by the public was precisely required to plug the budget hole. The net annual borrowing from the government corresponds to the cash deficit to be financed. The rest of the gross debt was financed internally, as we saw, by the government borrowing from itself. (This last point is important to understand in order not to be surprised by the fact that the increase in the gross federal debt is not equal to the deficit.)

The federal deficit ($1.3 trillion dollars in 2010), which is the main component of the gap to be financed, is mainly made of current, not investment, expenditures. What the federal government does, and has done for several decades, is to borrow in order to pay for current expenditures—borrow to pay the groceries, as it were. No ordinary individual or family or business would survive this way. Only a sovereign can—at least for a time.

We can check that the federal government has been borrowing to pay for current expenditures by comparing its total liabilities with its assets and calculating its net position. The resulting "net debt" or "net liabilities" of the federal government is another concept of public debt. It can be argued that this debt concept is more useful as it represents what the taxpayers would be left with, or left to pay, if the federal government were dissolved, however improbable this may be. The concept parallels the net value of an individual as the total value of his assets minus his liabilities. What is the net value of the federal government?

The federal government, as we have seen, owes $9 trillion to the public (as of September 30, 2010). Make this $9.1 trillion to include some adjustments such as accrued interest. But this does not exhaust the federal government's liabilities. To this figure, we must add its commitments of future pensions and benefits to its former and actual employees, which, as we have seen, are owed by the government to the funds meant to finance them. It is time to bring them back in the picture, like the GAO does, if we wish to get a better picture of federal liabilities.[7] These commitments must be calculated at their "present value," that is, as what would have to be invested now to honor the commitments as they come due; or, what amounts to the same, as the future payments discounted by the relevant rate of interest—the rate that would be earned if the money was invested now. The GAO calculates this present value to be $5.7 trillion. Add $1.6 trillion of miscellaneous liabilities, of which a chunk of $360 million in guarantees to Fannie Mae and Freddie Mac, two government-sponsored enterprises (GSEs) that failed at the beginning of the Great Recession and were taken over by the government. The total liabilities of the federal government thus amounted to $16.4 trillion as on September 31, 2010. This figure for "total liabilities" exceeds the gross federal debt reported on Chart 2.1 because it includes commitments for the future pensions and benefits of former and actual federal employees.

Against its legal liabilities of $16.4 trillion, the federal government holds $2.9 trillion dollars of assets. The main components of these assets are: the government's properties, plants and equipment ($829 billion); its loans (such as student loans) and the mortgage-backed securities it bought during the economic crisis (for a total of $943 billion); and its cash and other monetary assets ($429 billion). The difference between the federal government assets and its liabilities, what is technically called its "net position," is thus a staggering negative $13.5 trillion. (It is a fluke that the net position of the federal government is nearly equal to the $13.6 trillion of the gross federal debt, a different concept that excludes the present value of future pensions and benefits of federal employees.)

The negative net position of $13.5 trillion incorporates only the present value of the federal government's legal commitments to its own retired employees. We need to add the present value of future social insurance (Social Security and Medicare) net expenditures (forecasted expenditures minus forecasted revenues) for people already retired or contributing, which the GAO puts at $30.9 trillion. If we add the two figures, we get more than $44 trillion dollars in net liabilities. This is about three times GDP (gross domestic product).

Does this mean that the federal government of the United States is bankrupt? The answer would no doubt be affirmative if the federal state were not sovereign. Anybody whose balance sheet shows liabilities more than five times his assets ($16.4 trillion over $2.9 trillion, excluding Social Security and Medicare) would be five times bankrupt, as solvability requires assets to be at least equal to liabilities. What distinguishes a sovereign from an ordinary individual, family, or corporate body is that the former can have his debt paid by the taxpayers. The taxpayers can reimburse the uncovered liabilities with their future work and production.

In a sense, the taxpayers themselves are considered part of the sovereign's broadly conceived assets. The federal government recognizes this in its very official annual *Financial Report,* albeit in diplomatic terms, and without reporting the troubling fact on its balance sheet itself:

> It is important to note that the balance sheet does not include the financial value of the Government's sovereign power to tax, regulate commerce, and set monetary policy.[8]

And later in the report:

> Because of its sovereign power to tax and borrow, and the country's wide economic base, the Government has unique access to financial resources through generating tax revenues and issuing Federal debt securities.[9]

In other words, the sovereign's power allows him to tax, borrow, or print money, in order to appropriate the country's resources. The expression "set monetary policy" is just a euphemism meaning to print money. Printing money is like a tax because it means that the sovereign will be able to bid away goods and resources from individuals and corporations. As for borrowing, the official theory is that in a democratic country the taxpayers *are* the sovereign. We are asked to believe that *the citizens tax themselves to pay what they owe to themselves.* If you think that there is something fishy in this theory, you are right. We will return to the topic in chapter 6.

John Maynard Keynes and Democracy in Deficit

Deficits and a growing public debt is not a completely new phenomenon. What we are seeing today is the culmination of a process that started several decades ago. The name of one economist is intimately related to this evolution: John Maynard Keynes (1883–1946). Keynes was a British civil servant and lecturer at Cambridge University. Close to the British establishment, he was made a Lord in 1942. His most famous book, *The General Theory of Employment, Interest and Money,*[10] criticized accepted economic thinking about the business cycle, started a revolution in economics, and had a big impact on the way people and policy makers conceived of deficit and public debt; at least, such is the conventional wisdom.

We call "business cycle" the succession of economic booms and busts, expansions and recessions. Contrary to the "neoclassical" school of economics that had reigned before, Keynes argued that the business cycle can and should be controlled by the government. In his view, recessions are caused by a general deficiency of demand—or, which amounts to the same, a general oversupply of goods and services—and that the government should intervene with stimulus expenditures and deficit spending in order to restore growth when the economy stalls. Until at least World War I, most economists had thought that recessions were rapidly self-correcting, that government budgets should be generally balanced, or that unavoidable deficits in times of emergency (especially wars) should be compensated by surpluses in normal times. Historically, recessions did self-correct themselves after a short period: they lasted a few years at most. But Keynes thought that recessions could be better tamed with deficit spending. It followed that surpluses might be desirable in boom time, not necessarily in order to equilibrate the budget over a certain period of time, but in order to cool-off the economy and prevent inflation when the economy bumps on its limit. This limit is "potential output," the maximum that can be produced with the available resources.

Keynes believed that deficits could be easily financed by borrowing and building up the public debt. Having investors lend to the government instead of investing in stocks and corporate bonds was a way to socialize savings and to assure government control of the overall economy, of the macroeconomy. Indeed, Keynes created the whole field of macroeconomics, which analyzes the overall economy by looking at broad aggregates—total investment, consumption expenditures, general price level, and such—instead of adding up the microeconomic actions of individuals and firms. Keynesian macroeconomics amounted to a sort of top-down approach of the economy, compared to the bottom-up way of building microeconomics.

Analysts soon saw that Keynes's economics of aggregates was breaking the individualistic approach of economics and could have troubling political implications. J. Ronnie Davis, now an economics professor at the University of New Orleans, writes—referring to Henry Simons, a well-known economist of the 1930s:

> It might be added that Simons expressed a fear that the *General Theory* had possibilities "as the economic bible of a fascist movement." In the Foreword to the German edition of the *General Theory*, Keynes himself admitted that the theory of aggregates, which he said was the point of his book, could be much more easily adapted to the conditions of a totalitarian state [*eines totalen Staates*] than could "classical" theory.[11]

Be that as it may, it is conventional wisdom that Keynes's theory and policy prescriptions generated a real revolution in the free world. Did the Cambridge professor wield all the influence that he is credited with? This sort of question is always tricky, for we do not know what would have happened if John Maynard Keynes had never been born. Would another economic theory have come into vogue? Or would not other economists have proposed a theory similar to Keynes's? In reality, the idea that the recessions were caused by deficient demand was already in the air, as we find not only in pre-neoclassical economic thinking, but also among many American economists as well as in popular literature.

J. Ronnie Davis devoted his interesting book quoted above to the thesis that so-called Keynesian ideas were already endorsed by most well-known American economists before Keynes published his *General Theory* in 1936. Keynes would only have formalized them better in the context of a general theory. Davis writes:

> Around 1931 recognition of the inefficacy of countercyclical timing of normal expenditures led to the idea that "emergency expenditures" would "prime the pump"...Once prosperity was restored, the expenditures would be tapered off...The "Keynesian" policy paradigm which eventually crystallized out of the period 1930–36 represents the creativity not of a single mind but of many minds, among which one was Keynes.[12]

Popular culture was in tune. In *Brave New World*, the famous science-fiction novel published four years before Keynes's *General Theory*, Aldous Huxley echoes the simplistic idea that people must be led to consume in order to avoid overproduction. He imagines that a world where babies were conditioned to act accordingly:

> In the nurseries...the voices were adapting future demand to future industrial supply..."But old clothes are beastly," continued the untiring whisper. "We always throw away old clothes. Ending is better than mending, ending is better than mending...the more stitches the less riches."[13]

This is a strange idea, which can be easily debunked. Whatever is produced must be consumed because the income from production goes to the consumers or, through savings, to investors.[14] But this debate is not my topic here. I just want to stress how the Keynesian revolution, whether it needed Keynes or not to happen, did change the way we look at the economic world.

The concept of GDP or national income was (under different names) invented before Keynes, but it naturally found a central place in the new field of macroeconomics. It was systematically developed from the

1930s onward and started to be statistically measured first by the US federal government and then by other governments in the world. GDP is not a perfect measure of production, and represents a very imperfect measure of welfare, but a good grasp of the concept is essential to understand economic news and debates. For example, it will often be useful to compare public debt across countries or over time as a proportion of GDP, since different currencies or changing prices (due to inflation) vitiate simple comparisons of debt values. Unfortunately, many people who criticize GDP know little about its methodology and meaning.

GDP measures the total or aggregate production that is exchanged on markets in a given territory—such as the United States. This aggregate production is equal to "value added," a concept that avoids double-counting the value of inputs in a final consumption product. For example, it avoids counting wheat once when it is produced, another time in the value of flour, and a third time in the price of bread. The value of output is added at the different stages of production, but counting inputs only once. Since this final value is created by the factors of production (labor, land, and capital) and corresponds to what they earn (wages, rents, and return on capital), national income (the incomes of all factors of production) is by definition equal to GDP. So when we talk about GDP, we mean all final goods (excluding inputs, which are counted only once in the final products) produced and sold on markets, or equivalently all incomes that are earned, in a given territory. GDP is also equal to all expenditures on final goods and services—called "national expenditure"—since everything produced on the market will be consumed, or used to produce something else in the future, by somebody. (Inventories are considered as an investment, as production in waiting.) Thus, production equals incomes equals expenditures.

With these tools in our toolbox, let us return to our main strand. Before Keynes, the unwritten rule of public finance was that government budgets needed to be balanced. Only in times of emergency could a deficit be incurred, and it had to be compensated by subsequent (or preceding) surpluses so as to prevent an accumulation of public debt. A prudent management of public affairs required adherence to this principle. For a long time, it was pretty well respected.

Chart 2.2 shows the federal debt held by the public as a percentage of American GDP from 1797 to 2010. Taking the debt-to-GDP ratio allows a more meaningful comparison of the debt figures in different years. Just like an individual's debt takes a different significance if it represents a lower or higher proportion of his changing income, the burden of the government's debt may vary with the size of GDP and,

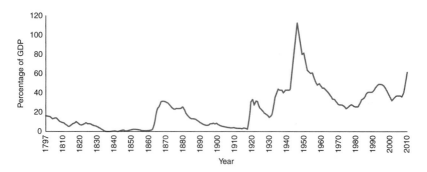

Chart 2.2   Federal Debt Held by the Public as a Proportion of GDP (1797–2010)

Source: Congressional Budget Office and Government Accountability Office, at http://www.gao.gov/special.pubs/longterm/debt/.

thus, the capacity of taxpayers to service and reimburse it. For GDP is what people earn, and it is with their contributions to GDP that they pay taxes. As we saw, the US government admits this, however troubling it may be to think of people as conscripts at the service of the state.

In 1797, the debt owed to the public by the new federal government, which had assumed the debt accumulated during the revolutionary war, amounted to 17 percent of the estimated American GDP. The 1787 GDP was only calculated a century and a half later, so it remains a rough estimate. Most of the data used in economics—like data in other sciences—are only estimated measures of the reality subsumed by a concept. The chart shows that the federal debt was gradually reimbursed until being totally paid off in the 1830s. Until the 1860s, it was never more than 2.5 percent of GDP. The Civil War pushed the proportion to 31 percent, but, again, it was gradually reduced in the decades that followed. It had been brought down to less than 3 percent of GDP when the federal government entered World War I. To finance the war effort, the federal debt held by the public rapidly jumped to 33 percent of GDP. It started diminishing again after the end of the war, albeit more hesitatingly, and was still 15 percent of GDP when the Great Depression hit. It jumped to 44 percent in 1934, where it plateaued until the US government entered World War II. An all-time high of 113 percent was reached in 1945. But again the debt held by the public decreased regularly as a proportion of GDP after the war, down to 24 percent in 1974.

The ratio of the debt held by the public to GDP moves not only when the numerator (the debt) changes, but also when the denominator (GDP) evolves through economic growth and the business cycle. For instance, if GDP grows, a constant value of the debt will translate into a diminishing ratio, thus hiding what happens to the debt itself and to the surpluses or deficits that underlie it. When we look at the data in dollars, we confirm that until 1930 the deficits were concentrated in times of war, and that the other years were characterized by surpluses meant to reimburse the debt. However, from 1931 until the end of World War II, the federal government incurred continuing deficits, and the deficits did not disappear after that war. From 1947 to 1960, surpluses and deficits alternated. Something had changed.

The worst was still to come. After the small surplus year of 1960, the deficit of 1961 marked the beginning of a new budgetary era. The decade of the 1960s would see deficits in every single year except 1969. Then, there would not be a single surplus until 1998. Between 1961 and 1998, only two surpluses were registered. Three more surplus years (1999, 2000, and 2001) followed, after which the federal government relapsed into red ink. There has not been a single surplus since 2001. During the five decades from 1961 to 2010, the federal government showed a surplus position in only five years, and the tendency of budget balances was clearly downward even before the large deficits that started with the recession year of 2008.

As expected, the debt held by the public grew in step with the deficits. If the water continues to flow, the bucket fills up. Brisk growth of nominal GDP hid the trend of the ratio for a while. "Nominal" GDP is GDP in current dollars, which includes real growth plus inflation. After World War II, the ratio of debt held by the public to GDP decreased until the mid-1970s, mainly as a consequence of inflation, which boosted the denominator. As we can gather from Chart 2.2, the debt was down to 24 percent of GDP in 1974, from its peak of 113 percent during World War II. From then on, the ratio doubled to 49 percent in the mid-1990s. A combination of high economic growth and the surpluses registered at the turn of the century brought the debt-to-GDP ratio down to 32 percent in 2001. But it immediately resumed its upward trend. It reached 36 percent in 2007, just before the Great Recession struck. Within the next three years, the ratio doubled to its 2010 level of 62 percent. It will have increased again by the time this book reaches the reader.

A similar story emerges if we consider the debt evolution in actual dollars. The value of the debt held by the public ballooned from the mid-1970s to 2007—and to now. It jumped from $344 billion in 1974 to $5 trillion in 2007, a fifteen-fold increase. It is true that there was some inflation during that period, so that one dollar at the end of the period was worth less than one dollar at the beginning—or, alternatively, one dollar in the mid-1970s was worth more than one dollar now. But even measured in "real" dollars, with inflation taken out, the debt followed a steep upward trend.

To measure something in real dollars, we need to use a price index, such as the consumer price index (CPI). Measured by the Bureau of Labor Statistics (BLS), the CPI tracks the "average" price of a consumer-preferred basket of goods and services from one year to another. Some attempts are made by the BLS to take into account quality changes (a TV or a phone today is not the same as it was in 1974), but the adjustments are subjective and imperfect. The data show that a standard basket of consumption costing $0.23 in 1974 costs $1 in 2010. In other words, there has been a 335 percent inflation (add 335% to $0.23 and you get $1, disregarding the rounding error) over these 36 years, or 4.2 percent (compounded) per year on average. Other ways of saying the same thing is that the cost of living has increased by 335 percent, or that the dollar has lost 77 percent of its value between these two years. Thus, calculating "in real dollars of 2010" (we also say "in constant dollars of 2010") the price of something bought in 1974 needs to be multiplied by 4.35 ($0.23×4.35=$1, neglecting the rounding error). It follows that the $344 billion of federal debt held by the public in 1974 is worth $1.5 trillion in real dollars of 2010. Using the BLS's original data, we can similarly calculate that the $5 trillion debt held by the public in 2007 was worth a bit more than $5.25 trillion in real 2010 dollars. Between 1974 and 2007, then, the debt held by the public in real (2010) dollars has increased by 250 percent.

This large increase in the federal debt occurred before the Great Recession, the latter only accelerating the trend. What happened that led to the federal debt held by the public to jump by 250 percent in real dollars between 1974 and 2007 and, as we saw previously, to its share in GDP to increase by 50 percent (from 24% to 36%)? Two economists from the Center for the Study of Public Choice (then at Virginia Polytechnic Institute, now at George Mason University), James Buchanan (winner of the 1986 Nobel Prize in economics) and Richard Wagner, asked the question in a prescient book published in 1977, *Democracy in Deficit: The Political Legacy of Lord Keynes*. A democratic government like the US federal government will necessarily fall into endemic budget deficits once the unwritten rule of budgetary equilibrium has been destroyed, and there is no perceived political cost in deficit financing. And Keynes taught that there is indeed no cost; that's his political legacy. Even if he was not alone in preaching the new gospel, he was a very efficient promoter. Politicians who are not held to the budget balance standard will run deficits because it allows them to offer their electors goodies at a zero tax price. A budget deficit is a politician's dream—at least until catastrophe hits—and bureaucrats (civil servants) will not object: the more public expenditures, the better treated and the happier they are. The state becomes addicted to deficits.

The school of economic thought represented by James Buchanan and the group of economists who converged at the Virginia Polytechnic Institute in the 1960s and 1970s (Gordon Tullock was another founder) proposed a new way of looking at public choice, public policy, and public finance. It came to be known as "Public Choice" economics. Three decades after the beginning of the Keynesian revolution, they led another revolution, "the Public Choice revolution."[15]

Buchanan and Wagner trace to 1964 the watershed year, when "the old rules of fiscal responsibility"[16] were abandoned: on that year, taxes were decreased for no other reason than that potential output was deemed too low. As I mentioned, the budget had already been in deficit since 1961. Another candidate for the watershed year is 1975, when the ratio of the debt held by the public to GDP started raising again. Historical cut-off points are always arbitrary, and we only need to understand that the endemic federal deficits started in 1961, pushing up the value of the debt held by the public, and that by 1975 the deficits were important enough to push up the ratio of the debt to GDP upward again. The mounting debt problem did not start with the jump in the price of oil in 1973–1974, nor with the recession of 1973–1975, but in the 1960s, when the federal government became a deficit addict.

State and Local Governments

The federal debt is not the only component of the US public, or sovereign, debt. States and local governments (cities, towns, counties, school and water authorities, and such) also borrow—issue bonds—to pay for investment projects and, sometimes, to fill a gap between current expenditures and revenues. Their debt must be added to the federal government's debt in order to provide a complete picture of what is owed by the American state, of which States and local governments are part. Even if they cannot print money like the federal government, States and local governments participate in sovereignty because they can force their citizens to pay (one way or another). In GAO's terms, they share the "sovereign power to tax [and] regulate commerce."[17] As Vermont's treasurer Jeb Spaulding recently said about his government's bonds, "the state has pledged its full faith and credit and all the potential revenues of that state to support these bonds."[18] In other words, the State of Vermont had pledged its citizens' incomes to reimburse the loan. American States are also sovereign in the more usual sense that out-of-state creditors would face obstacles in getting their money back in case of default.

Of course, a democratic sovereign—or any sovereign for that matter—faces limits as to how much he can extract from its subjects: he can take only so much political resistance, legal or illegal. Short of violence, black markets are one form of illegal resistance, very common when the tax burden gets too high. The sovereign does not want to kill the goose that lays the golden eggs, for he is after the eggs. To paraphrase Willie Sutton, why is the state after the taxpayers? Because that's where the money is.

At first sight, America's State and local governments may not seem to have a big debt problem. A Harvard University economist, Jeffrey Miron, recently reviewed the economic literature and evidence on this topic.[19] The States' gross debt was 18 percent of American GDP at the end of FY 2008 and ranged from 6 percent to 26 percent of gross state product (as State GDP is called). These figures incorporate the debt of local governments because they are perceived as benefiting from guarantees from their respective States, which also have legislative ways to control the profligacy of lower-level governments. If financial assets belonging to State and local governments (loans, holdings in public corporations, and such), which correspond to 16 percent of GDP, are deducted, their net debt is reduced to a mere 2 percent of GDP. This is not surprising as State and local governments generally run balance budgets. In fact, all States except Vermont are prohibited, by their constitution or by specific legislation, to incur deficits. They often find ways to bypass this constraint, but their global near-zero net debt shows that, on average, they officially behave. Eighteen States even show a positive net position. The worst ratio of net debt to gross state product was 10 percent in New York State. Even if we add the officially reported net liabilities of State and local employees' pension plans, the 2 percent of US GDP does not change materially. These ratios would make the federal government jealous.

This picture is misleading in many ways. State and local governments use a very high interest rate—around 8 percent—to discount their future pension liabilities when calculating the latter's present value. The California Public Employees' Retirement System (CalPERS) used a discount rate of 7.75 percent until very recently, but was on the path to reducing it to 7.5 percent.[20] (All rates of interest in this paragraph are nominal, that is, calculated in current dollars, without any correction for inflation.) This sort of discount rate corresponds to the historical rate of return on stocks and includes the risk premium that stocks carry over debt instruments (such as bonds). Since future pension payments are a contractual and certain liability, they should instead be discounted with a riskless rate of interest, which is much lower. A certain future should not be heavily discounted. Another reason to use a lower rate of discount is that State and municipal bonds (collectively called "municipal bonds" or "munis") have yielded an average of only 5.5 percent since 1953. This is presumably the marginal return that taxpayers obtain on projects financed by munis; otherwise their governments would not represent their interest well, for they would borrow at a higher rate than the returns they expect from the last (marginal) investment. No higher discount rate than this rate of return should be used to discount States' and local governments' future liabilities. Or consider the States' and local governments' yields on their own portfolios: according to *Bloomberg News*, the largest State retirement funds (those with more than $20 billion in assets) have had an annual return of only 4 percent during the past decade.[21] Economists forecast that even equities (shares of stock), which have a higher return because they are more risky, will not yield more than 6 percent in the foreseeable future.[22] In other words, a larger chunk of the pension liabilities of States and local governments—larger than what official figures suggest—is unfunded, that is, backed by no reserve of assets, but only by the taxpayers' future incomes.

According to estimates by Miron and others, the unfunded pension liabilities of State and local governments amounted to some 9 percent of GDP in 2008, which means a ratio of net debt to GDP of 11 percent, as opposed to the official 2 percent. Adding the unfunded liabilities for the health-care benefits of retired State and local government workers produces a total of over 15 percent of GDP. Although this ratio of net debt to GDP remains much lower than the federal ratio, it is sizeable, especially, since it comes on top of the federal government debt.

The situation may be much worse than what these figures suggest. Some estimates of the unfunded pension liabilities of State and local governments, and thus their true debt, are much higher, perhaps three times the 9 percent cited above. And the situation has deteriorated with the current low interest rates, which makes pension assets grow much more slowly. Gillian Tett, a *Financial Times* columnist, suggests that investors in munis may soon discover the time bomb in munis. "Fiscal woes," she writes, "are not just a matter for the Eurozone; investors had better keep watching the American periphery too."[23]

Another factor that has brought State budgets, and thus State debt, under pressure has been the growth of health-care expenditures, including Medicaid (medical coverage for the poor) and health care for public employees and retirees, which have increased their share of

State and local government expenditures from about 16.5 percent to 18.5 percent over the past two decades.[24] The recent spate of legislation targeting civil servants' trade unions and their power to negotiate extraordinary benefits has brought the issue to the forefront of debates. Note that the problem of employee benefits is also acute at the local government level. A few counties and cities have been recently defaulting, and some analysts suggest that "a municipal debt crisis looms in the near future."[25]

Adding Up and Taking Stock

Adding up everything is not as obvious as it would appear. Estimates and forecasts are necessarily uncertain. Many have not been calculated on the same basis. But we can provide some order of magnitude for the gross liabilities of the American state using the estimates reported in this chapter. These estimates show 13 percent of GDP in unfunded pension and related liabilities of State and local governments. Adding this to their gross liabilities of 18 percent (instead of the net liabilities as we did before), we get a ratio of 31 percent. This figure looks small compared to the 86 percent ratio of total federal liabilities to GDP in 2008 (the year of the estimates above), but it still adds up—to some 117 percent of GDP. And these estimates are for 2008; the numbers have jumped since. If we further add the net present value of Social Security and Medicare promises, which are equal to about twice GDP according to official figures, we can estimate that total federal liabilities amount to at least 300 percent of GDP; other estimates are much more pessimistic, putting the figure at 500 percent or even 900 percent of GDP.[26] Americans would have to work for free for several years to reimburse what their governments owe.

An interesting, but still imperfect, way to appraise the American public debt situation is to compare it with other countries using data from the Organization for Economic Co-operation and Development (OECD). The OECD is an intergovernmental organization of which the members are the representatives of 34 states (called "countries" in official parlance). Its members are recruited in Europe, North America, South America, plus Australia, New Zealand, Japan, South Korea, and Israel. OECD data are useful for international comparisons as the Organization's large staff of economists tries to make them comparable across countries, despite frequent differences in national statistics. We will review more international comparisons in the next chapter; just consider for now gross debt per capita—excluding the unfunded liabilities we have just analyzed, but including all levels of government.

The OECD reports that total gross public debt in America was already $28,856 per person at the end of 2007. At end of 2010 (the last year available when these lines are written), the total gross public debt corresponds to $44,616 for every man, woman, and child. The average American family composed of a husband, wife, and two children thus owes $178,464 through its sovereign. Except for Japan, this is the highest public debt per capita among all OECD countries.[27] It is true that the American economy is also richer than any other, and we'll look later at the debt in proportion of GDP; but these figures seem to confirm that a public debt problem exists in America.

It is of course important to distinguish between public debt and private debt. Federal Reserve figures[28] show that, at the end of civil year 2010, all outstanding debt securities from all governments in America totaled $12.5 trillion (three-fourths of which had been issued by the federal government). This was 22 percent more than the $10.2 trillion of residential mortgage loans in the whole country, which gives an idea of the weight of public debt in America. However, debt markets cover much more: they also finance businesses and consumer credit; and they are themselves part of the broader financial markets, which include shares of stock, mutual funds, and so on. Financial markets incorporate all the means to transfer money from people who want to save to those who want to invest or to consume more than they earn. The $12.5 trillion of government debt translates to 23 percent of all credit market instruments in the American economy. If we take the broader measure of financial markets and add all the assets (and thus all liabilities and equity) of broad categories of lenders (and borrowers) in the economy, public debt accounts for 8 percent of the total. As important as the public debt burden is, it is still only a fraction—albeit important and growing—of the total finance. These estimates of government borrowing however do not include the $7.6 trillion of mortgage debt guaranteed by housing federal agencies or the GSEs (mainly Fannie Mae and Freddie Mac).

Public debt is public debt, and private debt is private debt. The sovereign is not the only borrower. If one talks of the debt of "a country"—say "the US debt"—one has to be careful about what one means. Such confusing expressions can mean public debt, or the debt of all individuals, businesses, and governments located on the American territory, or only the part of the debt that is owned by foreigners. Here as elsewhere, we should always be careful to distinguish the state (or the sovereign) on the one hand, and private individuals, families, and businesses on the other hand.

Yet, the level of public debt does have an impact on the economy. The sovereign's solvency affects private lenders who hold government securities, for they would lose money, and perhaps risk insolvency themselves, if their creditor were to default. For that reason, banks, which are important holders of government securities, cannot usually issue long-term bonds (that is, borrow long-term on financial markets) at a better interest rate than their governments, whatever their own solvency. Investors reason that banks, whose solvability is tied to that of their governments, cannot be less risky than the latter.[29] The higher the level of public debt, the more impact it has on the economy. European sovereigns have experienced this problem. It is coming to America.

CHAPTER 3

LESSONS FROM EUROPE
(AND ELSEWHERE)

On everything, Europe blazed the path—from classical Greece where philosophy and science were discovered 25 centuries ago, to contemporary Greece where the recently forgotten art of openly cheating government lenders was rediscovered.

During the 2007–2009 Great Recession, states rescued their banks, fearful that the latter's problems would push the economy into a catastrophe similar to the 1930s Great Depression. Just as the Great Recession had painfully started to subside, a sovereign debt risk appeared in Europe. The first state to raise concerns was the Greek state, whose $398 billion of outstanding securities dwarfed the amount investment bank Lehman Brothers owed to its bondholders when it collapsed in the dark moments of September 2008.[1] The situation had changed radically: it was now the banks that were worried about their governments' solvency.

Who could have forecasted that just a few years ago? As we will see, all the signs were in the sky, but signs of unexpected events are often difficult to see. Who can forecast what will happen next, and how this might affect the whole world, the opportunities and the risks of most people, including you and me? We live in interesting, but dangerous, times.

Sovereign Bankruptcy

When an entity has more liabilities than assets, it is said to be insolvent. It will soon be forced by its creditors to sell off its assets and repay part of what it owes; in other words, bankruptcy is imminent. Except if a corporation facing bankruptcy can effectively reorganize under the protection of bankruptcy laws, or is acquired by another entity, it will be dissolved after its assets are disposed of. Liberal law regimes rightly forbid slavery and the dissolution of individual debtors, so personal bankruptcy is less exacting; yet, the bankrupt individuals' assets are seized (at least in part), and the proceeds of their sale are shared among his creditors.

It is a different story when a sovereign is insolvent. A sovereign cannot go bankrupt. Most of his assets cannot be seized. We saw how creditors have been trying, with much trouble, to seize assets belonging to the Argentine state in order to recoup the lost value of its securities. In a decentralized country such as the United States, subordinated levels of government can borrow on their own recognizance; local governments can even go bankrupt. Yet, they remain components of the sovereign and some of their assets cannot be seized: think of police stations or state capitols. In the same vein, the Eleventh Amendment to the Constitution bans any foreigner from suing a State before a federal court—although its interpretation may have been narrowed since World War II.[2] In any event, a sovereign cannot be dissolved, except by a revolution. Even in the case of a revolution, the concept and practice of sovereignty is such that the sovereign's throne is simply vacated and grabbed by another ruler or group of rulers.

Sovereigns can thus default on their debt at relatively low cost. Default means to stop paying interest, or to refuse to repay the capital lent when a bond matures, or to pay less than promised in either interest or capital. "Rescheduling the debt" is a way of doing the same thing by delaying payment or replacing the bonds with new ones worth less. All forms of debt restructuring amount to a partial default, even if it is made to look as a "voluntary" concession by the creditors. The creditors don't have much choice, as the sovereign tells them that either they accept reduced payments or they get nothing. The distinction between voluntary agreement on the part of the creditors and "a forced and disorderly sovereign default" is in large part arbitrary. As a German banker put it when the Greek state's private creditors were obliged to accept a large loss on the value of their bonds, "the participation in the haircut is as voluntary as a confession during the Spanish inquisition."[3]

To see how delayed reimbursement implies lower reimbursement, assume that a debtor issues a bond promising to repay $105 in one year. Assume that the current market rate of interest, or what you can get if you invest your money in other instruments for one year, is 5 percent. Thus, the present value of the bond is $100, for this is the amount you would have to invest now in order to get the same $105 in one year. If, just after selling the bond and taking the money, the debtor announces that he will only reimburse the $105 in two years, the present value of the bond is now only $95.24, for this is what you need to invest to get

$105 in two years. The bond can't be worth more because, for more money, you would get more than $105 in two years' time. The calculation is easy to make: invest $95.24 today at 5 percent interest, and you will earn $4.76 interest at the end of this year; reinvest this interest (you will then have $95.24 + $4.76 = $100 invested) and, at the end of the second year, you will get $105. The delay in repaying the bond has thus reduced its value from $100 to $95.24, a default of $4.76 compared to what had been promised when you bought the bond. Since everybody knows this, your bond will now trade on the market for only $95.24, which will confirm that the value of your bond has lost $4.76. Note that deferring interest payments also decreases the value of a bond.

A sovereign can not only default, but it can also in theory, and contrary to the rule of law, make its creditors "accept" their loss by retroactively changing the terms of the debt contract. The nonretroactivity of law used to be a major bulwark of the rule of law; indeed, Section 8 of the US Constitution prohibits "ex post facto Law." Retroactively changing the terms of the lending contract is what the Greek state did in 2012 with legislation forcing its creditors to abide by so-called collective-action clauses. These clauses, sometimes accepted voluntarily by debtors in bond contracts, oblige them to accept any restructuring agreed by a certain proportion (such as two-thirds) of other bondholders. But they had not been included in the vast majority of Greek bonds contracts, and the state imposed them retroactively.[4] Only a sovereign such as the Greek state could do this.

Sovereign defaults are not rare. The English, French, and Spanish states defaulted several times between the fourteenth and the eighteenth century. Economists Carmen Reinhart and Kenneth Rogoff even note that "the French monarchs had a habit of executing major domestic creditors," which they call "an early and decisive form of 'debt restructuring.'"[5] Reinhart and Rogoff have documented 250 cases of defaults (or rescheduling) on external debt (debt owned by foreigners) since 1800 and 68 cases of default on debt held domestically. In the nineteenth century, defaults were effected not only by many newly independent South American states but also by a number of European states, including France, German states, and, many times, Spain, Greece, and Portugal. The twentieth century witnessed a few European defaults, including Germany (twice) and Greece. In the 1980s, several Latin American states defaulted. The 1990s saw major defaults by a few Asian states and by the Russian state.

The US government effectively defaulted in 1790 when it deferred a portion of the interest on the debt it had assumed from the original 13 colonies. It defaulted again in 1933 when F. D. Roosevelt abrogated

the gold clause that, in most contracts, allowed creditors to be reimbursed in gold. The abrogation of the gold clause meant that the government could eventually reimburse its own debt in devaluated dollars,
as opposed to gold, thereby imposing a substantial haircut to its debt
holders.

American States have defaulted more often than the federal government. Between 1840 and 1843, eight states (Illinois, Indiana, Maryland,
Pennsylvania, Arkansas, Louisiana, Michigan, and Mississippi) and one
territory (Florida) defaulted. Three of those repudiated part of their
debt (Arkansas, Louisiana, and Michigan) and two repudiated completely (Florida and Mississippi). The debt of Confederate States was
repudiated by the Fourteenth Amendment of the Constitution. Many
Southern States defaulted again after Reconstruction. More recently, in
1933, the State of Arkansas reoffended.[6]

Local governments have also defaulted, both in the nineteenth century and recently. They can often resort to formal bankruptcy pro-
ceedings, but bankruptcy never means dissolution. Famous recent cases
of default include New York City in 1975 and Cleveland in 1978. One
of the largest municipal defaults was that of the Washington Public
Power Supply System in the 1980s. Between 1970 and 2009, rating
agency Moody's counted about 50 local government defaults. In the
wake of the Great Recession, a number of local governments declared
bankruptcy and defaulted. The recent bankruptcy of Jefferson County
in Alabama was one of the largest ever.[7]

The Debt Problem Predates the Great Recession

The sovereign debt crisis that followed the Great Recession looked
very serious because it involved developed Europe. The implicit story
in the public discourse seemed to go as follows: the Great Recession has
reduced GDP and, consequently, incomes and tax revenues; the crisis
also has increased government expenditures; the result is that government deficits have increased, pushing up the public debt to dangerous
territory. This story is misleading. In reality, many governments were
already insolvent before the Great Recession, and default was only a
matter of time. The economic crisis only revealed and exacerbated the
problem and brought the day of reckoning earlier.

The Great Recession started in America at the end of 2007. Its
name emphasizes that it was the most serious recession since the Great
Depression of the 1930s, and that it was not quite as severe as the latter. From the peak of the previous expansion, in the fourth quarter of
2007, until the trough of the second quarter of 2009, the US GDP fell

by 5 percent. Unemployment rose to more than 10 percent. The recession rapidly spread to Europe. In the European Union (EU), the recession started one quarter later (second quarter of 2008), but the drop of GDP until the second quarter of 2009 was a bit deeper. The causes of the Great Recession are still a matter of debate, and will probably remain so for a long time, as economists are still debating the causes of the Great Depression which took place 80 years ago. I have argued that one should first look at the crime scene, which is the government-supported residential mortgage market in America; a second cause can be found in the loose monetary policy of the Fed (and other central banks) from 2001 to 2004.[8]

The Great Recession was barely over when the European sovereign debt crisis struck. In Europe, state sovereignty is shared between national states and the supranational state, called the EU. As with other political collectives, the terminology is slippery: "the EU" is used as a political organization and sometimes as a territory —but apparently less often as a collection of people, perhaps because "Europe" conveys the nonpolitical meanings. I use "EU" to designate the political organization. Twenty-seven European states are members of the EU, of which seventeen share the same currency, the euro, and form the Eurozone (or "Euro area"). The Eurozone is composed of Austria, Belgium, Cyprus, Estonia, Finland, France, Germany, Greece, Ireland, Italy, Luxembourg, Malta, the Netherlands, Portugal, Slovakia, Slovenia, and Spain. The EU countries not part of the Eurozone are Bulgaria, the Czech Republic, Denmark, Hungary, Latvia, Lithuania, Poland, Romania, Sweden, and the United Kingdom.

Public debt is issued by each national state for its own purposes and, in the Eurozone, it is denominated in the common EU currency. Until the sovereign debt crisis hit, investors generally assumed that all sovereign bonds issued in euros were similarly riskless, whatever the national government that issued them. In other words, investors were willing to buy at roughly the same price any bond that carried the same nominal interest, whatever its issuing state. This translated into very small spreads (or differences) between the yields of, say, Greek and German government bonds (remember that the yield is the effective return, given the coupon interest rate or price at issuance and the price at which the bond trades on the market).

Investors are not a special class of exploiters. Look at the data. At the end of 2010, the US domestic financial sector held financial assets worth $64 trillion.[9] Financial assets are money and financial instruments (claims on money and ultimately on real goods and services). These financial assets took the form of not only direct holdings of stocks and bonds, but also mutual funds, shares of money market funds (mutual funds that invest in short-term securities), bank deposits, pension funds, insurance policies, and asset-backed securities sold or guaranteed by the federal government. In other words, these $64 trillion of American investors' money can ultimately be traced to individual American residents or the businesses that belong to them. In a very real sense, investors are mainly you and I. Even people who think they are not investors indirectly hold financial assets through their bank deposits, their pension funds, their mutual funds, their life insurance policies, or even through their governments (State governments, for example, hold federal securities).

When we read that investors have deserted some form of financial assets, we must understand that it refers to all people who own financial assets directly or indirectly. Most holders of financial assets count on financial intermediaries (banks, brokers, pension funds managers, mutual fund managers, insurers, etc.) to trade and hold financial securities for them, and the intermediaries earn their incomes trying to obtain the best returns for their customers. But when individuals lose confidence in their financial intermediaries, they take finance in their own hands, as it were, and retrieve their money. In the case of banks, this movement is called a bank run, or bank panic when many banks are involved. The beginning of such a panic appeared when many depositors withdrew their deposits from threatened European banks, vindicating the idea that the ultimate security holders and speculators are individuals. At the time of writing, such panics are contained.

When we say that in late 2009 and 2010 investors realized that the Greek state's debt was risky, we are referring to financial intermediaries not only in Europe, but also some in America and elsewhere. Through them, it is you and I, directly or indirectly, who tried to sell Greek sovereign bonds and the securities of any entity (Greek banks, for example) that would be hit by a sovereign default. The Greek state had to be bailed-out by a troika composed of the EU, the International Monetary Fund (IMF), and the European Central Bank (ECB). A few months later, the Irish state needed the support of the EU and the IMF to recapitalize the country's banks, left dangerously fragile by the economic crisis. Ireland's problem was quite different from Greece's: it started as a banking crisis, to which the government reacted by foolishly guaranteeing all banks' liabilities, including to bondholders; only then did the problem degenerate into a sovereign debt problem as investors stopped trusting the capacity of the government to finance its huge assistance program. The Irish public debt climbed from 29 percent of GDP in 2007 to 99 percent in 2010. It was soon discovered that the Portuguese sovereign had a debt problem similar to the Greek problem.

Not all European states had been unusually profligate, nor had they all amassed very large public debts. Denmark, with its 34 percent ratio of public debt to GDP in 2007, seemed secure. Other countries similarly stood below the OECD average of 56 percent (unweighted average, that is, the country average), including Finland, Switzerland, the UK, and the Netherlands. Exceptionally, a few states that also had relatively low levels of public debt before the Great Recession were also engulfed in the crisis: Ireland, Spain, and Iceland. The Spanish state, which had a relatively low level of public debt—42 percent of GDP—before the crisis, shot up to 67 percent in 2010. Even more than elsewhere in Europe, Spain's inflexible labor market wreaked havoc: unemployment climbed and stuck to more than 20 percent, with nearly half of the youngsters unemployed. The Icelandic state, not a member of the EU, was hit by a major bank crisis in the wake of the recession. The country's overextended banks went belly up and defaulted on their obligations to creditors and, for a time, to depositors in other European countries. Many local governments, especially in the UK, greedy for slightly higher interest rates, had deposited money in Icelandic banks, which they stood to lose until the matter was resolved in their favor by Iceland's Supreme Court in late 2011.[10]

Greece is more representative of typical European countries in that its debt problem can be traced long before the Great Recession. Chart 3.1 shows the evolution of the Greek gross public debt from 1970 to 2010. In the 1970s, it generally stood at less than 20 percent of GDP. It started exploding at the end of the decade and, by 1993, had reached 98 percent of GDP. High rates of GDP growth in Greece maintained the ratio at roughly this level until 2004. It then started creeping up again and had reached 105 percent by 2007. Remember, the Great Recession had not yet started.

The Greeks had developed the welfare state with a vengeance. According to press reports, people in more than 600 professions could retire at 50 with a state pension at 95 percent of their last working year's earnings. When in power, political parties packed the civil service with their supporters. As an example of bloated public services, Athens' underground was essentially free as there was no ticket control and few bothered to pay. The wage bill of the overground public rail system was six times its revenue from ticket sales, prompting a Greek politician to declare that it would be cheaper to put all commuters in private taxis. Tax evasion was generalized, generally accepted, and oiled by bribes when necessary—hence the officially small number

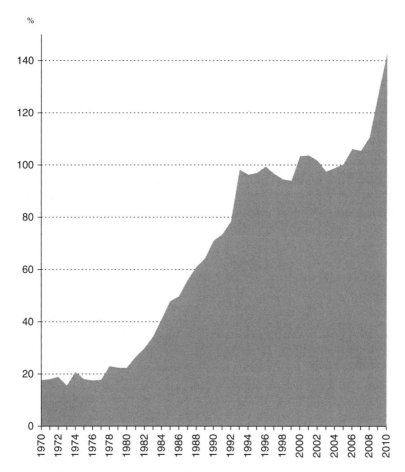

Chart 3.1   Greek Gross Public Debt as a Proportion of GDP, 1970–2010

Source: European Commission.

of rich people in Greece, even in plush neighborhoods, and the relatively low government revenues.[11] Since joining the Eurozone in
2001, Greece has seen its welfare state develop further. "More than
half of the rise in expenditures since 1999 stemmed from growth in
social transfers, writes the OECD, "which is only partly attributable
to the 2009 recession."[12] "Social transfers" are welfare and similar
payments made directly to individuals as income support. In fact,
the Greek state succeeded in joining the Eurozone and in avoiding
criticism by cooking up official statistics until just a few years ago.
It was discovered that public debt had been underestimated by some
11 percent of GDP. The 2009 budget deficit, forecasted at 2 percent
of GDP in 2008 and 13 percent one year later, was recalculated at
15 percent in 2010.[13]

Greek taxpayers did not want to pay for government expenditures, and the state was not able, or not willing, to enforce higher taxes. Corruption developed, as it always does when public greed takes over.

In many ways, Greece was just an exaggerated representation of the typical European country. Consider Chart 3.2, which shows gross public debt (all levels of government) as a proportion of GDP in selected countries just before the Great Recession as well as at the end of 2010.[14] In 2007, the gross public debt in the typical Euro-area country was 56 percent (unweighted average) of GDP, which amounts to nearly three-fourths of the level of 78 percent it reached in 2010. This is a fact: nearly three-quarters of Euro-area public debt was accumulated before the Great Recession and, in fact, before the mid-1990s. Neglecting the extreme case of Japan (a special outlier), Greece and Italy came second and third among OECD countries in 2007, with ratios of 115 percent and 112 percent respectively. Note how Belgium (88%), Portugal (75%), France (73%), and even Germany (66%) were also pulling up the Euro-area average. In all these countries, the level of public debt was 75 percent or more than what it would reach after the Great Recession. Compared to them, Iceland, Spain, and Ireland were in a good position. Note how, before the Great Recession, the ratio of gross public debt to GDP was 62 percent in America, putting the country over the Euro area and OECD averages. In America, 66 percent of the public debt was accumulated before the recession. In both Europe and America, then, the debt was not created by the 2007–2009 recession, which merely revealed the depth of the problem.

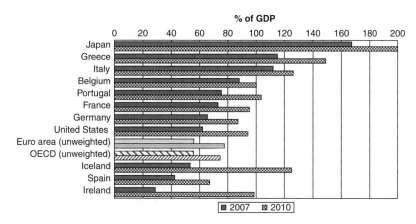

Chart 3.2 Government Gross Debt as a Proportion of GDP, Selected Countries, 2007 and 2010

Source: OECD (2011c).

Since the end of 2010, public debt has continued to increase, even if more recent comparative figures were not available at the time of writing. Could it then be argued that the proportion of the public debt caused by the Great Recession is actually higher than the above figures suggest? No, because most of the economic problems after 2010, when growth had resumed, were caused by the very sovereign debt problem, which provoked a European relapse into recession. Most of the public debt was accumulated before the Great Recession, which pushed European countries above the debt crisis tipping point, which in turn worsened the debt further. The new wave of debt increase was caused not by the Great Recession itself, but by the impact of the growing debt (and by mistaken policy responses). Note that the debt-to-GDP ratios underestimate the importance of the prerecession debt as reduced GDP after the recession boosts the postrecession debt ratios and exaggerate the difference with the dampened prerecession ratios. If we exclude tax evasion and the cooked statistics in Greece, the same structural causes that brought the Greek state to default seem to be at work in other European countries and in America.

What are these causes? The immediate cause lies in the endemic deficits that have developed since the mid-1970s. The deficits were themselves the product of the persistent gap between public expenditures and revenues. Since tax revenues increased, the main blame must be put on the growth of public expenditures. This growth has been a defining characteristic of the twentieth century. Look at a few typical European countries: Austria, France, Germany, Italy, Norway, and Sweden. Around 1870, government expenditures in these countries were between 5 percent and 14 percent of GDP. Northern Europe was closer to the lower limit, France and Italy closer to the top, and Germany and Austria stood about in the middle of the range. Just before the Great Recession, all these countries had public expenditures of over 40 percent of GDP and sometimes over 50 percent. In America, total government expenditures increased from about 8 percent of GDP before World War I to 38 percent in 2007.[15]

State Greed

It is a mistake to think that sovereigns are not greedy. Greed is as much a feature of public life as of private life, even if the public variety is often hidden under the mantle of public welfare.

Sovereigns, like ordinary individuals and corporate bodies, default when it is in their interest to do so. Between 1826 and 1964, the Greek state defaulted five times on its external debt and once on its domestic debt. It was in actual default (that is, in a situation where it had not paid, or settled with, its creditors) during 90 of these 139 years. Its debt as percentage of GDP stood over 150 percent of GDP most of the time from the mid-nineteenth century until the first decade of the twentieth.[16] Although already a model of sorts, Greece did not represent the only greedy state in Europe. Except in the UK, Belgium, and Northern Europe, many central governments defaulted (or rescheduled) at least once between the beginning of the nineteenth century and 2008. The French state did it once, and so did the Dutch and the Italian states, the last two remaining in default during several years. Portugal, Germany, and Austria each defaulted half a dozen times and spent many years in default during each episode. Spain defaulted 13 times and was in default nearly a quarter of the time over the whole period.[17]

Most of these episodes of default occurred in the nineteenth century, but this does not mean that it cannot happen again. In the meantime, two fundamental things have changed in old Europe, which have a bearing on actual and future defaults.

The first major change was the development of the welfare state from the late nineteenth century on. The idea that the state is responsible for the welfare of its citizens or subjects was probably not a creation of the nineteenth century, as many rulers had practiced it before. The wheat and entertainment—*panem et circences*—that Roman emperors made available to the Plebs was an earlier attempt by the sovereign to buy the support of the ruled by providing for their contentment. This Plebs-corruption motive did not completely disappear with the contemporary welfare state. German chancellor Otto von Bismarck, who created the first modern welfare state in the late nineteenth century, wanted the popular classes to trust and support the state. The "Motive" accompanying his first accident insurance bill declared:

> That the state should assist its needy citizens to a greater degree than before is not only a Christian and humanitarian duty, of which the state apparatus should be fully conscious: it is also a task to be undertaken for the preservation of the state itself. The goal of this task is to nurture among the unpropertied classes of the population, which are the most numerous as well as least informed, the view that the state is not only a necessary but also a beneficent institution.[18]

The formalization of the idea that the goal of the state is to maximize the welfare of the population only came with theories of social welfare—especially in the field called "welfare economics" developed in the twentieth century. Activities and expenditures of the state were to be devoted to the population's welfare, or what the sovereign defined as such. Since welfare can always be improved, including the welfare of those threatened by the state itself, public expenditures could go nowhere but up.

The second major change in Europe was the establishment of the EU in 1993 and, in 1999, of a common currency, the euro, for the majority of its member states (now 17 out of 27) and their citizens. Only one major EU country, the UK, remained outside the Eurozone. These developments had been preceded by the creation of the European Coal and Steel Community in 1951 and the European Economic Community in 1957.

Many analysts saw the developing European institutions as the foundation of a free-trade zone. The benefits of free trade are difficult to overestimate. For the same reasons that individuals and their firms should be left free to trade between American States or among regions of France, governments should not prevent them from trading across Europe. Free trade, which is just the name of free exchange across political borders, allows individuals, as consumers, to buy goods and services from the cheapest source and, as producers, to specialize in what they can produce the most cheaply. The result is that any consumer can consume more, given the available resources and what everybody else is consuming—the very definition of economic efficiency. Imagine how less wealthy (or poorer) you would be if you could not exchange what your labor produces with what your suppliers produce. Imagine how handicapped you would be if you could not freely move to another State in America when opportunities call for it. Free exchange is a necessary condition for economic efficiency. Besides the historical fear of wars, there were thus good reasons for the development of supranational institutions in Europe. It is highly questionable whether free trade required the centralized and bureaucratized organization that became the EU, or even if it required a customs union around a free-trade zone, but there is no doubt that the abolition of protectionism among European countries was the goal pursued by many supporters.

From its beginning, however, the movement toward European integration had another, inconsistent thrust. Many promoters aimed at establishing a new supranational state that would do the same things that national states do: determine the conditions under which individuals can exchange and redistribute income from some to others. In other words, they wanted a supranational state apparatus that would regulate commerce and play Robin Hood across the continent. The tension between free trade and central redistribution challenges any federal project; in the United States, it fuels the conflict between State rights and the central government.

A common currency eliminates the foreign exchange risk that stems from changes in the relative prices of different currencies. A currency union, however, is not without problems; it does not by itself solve deep competitiveness and confidence problems. When, say, Germans and Frenchmen used different currencies, the latter's exchange rate (the price of one currency in terms of another) was, by and large, determined on the foreign exchange market, that is, by the interaction of people who wanted to buy francs with marks and those who wanted to sell francs for marks. Any general imbalance between the two economies was reflected in the relative prices of their currencies. If the French wanted to import more from the Germans, the franc would lose value (since it would be sold in order to purchase marks), which would automatically slow down and eventually stop the growth of imports. The lower franc would signal the lower competitiveness of the French economy, which would lead German investors, *ceteris paribus*, to lend less to the French and invest less in France. Lending less to the French meant that the rate of interest on French bonds sold to Germany would have to increase to motivate some Germans to continue lending. Thus, both exchange rates and interest rates cooperated to equilibrate what is called the balance of payments between the two countries.

With the creation of the euro as the common currency, the exchange rate adjustment mechanism stopped working. A single currency freezes the exchange rate, converting a more or less flexible rate into a fixed one. I say "more or less" because central banks often try to manipulate the exchange rate, although they cannot long maintain it at unrealistic levels. The value (that is, the price) of a currency incorporates the degree of market confidence for the economy it encompasses, a fact well connoted by expressions such as "a strong dollar" or "a strong mark." With the abolition of the exchange rate, confidence or lack thereof must be signaled entirely by other indicators: balance of payments surplus of deficits, interest rate levels, employment, and inflation. One price, the exchange rate, does not adjust anymore, increasing the burden of adjustments on other prices and on real quantities (jobs, for example). If the currency does not depreciate to solve a competitiveness problem, wages must fall or unemployment must rise. Abolishing competing currencies does not suppress the reality underlying the information that their relative prices embody. A common currency does not solve balance of payment issues, which are really issues of competitiveness and confidence; it just pushes them under the rug and eliminates one of the mechanisms that can help resolve them. We saw this in the European sovereign debt crisis when capital started fleeing out of troubled countries to be invested in others (including in American government securities). In many cases, the capital flight was simply the result of ordinary people withdrawing their savings to put them in foreign banks.

Another important adjustment mechanism stopped working: the differential yields on sovereign debt. Before the euro, government bonds in different EU countries were priced by financial markets as different financial products, not only because they were typically denominated in different currencies that could rise or fall, but also because their reimbursement clearly depended on the issuing state's financial health. With the euro, investors reasoned that all bonds denominated in euros carried the same little risk and sovereign bonds converged to nearly the same rates. Profligate governments in Greece, Italy, Portugal, or France could now run deficits and accumulate public debt without fear of a rise in the rate of interest at which they were borrowing. A state could live with irresponsible budget policies and avoid the consequences. At worst, its Eurozone neighbors would come to its help, perhaps to preserve the reputation of the euro or to prevent the country from leaving the currency union. But the investors were not fooled forever, and when they finally realized that there was no sacred cow and that subsidies would not necessarily be forthcoming, the spreads between the sovereign bonds widened. The sovereign debt crisis was underway.

It should have been obvious, when the Eurozone was created, that every state's incentives would be to run deficits and dilute their risk in the Eurozone. Eurozone states were like a group of diners ordering food at a restaurant after agreeing that they would split the bill equally: it becomes rational for each diner to indulge in his most expensive tastes, for he will pay only a fraction of the additional cost, and he knows anyway that the others will do it even if he restrains himself. In order to align the incentives correctly, the EU attempted to ceil the deficits of Eurozone states at 3 percent of GDP, but since sovereignty still belongs to European states as opposed to the EU, the attempt did not succeed. The sovereign can do what he wants, cheat as he wills, and for as long as he can—up to a point.

State greed is a defining characteristic of the nation-state. The state tries to protect its citizens' or subjects' interests against the interests of the citizens or subjects of other states. In fact, the state protects the interests of the domestic clienteles he needs the most and, of course, not the interests of everybody, which is impossible: even domestically, the state harms some in order to help others. But I want to emphasize here the external behavior of the state. After the late 2011 EU meeting that decided, over the dissent of the British government, to move along with a new fiscal alliance (overseeing member states' budgets), Prime

Minister David Cameron said it concisely: "I went to Brussels with one objective, to protect Britain's national interest, and this is what I did."[19] The Norwegian state's sovereign wealth fund, which invests revenues from oil taxes, recently announced that it would reduce the proportion of European securities in its portfolio in the hope of increasing returns.[20]

The welfare state is as greedy as any other state. It tries hard to avoid redistributing to clienteles whose support it does not need—foreigners, for example. It uses nationalist sentiments and propaganda to justify this arbitrary solidarity. People prefer to redistribute among themselves—within their families, tribes, ethnic groups, and nations. An appeal to primitive solidarity, redistribution becomes more difficult as the state becomes larger and more supranational, as the empire's borders extend. Citizens who seem to approve redistribution within their own countries, suddenly become less altruistic when the needy—even much poorer than themselves—speak another language and live over some national border. Hence, when it appeared that southern countries would need overt subsidies from the rest of the Eurozone in order to avoid default, the redistributionist rhetoric stopped to work. The majority of Germans, despite their devotion to their own welfare state, were not happy to support the poor Greeks. Why, asked some, would poor Slovaks (from the poorest country in the Eurozone) pay to support the Greeks?[21] A brutal fact was thus revealed: there is no way to maintain both democracy and a vast redistributive empire. A democratic Europe can only survive and prosper as a free-trade zone; the EU is doomed to failure as a pan-European welfare state and subsidy union.

The immediate lessons of the unfolding debt crisis in Europe are pretty clear. Sovereign states are powerful and privileged debtors that will default when they can get away with it. Their current debt problems do not stem mainly from the Great Recession, but have accumulated over decades of greedy profligacy. European welfare states have played a major role in this greedy march of the state.

Public debt can accumulate over decades without apparent detrimental effects, but when it reaches a certain threshold, an avalanche of problems suddenly starts rolling. Carmen Reinhart and Kenneth Rogoff have studied this process for 44 countries over two centuries. They found that when public debt reaches about 90 percent of GDP, economic growth falls, the capacity of the state to raise revenues and service the debt is reduced, and a vicious circle develops where more debt causes lower economic growth, which in turn generates more debt and so on.[22] Japan, Greece, and Italy were already above the 90 percent threshold before the Great Recession, Belgium was very close, Portugal and France were getting there. In 2010, as the Great Recession was replaced by the sovereign debt crisis, several other countries passed the historically fatidic threshold: not only Belgium, Portugal, and France but also Iceland, Ireland, and the United States. The avalanche risk is spreading.

CHAPTER 4

THE HIDDEN WELFARE STATE

Conventional wisdom sees a major difference between Europe and America: European states are welfare states and spend mainly on "social" functions, whereas the American state devotes most of its expenditures to national defense, law and order, and other traditional functions of government. Theda Skocpol, a Harvard University political scientist, is representative of these beliefs when she claims that America is deprived of a European sort of welfare state: "The US," she writes, "has never come close to having a 'modern welfare state' in the British, the Swedish, or any positive Western sense of the phrase."[1] If this is true, we may think that the European sovereign debt problem is due to their welfare state, and that such problem does not threaten America. But these beliefs are at best seriously misleading.

Federal Social Spending

Many people seem to think that federal expenditures go mainly to warfare and to law and order. The federal budget figures are publicly available for anybody to see,[2] and are summarized in my Chart 4.1. In federal budget parlance, expenditures are called outlays, but I will use the terms expenditures and outlays interchangeably. I am presenting the figures for FY 2007 in order to bypass the special problems created by the 2008–2009 recession.

The US federal government spends a fair amount of its budget—20 percent—on national defense. Yet this is still only one dollar out of five, and national defense is not the largest broad category of expenditures, or "function" as they are called in OMB data. On which function does the federal government spend most? The answer may surprise many voters who typically know little about public policy: it is on Social Security, where 22 percent of federal expenditures go, mainly for old-age pensions. Even if we add international affairs to national defense, we don't

	Billions of dollars	% of total expenditures
National defense	551,271	20.2%
International affairs	28,482	1.0%
Natural resources and environment	31,716	1.2%
Agriculture	17,662	0.6%
Transportation	72,905	2.7%
Education, training, employment, and social services	91,656	3.4%
Health (excluding Medicare)	266,382	9.8%
Medicare	375,407	13.8%
Income security	365,975	13.4%
Social Security	586,153	21.5%
Veterans benefits and services	72,818	2.7%
Administration of justice	41,244	1.5%
General government	17,425	0.6%
Net interest on public debt	237,109	8.7%
Others	-27,519	-1.0%
Total	2,728,686	100.0%

Chart 4.1   Outlays by Function, US Federal Government, 2007

Source: OMB (2011b).

get a higher share than for Social Security. To boost national defense at the top, we would need to combine veterans benefits and services (3% of federal expenditures) to defense and international expenditures.

The third highest share of federal government expenditures after Social Security and national defense goes to another welfare-state function: Medicare, the public health insurance program for the elderly, consumes 14 percent of annual federal expenditures. I call "welfare-state function" any function that is necessary for the state to pursue its mission of maximizing the welfare of the population. Welfare-state functions exclude more traditional law and order functions, as well as standard "economic" interventions. And here is another surprise. Adding Medicare to other federal expenditures on health—which comprise mainly Medicaid, the public health insurance program for the poor—takes the percentage up to 24 percent. Together, health and Social Security make up for 46 percent of total expenditures, more than twice what is spent on all national defense and related functions.

We still haven't considered the next largest expenditure function: income security. Besides federal employee retirement and disability (more than one-fourth of the category), this function covers food stamps, housing assistance, and unemployment compensation. Some 13 percent of the federal government's budget is spent on income security. Adding income to Social Security and health (including Medicare) accounts for 58 percent of federal expenditures, which is nearly 150 percent more than national defense expenditures writ large (24% when everything is included).

We may add the function "education, training, employment, and social services," which is clearly part of the welfare-state mission, even if we are so used to government intervention in these fields that they often don't register in our minds as related to the welfare state. Adding them would give us more than 60 percent for the proportion of the federal government's budget spent on welfare-state functions.

Not only does the federal government spend much more on welfare-state sorts of expenditures than on any other sort of program, but the share of these expenditures has also been growing over time. In 1962 (the first year for which these data are reported separately), the federal government spent only 24 percent of its budget on welfare-state functions, compared to 62 percent in 2007. With the recession and the increase in federal income security expenditures, this proportion had jumped to 66 percent by 2010. The federal government now devotes two-thirds of its expenditures to welfare-state functions.

Other federal government expenditures pale into insignificance—although their absolute levels are in the tens of billions of dollars. Everything related to "economic intervention" in a narrow sense—transportation, natural resources, environment, and agriculture—make up for less than 5 percent of expenditures. And note how the administration of justice—all federal law enforcement, federal prisons, and so on—accounts for only 2 percent of federal expenditures. "General government," which includes running Congress and the White House, is even less. (The negative amount in "others" comes from offsetting all remaining federal expenditures with receipts that accompany certain functions, such as the federal employees' contributions to their retirement benefit premiums.)

At 9 percent of federal expenditures, interest on public debt comes right after welfare-state functions and national defense. In 2007, $237 billion or nearly one in every 10 dollars of revenue went to pay interest on the federal debt. Ten percent of what you pay in taxes to the federal government is used to pay interest on past expenditures. This proportion is lower than in many other countries because federal securities are deemed safer, and benefit from much trust from investors. The question is, how long will this last?

Two Welfare States

Federal outlays are only one part of total government expenditures, which also include State and local government expenditures. In 2007, federal expenditures made up nearly two-thirds of the total—including federal grants to State and local governments. In normal times, the federal government subsidizes about one-fifth of State and local expenditures (a proportion that moved closer to one-fourth in the wake of the Great Recession). Viewed another way, State and local governments' expenditures including federal grants make up 45 percent of total government expenditures, but 20 percent (or nine percentage points) of these come from the federal government, bringing State and local expenditures from own source to slightly more than a third of the total. To summarize: on $100 of government expenditures in America, $55 come from the federal government excluding grants to State and local governments, $9 are made up of such grants, and the States and local governments spend $36 from their own revenue sources. To compare the American state with more centralized European states, we of course need to consider public expenditures from all levels of government. This is what Chart 4.2 purports to do.

The chart compares the proportion of expenditures by function in total government expenditures (all level of governments) between

		Euro10	US
1	General public services†	14%	14%
2	Defense	3%	11%
3	Public order and safety	4%	6%
4	Economic affairs	8%	10%
5	Environment protection	2%	*
6	Housing and community amenities	2%	2%
7	Health	14%	21%
8	Recreation; culture and religion	2%	1%
9	Education	11%	17%
10	Social protection	40%	19%
11	*Welfare State expenditures (7+9+10)*	65%	57%
12	*Welfare State expenditures as a proportion of total gov't expenditures in the typical Euro10 country (unweighted)*	63%	

EU10: Austria, Belgium, France, Germany, Ireland, Italy, Luxembourg, Netherlands, Portugal, and Spain.
† Includes interest on public debt
* Not available

Chart 4.2 Government Expenditures by Function, Eurozone and United States, All Levels of Government, in Proportion of Total Government Expenditures, 2007

Source: Database of the Organization for Economic Co-operation and Development, National Accounts, Table 11: Government Expenditure by Function (extracted November 2011).

Europe and America. I use the 2007 figures to focus on the situation before the Great Recession, in more "normal" times. The European countries chosen are the 10 major ones among the 17 in the Eurozone: Austria, Belgium, France, Germany, Ireland, Italy, Luxembourg, the Netherlands, Portugal, and Spain. The other seven Eurozone countries are excluded because no data are available (Cyprus, Estonia, Finland, Greece, Malta, and Slovenia) or, in case of the Slovak Republic, because it is small, only recently a member the EU, and likely not representative of what people generally think of modern Europe. Let's call this group of 10 important Eurozone states "Euro10."[3]

The data of Chart 4.2 are extracted from the international System of National Accounts,[4] which tries to compare broad economic magnitudes (such as GDP) across countries. The national accounts recast government accounts into a more general and consistent form of economic accounting, and recalculates them over the civil year (as opposed to fiscal years). It should be noted that the OECD classification of government functions in Chart 4.2 does not exactly parallel that of the OMB statistics given in Chart 4.1.[5] For example, the OECD's "general public services" include many components absent from the OMB's "general government," such as the interest on public debt and general transfers to States and local government. However, the two classifications are close enough to be consistent with what we know thus far: for example, the proportion of defense expenditures in America drops by about one-half when State and local expenditures are added; on the contrary, public and safety expenditures, which are often financed locally, go up.

In each of the two categories "defense," and "public order and safety," the American state (all levels of government) spends more, relative to total expenditures, than our ten Eurozone countries. Adding "general public services" (which include interest on the public debt), we find that the American state spends 31 percent of its budget compared to 21 percent for the Euro10 in what may be thought of as the traditional missions of the state. Not surprisingly, defense explains virtually all the difference between America and Europe.

The "economic affairs" category includes expenditures on much of what would pass for standard economic intervention: labor, agriculture, fuel and energy, mining, manufacturing and construction, transport, communications, tourism, most R&D, and so on. Slightly more is spent on such interventions in American governments' budgets (10%) than in the budgets of European states (8%). This is not as surprising as it may look: Europeans generally underestimate the extent of intervention and regulation in America, just as Americans often overestimate government intervention in Europe.

The biggest surprise comes again from welfare-state functions. It is true that, if one looks only at social protection expenditures, also known as income support (disability and old-age pensions, welfare, unemployment insurance, housing assistance, and such), Euro10 governments spend twice as much of their budgets (40%) as American governments do (19%). However, income support in cash transfers is not the only function of the welfare state. Another major one is health. Many will be surprised to observe that American governments spend 50 percent more of their budgets on the health function than Euro10 governments: 21 percent versus 14 percent.

The high level of public health expenditures in America is a well-known fact among students of that field. Mainly through Medicare and Medicaid, the American state spends more on public health insurance, as a proportion of GDP, than most countries. Half of health expenditures in America are financed by public programs. The latest OECD figures (which cover the years between 2007 and 2009), show that only in the Netherlands, France, Germany, and Denmark, did public health expenditures exceed the American proportion of 8.3 percent of GDP. The proportion is 7.9 percent in our typical Euro10 country, and 6.6 percent over all OECD countries (including the United States).[6] (Note that these proportions are to GDP, not to budget expenditures as in the previous paragraph.) US governments spend more for health on one-third of their population[7] (the old and the poor) than most other welfare states do to cover all of theirs. Many overlook this fact because they focus on *total* health expenditures, public and private, and assume that the higher American ratio to GDP is explained by private expenditures only.

A few examples may be useful to illustrate the extent of health subsidization by the federal and the State governments. Since the late 1990s, nearly half the births in America have been financed by Medicaid.[8] One out of every two Americans has been delivered with government money! Some 40 percent of long-term care services in America are financed by the same program.[9] The welfare state takes care of people from the cradle to the grave or, to be more precise, from the uterus to the grave. Among the smaller public health programs, CHIP (Children's Health Insurance Program) provides health insurance to children in low-income families.

This is not yet the end of the story. Today's public expenditures in education should also be considered a function of the welfare state. We are far from the days where local governments assured some basic primary education. In proportion of GDP, US governments' spending on primary and secondary education (plus vocational training) has tripled since 1962, while the proportion on higher education has doubled.

Education is now part of what the state does in order to fulfill its official goal of maximizing the welfare of the population, as opposed to merely providing some basic equality of opportunity. As we see in Chart 4.2, more of government budgets go to education in America (17%) than in our Euro10 countries (11%).

Adding up all these functions of the welfare state—social protection, health, and education—we obtain the total welfare-state expenditures calculated on line 11 of the chart. The gap between our Euro10 welfare state and its American correspondent has been reduced to a mere eight percentage points: the first spends 65 percent of its budget on welfare-state functions, the second 57 percent.

The gap is further reduced when we take the unweighted average of the Euro10 countries, shifting from the "average" to the "typical" country. This approach reduces the influence of large countries such as France and Germany, which have higher government expenditures, weigh more the total, and misrepresent the typical country. As shown in line 12 of Chart 4.2, our typical Eurozone state spends 63 percent of its budget on welfare-state functions, instead of the 65 percent calculated when larger countries skew the average. Thus, only a six-percentage-point difference (between 63% and 57%) separates the proportion of money spent on welfare-state expenditures in the typical Eurozone country and America; or, we may say, the European welfare state is only 10 percent larger in Europe than in America. There is even one Euro10 country where welfare-state expenditures are lower than in America: the ratio is 52 percent in Portugal.

It is thus not necessary to invoke tax expenditures (tax deductions for private health insurance, mortgage interest, etc.) or more progressive American taxes to conclude that America has a welfare state comparable to Europe's. At any rate, these arguments would only strengthen my claim.[10]

Some welfare-state expenditures are not included in lines 11 and 12 of Chart 4.2. I have neglected the function "housing and community amenities" because it includes expenditures such as water supply and street lighting, which, although they could conceivably be privatized, can also be thought as characterizing the night-watchman state, the opposite of the welfare state. Thus, my totals do not include some welfare-state activities like housing development. I have also chosen not to include expenditures on "recreation, culture and religion," even if many of those, such as support for recreational activities and perhaps public broadcasting, respond to the mission of the welfare state. Including the neglected expenditures would not change my comparative results in any significant way.

These results call for some caveats. Since the total expenditures of the average Euro10 state correspond to a higher proportion of GDP than do government expenditures in America, the gap gets amplified when welfare-state expenditures are compared directly to GDP. It can be calculated that (in 2007), welfare-state expenditures were 30 percent of GDP in our Euro10 countries compared to 21 percent in America. The 10 percent gap calculated previously is thus amplified to a 43 percent difference (30 percent is 43 percent higher than 21 percent). Moreover, the political culture remains less welfare-statist in America than in Europe. The American welfare state is far from obliterated, but one could say that the glass is half full.

These caveats are, in turn, attenuated by the fact that a generally higher GDP per capita in America implies that lower social expenditures as a proportion of GDP often translate into higher amounts in actual dollars. Peter Baldwin, a historian at UCLA, reports that social expenditures per capita in US dollars (corrected for purchasing power parities) are higher in America than in Portugal, Greece, Spain, Ireland, and Iceland. (The correction for purchasing power parities, or PPP, aims at compensating for higher consumer prices in Europe, as opposed to simply converting euros to US dollars at the prevalent foreign exchange rate.) US governments spend less welfare-state money in proportion of GDP, but the fact that GDP is higher in America means that recipients end up with more actual subsidies—or with paying more actual taxes in dollars.[11]

All this said, three important facts remain:

1. Before the Great Recession, all governments in America spent on welfare-state functions only slightly less of their budgets (57%) than the typical Eurozone country (63%).
2. Even if the weight of welfare-state expenditures was lower in the American economy than in Europe—21 percent of GDP compared to 30 percent—the allocation to the welfare state of one dollar out of every five that people produce and earn is very significant. And this sometimes means higher support in actual money for the American recipient than for his European counterpart.
3. As I measured the welfare state above, the recent trend has been toward a slight increase of its relative size in America. From 1995 (last available data) to 2007, the American welfare state has gained one percentage point in GDP whereas our typical European government has lost one.

The Look and Feel of the Welfare State

Beyond detailed statistical comparisons, the American state has the look and feel of a welfare state. Differences between the state in Europe and in America are often exaggerated, by both Europeans and Americans. Peter Baldwin calls this "the narcissism of minor differences."[12] For example, the richest 10 percent pay a higher proportion of income tax revenues in America than in all major European countries, and these taxes are more progressive in America than in most of these countries. The effective tax rate on corporations is higher in the United States than in any of the major countries in Europe, although France and Germany come close. It has been estimated that 49 percent of the American population lives in households receiving government benefits through either means-tested or general programs.[13]

Similarities sometimes become more striking if, instead of comparing the whole diversified America with Europe, we compare individual American states with European countries. Other surprises await us. Minimum wages (calculated in dollars corrected with PPP) in Washington, Oregon, Connecticut, and Vermont are higher than in France and all major European countries; Maine is not far behind France. Such examples are not representative of the general situation of Europe and America, but they suggest that, in certain American States, the welfare state is even more similar to the European variety. In Vermont and Maine, private health insurance companies have long been forbidden from discriminating among customers according to their health condition, providing a sort of public health insurance to whoever is willing to pay for it.[14] Except for redistribution as a function of income and age, the price the insured pay is then similar to what participants in a public regime pay through contributions and taxes. In fact, it may very well be lower because of the superior efficiency of market competition over bureaucratic processes. Moreover, the State of Vermont offers its own health insurance programs to uninsured residents.[15] Since 2006, the State of Massachusetts imposes an individual mandate to purchase health insurance, with subsidies to those who cannot afford it.[16] Any American who, because of his health condition, is unable to obtain affordable health insurance can solve his problem by moving to one of those States. This diversity was part of the genius of American federalism, until Barack Obama tried to impose nation-wide uniformity with a federal regime copied on Massachusetts.

The recognition that the American welfare state has been converging to the European model has made headways in academic circles. Welfare states "are increasingly dominated by pension and health expenditures,"[17] observes Jens Alber, a German social scientist. He also observes that "once the impact of taxes and publicly mandated schemes is taken into account, the US no longer falls far behind most European countries."[18] The title of a 1997 book by Christopher Howard, a professor at the College of William and Mary, emphasizes that America is a "hidden welfare state."[19] Howard correctly includes education in the functions of the welfare state.

Differences exist between America and Europe, but they must not be exaggerated. The welfare state is less extensive in America, but it is more a question of degree than a difference in kind. The American welfare state relies more on selective, means-tested income transfers, as opposed to automatic benefits. In America, people are expected to support themselves, and don't have a guaranteed access to a minimum income financed by the state. This has become more obvious with the American reforms of the last few decades, which, in many States, prevent individuals from being long-term welfare recipients. In fact, the same trend toward more selective social programs and a new emphasis on individual responsibility have recently appeared in Europe, and Jens Alber detects a convergence in policy discourse between the two sides of the Atlantic. No doubt the trend toward selectivity will continue as the exploding public debt creates pressure for budget austerity, both in America and in Europe.

Convergence

If the differences between America and Europe are exaggerated, if the welfare state is similar on both sides of the Atlantic, when did the convergence occur? The late economist Harold Vatter argued that the mixed economy, of which he was a fan, appeared in America with Franklin D. Roosevelt's New Deal of 1933. The mixed economy is a mix of capitalism and socialism and, in Vatter's own evaluation, is closely related to the welfare state: his characterization of the mixed economy include "an absolute and relative jump in government expenditures and transfer payments to persons ... a vast socialization of material security for the individual, a distinct drop in the importance of 'private consumption'" (in favor of government-decided consumption in health, social services, etc.).[20]

On the road of the welfare state, Vatter cites the Employment Act of 1946 which "reflected a new, transformed outlook."[21] This law declared that "it is the continuing policy and responsibility of the Federal Government ... to promote maximum employment, production, and purchasing power."[22] The Keynesian state is a natural ally of the welfare state, for managing the business cycle—cycles of booms and bust—is deemed necessary to guarantee the population's total welfare. Recall that Keynes wanted government to fine-tune the economy with fiscal and monetary policy in order to maintain full employment. The

1966 *Report of the Council of Economic Advisers* (CEA) lauded the success of the new policies:

> Twenty years of experience have demonstrated our ability to avoid ruinous inflations and severe depressions. It is now within our capabilities to set more ambitious goals. We strive to avoid recurrent recessions, to keep unemployment far below the rates of the past decade, to maintain essential price stability at full employment, to move towards the Great Society, and, indeed, to make full prosperity the normal state of the American economy. It is a tribute to our success under the Employment Act that we now have not only the economic understanding but also the will and determination to use economic policy as an effective tool of progress.[23]

Further experience was to show that these self-congratulations were presumptuous.

Although data are sparse, we can get a glimpse at how the American welfare state has grown by considering the evolution of social benefits to persons, shown on Chart 4.3. These data mainly comprise government expenditures on Social Security, Medicare, Medicaid, and unemployment benefits; they do not include education and, in general, have a smaller coverage than the OECD's comparative data examined on Chart 4.2. However, the data on social benefits to persons have the advantage of going back to 1929, contrary to other statistical series available. I consider the ratio of these expenditures to GDP (bottom curve) and to total government expenditures (top curve). The two measures generally move together, and the choice between them depends on what one wants to focus on and on what the growth of GDP or the growth of expenditures reveal or hide.

From 1929 (the year when the Great Depression began) to 1933 (the trough of the depression), the share of social benefits to persons in GDP was multiplied by three. Both a GDP drop and an increase in the actual amounts of social benefits explain this evolution. The amount of social benefits in dollars (not shown on the chart) increased by more than 40 percent, which corresponds to an even steeper increase in constant dollars as prices dropped during the depression. So Vatter is not totally right to say that the American welfare state was born in 1933, for it had already started under the Hoover Administration (1929–1933). With Roosevelt, social expenditures doubled again in dollars over a few years. By 1936, social benefits had reached 3.2 percent of GDP, four times the 1929 ratio.

Not too much significance should be put on the fluctuation of the curves between 1936 and the end of World War II in 1945. The ratio

Chart 4.3   Social Benefits to Persons, United States, 1929–2010

Source: BEA, National Income and Product Accounts, Table 3.1: Government Current Receipts and Expenditures (extracted December 8, 2011).

of a value to GDP has the advantage of showing some perspective, but carries the corresponding drawback of being subject to changes in the denominator. In dollars, social benefits remained approximately constant throughout the war. In 1945, the last year of the war, however, veterans' benefits pushed up the ratio of social benefits to GDP. In 1946, the ratio had increased by 40 percent more than its New Deal peak. This was the second jump of social benefits in relation to GDP. With ups and downs due mainly to the business cycle, the ratio maintained this level until the mid-1960s. By that time, veterans' benefits had started easing, but the Social Security system, created in 1935, was costing more and more.

The chart shows clearly the third era of growth in social benefits, which lasted from the mid-1960s to the mid-1970s, when the ratio of these benefits to GDP doubled. From 1965 to 1975, social benefits paid to individuals in America climbed from 4.7 percent to 10 percent of

GDP. Fuelled by Lyndon B. Johnson's "war on poverty" and "Great Society" programs, payments of social benefits quintupled in dollar value. Medicare and Medicaid were created in 1965. Social Security expenditures more than tripled, unemployment insurance benefits went up eightfold. On our chart, the growth of the American welfare state is also easily visible in the ratio of social benefits to total government expenditures. Although not confined to America, the growth of the welfare state during the 1960s and 1970s remains striking.

The American welfare state moved more slowly between the mid-1970s and the onset of the 2007–2009 Great Recession. The ratio of social benefits to GDP was still on an upward trend, though, and reached 12 percent in 2007. Since GDP grew briskly over most of that period, the creeping-up can be seen better in the ratio of social benefits to total government expenditures, which increased from 33 percent to 38 percent between 1975 and 2007. Recall that education expenditures and social expenditures that are not directly paid to individuals are not included in the measures under consideration here: all welfare-state functions included, the ratio would be closer to the 57 percent of Chart 4.2.

As obvious from Chart 4.3, the Great Recession will have marked the fourth great push of the American welfare state. In 2010, social benefits paid to individuals amounted to more than 15 percent of GDP. On each dollar produced and earned in the economy, the American welfare state took $0.15 in taxes and redistributed it in direct support to some individuals.

To summarize, some of the growth of the American welfare state occurred in the 1930s, but a major episode occurred in the 1960s and 1970s, and another steep climb can be observed during the recent recession. No surprise that today's American welfare state is not as different from European welfare states as most people imagine.

The growth in the welfare-state expenditures explains almost all the growth in government expenditures at least since the 1950s. In relation to GDP, other expenditures have decreased. Consequently, the growth of the public debt is traceable to the growth of the welfare state. Two economists from the Federal Reserve Bank of St. Louis, Kevin L. Kliesen and Daniel L. Thornton, summarize their research on this topic:

> This analysis suggests that the increase in the debt over the period 1975–2007 was not only a consequence of increased government spending without increased revenues, but also that the government increased payments to individuals through Social Security, Medicare, and other payments without sufficiently reducing spending elsewhere in the budget.[24]

Rational Ignorance

Why do so many Americans ignore where their own government spend their money? Why don't they see how they have a welfare state that differs only in degree from its European counterpart? All the information is available. Information on governments' expenditures and other activities has always been easy to find especially in America, and the revolution in information technology has made it even more accessible. Equipped with a computer, one can theoretically find all the information I have presented in this chapter. For the technophobe with more time on his hands, the information is available in public libraries.

The solution to the conundrum of public ignorance in the midst of a plethora of information is, on reflection, quite simple. Economists call it "rational ignorance."

Information has a cost in the sense that its production uses real resources (labor, equipment, etc.) that could be used to produce something else that people value; this is why some information is not produced. Information—even those already produced—also costs something to the consumer, either in terms of a price to reimburse information producers (books and many databases come at a price) or, when a third party like government pays, in terms of the time and expertise necessary to find, read, and understand what's available. When something has a price, either in terms of money or time, the quantity demanded of it is not infinite. Once produced and made available, information will only be accessed by those individuals who think the benefits are worth the cost. This cost may be high. Retrieving BEA (Bureau of Economic Analysis) information from the Web carries a low cost if you know what you are looking for. You do need a computer and Internet access, but once this is paid for, the *marginal* (that is, additional) cost of retrieving the information you are looking for is only a few minutes of your time. But for this to be true, one has to know what information exactly one needs and how to interpret it. This may take several hours if not days of study. Sometimes, a graduate degree in economics may be necessary, which makes for a high fixed cost. For the ordinary citizen, these high costs will be paid only if the benefits are worth it.

Now, what are, for the ordinary citizen, the benefits of understanding where the state spends his money and how that compares to other countries in the world? In most people's preferences, the benefits are so infinitesimally small that they are nil for all practical purposes. Consider the following. When an individual buys a car, he has an incentive to pay for information up to a certain point, for he will then be better able to make the best decision in accordance with his preferences and budget, and thereby gain a direct benefit for himself. The more information he gets, the higher the likelihood he will get the car that is just right for him. Once the supplementary benefits are not worth the additional costs, he will stop inquiring, and buy the car. The situation is very different in politics. Whatever information he obtains, the ordinary citizen still has only one vote. Only if there would have been a tie without his vote will his information actually get him what he wants. Otherwise, his vote is wasted. An individual vote is wasted if it did not break a tie. But the probability that, without an individual vote, there will be a tie in a general election is tiny, and the more voters there are, the tinier it is. In practice, a tie never happens. We can, on the basis of some realistic hypothesis and using probability theory, calculate that, with an electorate of ten million voters, the probability of a tie is equal to a number much lower than one divided by the number of elementary particles in the universe—a probability so small that it is, for all practical purposes, undistinguishable from zero.[25]

Contrary to the pundit, the high-level activist, or the organized interest group, the ordinary citizen-voter has no influence on political outcomes and, thus, will gain no benefit from paying the cost of information on public issues. Of course, many voters taken together may have an influence, depending on their number. But a rational individual only acts when his own action can change the result toward what he wants. A voter has no chance of doing this, no more than a grocery shopper can hope to change the market price of tomatoes if he buys one more. Hence, the ordinary citizen remains rationally ignorant and votes blind. Examples of this are everywhere.

It is true that benefits are subjective, and that they don't need to translate into an action being decisive in the results of an election or referendum. Even if one has no impact on an election result, one may like to play the game. A grocery shopper may buy one more tomato because he likes them. An individual may enjoy expressing himself through voting, or he may find it fun to cheer with a crowd, but little information is necessary for that purpose. Some individuals may consider information good by itself, and derive pleasure from pursuing knowledge and the truth—the reason why you are probably reading this book. But this does not change the fact that no voter has any incentive to get political information *in order to* change the political outcome of the vote. Ignorance of information is built into the system. A political information deficit is unavoidable.

Hence the typical voter is not really interested to know that three-fifths of government expenditures in America go to welfare-state activities, or that there is not, from that point of view, a big difference between Europe and America. This is why this book will not be a best seller—and if it is, it will be for other reasons than my readers wanting to influence electoral results.

How American governments spend taxpayers' money does, however, have a direct bearing on the public debt situation. We are back to the issue raised in the beginning of this chapter. If the welfare state, which explains the growth of government expenditures, is nearly as developed in America as it is in Europe, should we not expect the sovereign debt problem to be, or to become, as severe here as it is there?

CHAPTER 5

FEDERAL OUTLOOK: THE NAKED EMPEROR

Prediction is difficult, especially about the future.

—Unknown author

The epigraph above is often attributed to the late Danish physicist Niels Bohr, but some claim that it was authored by his fellow citizen cartoonist Robert Storm Petersen or by American novelist Mark Twain. The humor comes from the fact that scientist do try to predict both the past and the future, and that they are indeed more successful in the former than in the latter. The failure at predicting the future is especially notable in the social sciences, but is not unique to them: although physicists regularly hit the mark, astronomers and meteorologists, to name only those, are often far off.

Predicting the past is the standard method of scientific inquiry. The method consists in formulating a theory that aims at predicting what happens if certain conditions are met, say, what happens if demand increases while supply is constant. But man does not live by logic alone, and theories must in some way be tested to make sure that their conclusions are consistent with reality. Consequently, the scientist collects data about past episodes when demand increased and other things remained more or less constant, and checks whether price and quantity supplied increased as predicted by the theory. In other words, he checks if his theory predicts the past correctly. Only then can he hope that it will correctly predict the future.

Predicting the future is difficult because we must be sure that the same cause and the same environment obtain. Thus, the future is often surprising, especially in social affairs. So will be the evolution of the sovereign debt problem. Between the time these lines are written, in the early spring of 2012, and the time this book hits the bookstores, new events will occur that will modify the predictions reported or made here. The present, which is the future of the past, is already surprising. Who would have said that the European and the American public debt would become so problematic? Yet, we have good reasons to believe that some general predictions are very likely to materialize, just as other economists were able forecast that the abolition of the budget equilibrium constraint would lead to mounting deficits and public debt (see chapter 2). At least we can point to the dangers ahead.

Uncle Sam's Solvency in Doubt

For a few years, economists have been warning about the impending catastrophe in the US federal debt and other future obligations. In 2003, Jagadeesh Gokhale, then a Fed economist, and Ken Smetters, who was deputy assistant secretary for economic policy at the Treasury Department, published a book estimating the size of the "fiscal imbalance" of the federal government; they reviewed their estimates in a 2006 article.[1] The fiscal imbalance is the present value of the difference between forecasted federal expenditures and revenues, taking into account all actual debts and assets of the federal government. It includes not only the debt held by the public but also the commitments that the government has made through Social Security and Medicare. The two economists calculated that, by 2010, the fiscal imbalance would amount to $79 trillion (in dollars of 2004), or about five times today's GDP.

Another economist on record is Laurence Kotlikoff, professor of economics at the University of Boston, who in 2006 published an article nowhere else than in the journal of the Federal Reserve Bank of St. Louis.[2] Kotlikoff closely analyzed the federal government's solvency, relying partly on data from Gokhale and Smetters. The title of Kotlikoff's article asked the blunt question, "Is the United States Bankrupt?" (he meant of course "the United States government"). His answer was that "the U.S. government is, indeed, bankrupt, insofar as it will be unable to pay its creditors."[3] "Countries can and do go bankrupt," he wrote. "The United States...seems clearly headed down that path."[4] In the fall of 2012, Kotlikoff declared that in effect the debt problem of the US government is worse than that of the Greek state.[5]

Other economists have issued similar warnings; Jeffrey Rogers Hummel of San Jose State University is foremost among them.[6] He believes that it is likely "that the United States will be driven to an outright default on Treasury securities, openly reneging on interest due on its formal debt and probably repudiating part of the principal," He suggests that "the unwinding could move very fast, much like the sudden collapse of the Soviet Union." In early 2012, *The Economist* echoed these fears as voiced in a Mercatus Center symposium.[7]

Official Forecasts of Insolvency

Such dire appraisals are supported by the official calculations of two independent agencies of the US government, the CBO and the GAO, which were already mentioned in chapter 2. The GAO is an independent executive agency created in 1921 with an auditing mission, and is run by the comptroller general of the United States. The CBO is a nonpartisan agency created by Congress in 1974 to provide objective analyses of programs covered by the federal budget. The predictions of these agencies are realized with economic models which are mathematical representations of the multiple interactions among budget components and the general economy. Past data give the parameters of the models' equations—for example, by how much have health-care expenditures increased with incomes. Future conditions of the environment are then adjusted—for example, how is health-care technology likely to evolve—and the model is run on a computer to simulate the effect of the changed conditions and the passage of time. One can visualize such a model as a number-crunching machine that takes as input what basic future conditions are forecasted to be, simulates the evolution of the economy on this basis, and produces as output a set of predictions for expenditures, revenues, deficit, and debt, over a number of years in the future. The number-crunching machine is more sophisticated than tea leaves, but it depends on the data fed to it and on the theories with which it crunches the data. The future will still hold surprises, but modeling at least forces us to think about it in an organized way. Official economic forecasters are prudent with their predictions, emphasizing their uncertainty. Yet, the CBO's and GAO's projections provide an official admission of the coming (if not actual) insolvency of the federal government of the United States.

Every year, the CBO publishes a long-term budget outlook, which makes predictions to 10, 25, and 75 years in the future.[8] The CBO presents two different scenarios, one called the "extended-baseline scenario," and the other one, the "alternative fiscal scenario." The GAO entertains similar, but not identical, scenarios, which also bear similar names.[9] For example, GAO is less optimistic than CBO on the future increase of health-care costs. In this chapter, I rely mainly on the CBO's crystal ball, adding some GAO numbers when the other agency is silent. The picture of the future they paint is bleak, even when painted with the rosier colors of the most optimistic scenario.

The first scenario (called extended-baseline) is the most optimistic. It assumes that Congress will maintain current law as is, extending today's baseline. On the revenue side, the temporary tax cuts enacted since 2001 will expire as planned, thereby generating large revenue increases as economic growth (hopefully) returns to its long-long trajectory. In this scenario, the CBO assumes that "many adjustments that law-makers have routinely made in the past—such as changes to the AMT and to the Medicare program's payments to physicians—will not be extended again."[10] The extended-baseline scenario also assumes that Medicare expenditures and the subsidies to buyers of health insurance in the new federal exchanges (created by the Affordable Care Act of 2010, or "Obamacare") will be relatively well controlled as the government claims so. When the higher revenues and the better-controlled expenditures start to materialize in a few years, the primary budget deficit will be more or less eliminated, and the federal debt as a proportion of GDP will stop increasing. ("Primary" surplus or deficit and primary spending exclude the interest on the public debt. The existence of a primary surplus indicates that at least part of the interest is paid out of current revenues and does not need to be added on top of the previous debt.) The extended-baseline projections suggest that in three-quarters of a century (in 2085) the federal debt held by the public will have stabilized at 84 percent of GDP, compared to 69 percent in 2011 and an average of 37 percent over the past 40 years. By then, federal revenues—that is, essentially federal taxes—will have gradually increased to 30 percent of GDP, from their average of 18 percent over the past 40 years. As the average tax take over GDP represents the overall average tax rate on people's incomes, this means that the federal average tax rate will have increased by two-thirds (from 18% to 30%).

The second scenario, called alternative fiscal scenario or simply alternative scenario in CBO's jargon, presents an even bleaker outlook. It is more realistic because it assumes that what will remain unchanged is the sort of budget policies that have been followed over the past few decades, not necessarily current law with its temporary extensions. As the CBO admits, "many analysts believe that the alternative fiscal scenario presents a more realistic picture of the nation's underlying fiscal policy than the extended-baseline scenario does."[11] The alternative fiscal scenario, the CBO explains, "incorporates several changes to current law that are widely expected to occur or that would modify some provisions of law that might be difficult to sustain for a long period."[12] The alternative scenario is thus a policy-constant, instead of a law-constant, scenario. It's a good idea: in today's world, where the "lawmakers" compulsively create and change laws all the time, there is no such thing as constant law. In the alternative scenario, the temporary tax cuts that have been extended many times will continue to be extended, so that the global effective tax rate (tax revenues over GDP) remains at 18 percent. In fact, they have already been extended again since the CBO's 2011 forecast. As for the major federal expenditures, they will continue to grow with GDP as before. Consequently, the public debt and the interest paid on it will continue their upward trend.

Chart 5.1 depicts this alternative CBO scenario for 2021 and 2035. For 2085, the CBO stopped providing a forecast for interest spending, saying that the debt-to-GDP ratio will be "greater than 200 percent in 2037 and later."[13] For that year, I use instead the GAO's estimates. Since the GAO is more pessimistic than the CBO, mixing up the CBO and GAO forecasts this way is not methodologically correct, but it fills some blanks left by the CBO and helps think through the issues. This combined forecast points to a very difficult future indeed.

Federal government spending was 21 percent of GDP in 2007, before the Great Recession. Fueled by social expenditures related to the economic slowdown that started at the end of 2007 and by the stagnation of GDP, the ratio was up to 24 percent in 2010 and stayed roughly the same in 2011. Federal spending is forecasted to continue creeping up by another two percentage points during the next ten years, and then at an accelerating rate as the deficit increases and compounded interest piles up. By 2035, total federal spending is predicted to reach 34 percent of GDP. By 2085, nearly half of federal government expenditures would be devoted to paying interest to holders of the debt, and their total would amount to 75 percent of GDP, or three-fourths of everything American residents produce and earn. This ratio of spending to GDP is much higher than anything experienced in developed countries. America would not be America anymore.

	Past 40 years	2011	2021	2035	2085
Total spending	19%	24%	26%	34%	75%
Of which: Interest on debt held by the public	–	1%	4%	9%	45%
Revenues	18%	15%	18%	18%	18%
Deficit	-1%	-9%	-8%	-16%	-57%
Debt held by the public	37%	69%	101%	187%	929%

Chart 5.1 Official Forecasts for the Federal Government (Proportions of GDP)

Source: Alternative scenario, CBO (2011a) and GAO (2012), with online data from respectively Fall 2011 and Spring 2012. Forecasts for 2021 and 2035 are from CBO; the 2085 column is from GAO—see text.

What are the underlying expenditures that would push total spending to such levels? Under the two CBO scenarios, all the projected growth in primary spending comes from Social Security and health programs (Medicare, Medicaid, CHIP, and the insurance subsidies that will be provided by Obamacare). Until 2035, 80 percent of the increase will come from health programs. The increase in the cost of these programs is caused by the aging of the population, and the growth of health-care cost per capita regardless of age; until 2035, both factors exert the same influence on the growth of the programs but, from then on, the second one accounts for a larger share of the increase as the proportion of old people stabilizes.

As for the differences between the two scenarios—the alternative scenario represented in Chart 5.1 and the extended-baseline scenario—the major one is the assumption by the latter that the federal government will ration health care by reducing payments to doctors treating Medicare patients and by limiting the growth of insurance subsidies on federal exchanges. In both scenarios, Social Security will be in similar trouble. Since 2010, the system has been paying out more than the contributions it takes in. Its trust funds (funds in which contributions are put and from which pensions are paid) are thus diminishing and will, under both CBO scenarios, be exhausted during the 2030s. From then on, the Social Security Administration will have no legal authority to pay the full benefits to the 97 million individuals who will be entitled to them. The demise of Social Security in about a quarter of a century gives an idea of the looming catastrophe.

In the alternative scenario presented on Chart 5.1, the overall federal tax rate is assumed to stay constant. As a consequence, the jump in federal expenditures is bound to create an unsustainable level of debt. Consider the increase in primary spending from 23 percent of GDP in 2011, a level that already seems unsustainable, to more than 25 percent in 2035, and 30 percent in 2085. This increase will have to be financed exclusively with debt, since revenues are assumed ceiled at their historical rate of 18 percent of GDP. Imagine a family borrowing to buy a car, never making any payment either to reimburse the capital or to pay any interest: the capital due would increase every year by the interest arrears. Assume moreover that the family continues to spend more than it earns, even not counting the accumulating interest. No creditor would let this happen, of course, and such a profligate family would soon face bankruptcy. This is the situation of the federal government. But the sovereign cannot go bankrupt. According to the official forecasts of Chart 5.1, the federal debt held by the public will hit 101 percent of GDP in less than ten years, which is close to its 113 percent peak of World War II and to Greece's 115 percent just before the Great Recession; in 2035, about 25 years from now, the federal debt will amount to 187 percent of GDP; and it will reach to a staggering 929 percent in 2085, higher than in any country today, and quite probably much more than any sovereign has ever been able to reach.

To avoid such an unsustainable federal debt, either expenditures have to be cut or taxes increased. In its extended-baseline scenario (the "optimistic" one), which assumes that existing law will continue to apply, the CBO calculates that expenditures would increase a bit less than in the alternative scenario, and that automatic tax increases would fill most of the gap. In that scenario, the ratio of federal debt to GDP is stabilized at 75 percent by 2085, which is still high but only marginally higher than the current 69 percent. It is worth noting that the CBO's extended-baseline scenario used to be more pessimistic: in the 2009 and 2010 outlooks, the 2085 debt held by the public reached 283 percent and 113 percent respectively. Congress's 2011 efforts at controlling future expenditures explain the new optimism. Yet, this optimistic case assumes that federal revenues in proportion of GDP increase by two-thirds, that is from the historical 18 percent of GDP to an incredible 30 percent.

This increase in the global federal tax rate would happen automatically, under existing law (the extended-baseline scenario), for several reasons. First, the tax system is built in such a way that, even without inflation, economic growth automatically brings taxpayers into higher tax brackets and thus higher tax rates. If you earn more, your federal income taxes increase more than proportionally to your income as you change brackets by the effect of progressivity. The income tax is largely indexed to inflation, but increases in real income (after inflation) do push the taxpayers to higher brackets.

Second, there is the Alternative Minimum Tax (AMT) enacted in 1969. Except for temporary offsets adopted in extremis and renewed ad hoc by Congress, the AMT catches a larger and larger number of taxpayers as time passes. The AMT is a parallel income tax system meant to ensure that taxpayers who take advantage of the many deductions, exemptions, and other loopholes created by Congress itself don't end up paying less than a minimum federal income tax rate. It's a bit like if Congress said: "You can reduce your 30 percent average tax rate if you have more children, support higher medical bills, give to charities, and so on; but if you reduce it to less than 26 percent, you have to pay the AMT of 26 percent (28% after a certain threshold)." The AMT does just that: it establishes a sort of minimum rate (26%) on taxable income, and the taxpayer has to pay the highest of the AMT rate or the rate calculated through the ordinary income tax calculations. To further illustrate the complexity of the system, the AMT rate is limited to 15 percent on long-term capital gains and qualified dividend income. Most taxpayers don't know all this because, in 2011, only 3 percent of taxpayers had to pay the AMT rate. The trick is hidden behind tax calculations, especially if one uses tax software. The AMT system was adopted because it was perceived as a tax-the-rich measure—and because, as usual, citizens remain ignorant of such complicated matters. But as incomes increase, more and more taxpayers are pushed over the AMT threshold (or "exemptions"), which is around $100,000. This applies even if increases in income are merely nominal, that is, caused by inflation, as the parameters of the AMT are not indexed. It is to postpone biting tax increases generated by the AMT that higher temporary exemptions have been granted through annual "patches" voted by Congress.[14] Since the extended-baseline scenario assumes that temporary measures like these patches will not continue, the AMT would catch more and more taxpayers. Just by the normal increase in nominal revenues, part of which comes from inflation, half of taxpayers would be considered rich and fall under the AMT in 2035. The AMT is quite a vicious system for the taxpayer; for the government and its creditors, it is a bonus that would help much in stabilizing the public debt in relation to GDP.

A third component of the federal tax system that has benefited from temporary breaks over the past few years is the Social Security payroll tax. This tax generally represents 12.4 percent of taxable earnings, split evenly between employer and employee, except for the temporary reduction of two percentage points granted to employees in 2011 (and 2012). The optimistic—extended-baseline—scenario assumes that all such temporary breaks will not be continued.

Current law, then, would automatically produce much higher tax revenues if the extended-baseline scenario comes to pass. The average federal tax rate would increase by about 17 percent in the next ten years (from 18% to 21%), and then by another 50 percent (to 31%) by 2085. This result would be obtained automatically if the federal government did nothing but just maintained current tax law. Give Leviathan an inch, he will take a mile.

Would such large tax increases be politically feasible? Could the political system, by persuasion or by force, bring Americans to obey? Since World War II, federal receipts have very rarely exceeded 20 percent; as we saw, the average over the past 40 years has been 18 percent. Even at the peak of World War II, it did not reach over 21 percent. It is difficult to believe that Americans would accept to pay more than this on a permanent basis. Indeed, this is why the alternative scenario depicted in Chart 5.1 appears more realistic to many.

Another way to look at the situation is to use CBO's and GAO's data on the so-called fiscal gap. The fiscal gap is the difference between the present value of all future (over the next 75 years) revenues and expenditures of the federal government if the ratio of the federal debt to GDP is to be kept constant. In the alternative scenario, the fiscal gap is estimated at 8 percent of GDP, which means that closing the gap would cost 8 percent of total GDP (in present value) over the period considered, either with higher taxes or with reduced spending. This (rounded) estimate is the one provided by both the CBO's 2011 long-term budget outlook and by the GAO's 2012 long-term fiscal outlook (the latest available outlooks at the time of writing).[15] This estimate is close to the 9 percent "fiscal imbalance" estimated by Gokhale and Smetters.[16] Fiscal-gap calculations are especially useful as they take into account all promised expenditures, and not just the recorded deficits and official debt.

The CBO and the GAO calculate the immediate and permanent increase in revenues as proportion of GDP (which we can call the global tax rate) or the immediate and permanent decrease in primary spending that would be needed to close the fiscal gap. The two agencies arrive at different numbers because they make different estimates for the future profile of tax revenues, outlays, and debt growth (the GAO's outlook is slightly more pessimistic), but the differences are relatively small. From the CBO's figures, it can be seen that eliminating the fiscal gap to 2085 would require an immediate and permanent cut of 31 percent in noninterest spending or, alternatively, an increase of 44 percent in revenues (that is, in the global tax rate, since this is what revenue over GDP corresponds to). The GAO's estimates are respectively 32 percent and 46 percent. It's worth quoting the GAO's report:

> For example, under our Alternative simulation, the fiscal gap is 8.2 per-cent of GDP (see table 1). This means that, on average over the next 75 years, revenue would have to increase by more than 45 percent or noninterest spending would have to be reduced by about 32 percent (or some combination of the two) to keep debt held by the public at the end of the period from exceeding its level at the beginning of 2012 (roughly 68 percent of GDP). Even-more significant changes would be needed to reduce debt to lower levels.[17]

The CBO emphasizes that its own estimates convey what is required as "an immediate and permanent reduction is spending or increase in revenues,"[18] and this is apparently what the GAO's estimates also represent. Both agencies stress that the changes will have to be larger if they are not made immediately (in 2011 or 2012), and that the more they are delayed, the bigger they will need to be.

These figures are consistent with a rougher sort of estimate that disregards present values and *immediate* changes, to focus instead on the *ultimate* revenue boost or spending cut that will be needed to close the fiscal gap. Chart 5.1 suggests that the ratio of federal revenues to GDP would have to rise to 30 percent in 2085 from its historical figure of 18 percent, in order to cover primary expenditures amounting to 30 percent of GDP (that is, 75% minus interest payments); this would mean an eventual increase in the global tax rate of 67 percent (compared to the immediate increase of 44%–46% reported above). Alternatively, if the growing gap between revenues and expenditures is resolved by cutting noninterest spending, cuts amounting to 37 percent would be needed, that is, the 30 percent of 2085 would have to be reduced to 19 percent (compared to the 31%–32% cuts mentioned above). The higher estimates reflect the fact that taking action later than now would require higher tax increases or spending cuts, because the problems continue to deepen and debt to accumulate in the meantime.

The requirements of an immediate and permanent spending cut of 31–32 percent, or an immediate and permanent tax increase of 44–46 percent, are conservative estimates in many ways. They would only stabilize the ratio of federal public debt to GDP; larger changes in outlays and revenues would be required to reduce the ratio. Also, larger changes will be required if such radical measures are not taken right now (in 2011 or 2012), and they certainly will not be. Moreover, the forecasts do not take into account the lower tax base, and the higher welfare-state expenditures, that would follow from reduced economic growth—as we will see in the coming section. It thus appears reasonable and still conservative to round up figures and say that closing the fiscal gap would require a one-third cut in noninterest federal spending, or a 50 percent increase in the global federal tax rate. These would have to be realized now.

The Ghosts in the Closet

However we look at it, the gap between federal revenues and expenditures appears unbridgeable. And there are many ghosts in the closet, which make the optimistic extended-baseline scenario (which relies on high taxes) absolutely unsustainable, and worsen the alternative scenario (which implies a very high level of debt).

The biggest ghost in the closet is the impact that government borrowing (as long as it can borrow) or higher taxes will have on the economy, and thus on the size of the tax base on which rests the capacity to tax or to borrow. The government's capacity to borrow ultimately rests on its capacity to levy future taxes. Taxes—either actual or future—are the key to any government activity. For government, persuading lenders to buy its bonds amounts to persuading them that it will be able to tax enough in the future. (Interestingly, the rest of the world, which buys nearly half the federal government securities, bets on future tax increases on Americans to partly finance its own retirements!)[19] If budget policies undermine economic growth, they cut the branch on which the sovereign and its lenders sit. The official (CBO's and GAO's) forecasts reviewed thus far do not take this phenomenon into account. The CBO openly admits it:

> CBO's projections in most of this report understate the severity of the long-term budget problem because they do not incorporate the negative effects that additional federal debt would have on the economy, nor do they include the impact of higher tax rates on people's incentives to work and save.[20]

When the government borrows, it pushes up interest rates compared to what they would otherwise have been. The effective interest rate on a bond is referred to as its yield. For short-term bonds that are issued at a discount (the difference between their face value and their price) and offer no explicit interest, yield is the annualized percentage difference between the price you paid for the bond and its value at maturity. For bonds that have "coupons"—that is, fixed, regular interest payments based on their face value at issuance—the yield must take into account how changes in the bond's price affect the annualized return given *both* the coupons and the bond's value at maturity. Although the nominal interest rate imbedded in the coupon can be calculated by dividing the interest coupon (say, $50) by the bond's face value (say $1000, for a nominal interest rate of 5 percent), this nominal rate is immaterial once a bond trades on the market at a price different from its face value.

The federal government is a major participant in the loanable funds market: according to Fed figures, its outstanding securities accounted for about 18 percent of all credit market debt at the end of 2010.[21] This proportion would jump to nearly one-third if we include the mortgage securities guaranteed by federal agencies and the GSEs. In the wake of the economic crisis, the flow (as opposed to the stock) of federal borrowing in proportion of all market debt became much higher than the historical stock ratio: in fact, the federal government was borrowing everything available. With such a share of the market, only by offering a higher return can the government persuade potential lenders to part with funds they would otherwise have used for consumption or for investment elsewhere. This of course does not mean that the federal government pays more than others to borrow; on the contrary, as its securities are thought to be safer, it pays less. At the end of December 2011, for example, ten-year Treasury notes yielded about 2 percent, whereas corporate bonds rated Aaa by Moody's yielded double. What I mean when I say that the government has to offer a higher return is that government borrowing pulls up all interest rates *compared to what they would have been otherwise*. It is the same as for any other good: somebody who wants a large chunk of available tomatoes would have to offer more in order to persuade some people to part with their tomatoes, pushing up the tomato price for everybody. Understanding how any demand bids up prices is basic to understanding the economy.

When government borrowing pushes down bond prices (because of the increased supply of bonds), and thus pulls up interest rates, it makes unprofitable some private investments (in physical capital) that would otherwise have been profitable. Investments yielding less than the new, higher return on government securities will not be undertaken. Thus, interest rates pushed higher by government borrowing reduce private investment. We say that government borrowing "crowds out" investment. Lower investment means in turn lower production and lower income, and consequently lower GDP.

Similarly, the higher taxes envisioned in the extended-baseline scenario, and the tax increase necessarily to close the large fiscal gap of the alternative scenario, would have a detrimental impact on GDP, albeit through a different route. Higher taxes make working less attractive because the take-home pay is lower. When individuals face higher effective marginal tax rates on their incomes—when they earn less for their work—they generally reduce their labor supply and produce less. The marginal tax rate is what you pay out of an additional dollar you work for and earn. It directly influences your decision to work more or to take more leisure. Think about it this way: if you lose less in income when you enjoy more leisure, you will choose more of the latter. Empirical research shows that most people faced with the prospect of getting less income out of their work choose to work less, not more. Each individual who reduces his own production pushes GDP down, since GDP is nothing but the sum of all individuals' outputs and incomes. The CBO estimates that the higher taxes implied by its extended-baseline scenario would, on average, increase the effective marginal tax rates on labor income by some 40 percent. If people work less, produce less, and earn less, the federal government has a lower tax base to extract money from.

This process illustrates the important economic concepts of "rational expectations" and "Ricardian equivalence." Individuals have rational expectations in the sense that, in order to improve their situation or to minimize an inevitable deterioration thereof, they adapt their behavior to what they expect to happen. When taxpayers expect higher marginal tax rates, they will adapt their behavior. They expect their work efforts to pay less, so they will work less, regardless of what fiscal policy aims at. Ricardian equivalence, a phenomenon named after British economist David Ricardo (1772–1823), states that substituting debt to taxes will lead to equivalent results because taxpayers, who hold rational expectations, will expect their future taxes to increase (in order to service and reimburse the debt) and will thus react just as they would to current taxes: spend less and work less. In this sense, future taxes are equivalent to current taxes.

Higher taxes or more government borrowing would thus reduce GDP. The CBO does not take this factor into account in the forecasts we have reviewed. But the agency separately estimates that government taxes and other policies implied by its extended-baseline scenario would reduce GDP growth until, in 2035, its level is 1 percent lower than it would otherwise have been. In the alternative scenario (that of Chart 5.1), high borrowing would push federal debt close to 200 percent of GDP in 25 years, dampen economic growth, and reduce the 2035 GDP by 2 percent–10 percent.[22] Such reductions of GDP, which would be even steeper in 2085, would have major consequences.

The CBO's fears relate directly to Reinhart and Rogoff's historical calculations. The two economists have calculated that, in advanced countries over the past two centuries, a ratio of public debt to GDP over 90 percent has been associated with an annual average growth rate of four percentage points lower than with public debt ratios under this threshold. On average, this gap translates into a negative growth rate. The two economists admit that the causal relationship is bidirectional: lower growth pushes the tax revenues down and the public debt up, but it is also clear that more public debt dampens growth as it signals higher future taxes. Reinhart and Rogoff point to other econometric evidence that high public debt dampens economic growth even when other causal factors are statistically accounted for.[23] In more recent work with Vincent R. Reinhart, the two economists focus on the "debt overhang" episodes during which, since the early 1800s, the level of public debt in 22 advanced countries exceeded 90 percent for at least five years. They find that, on average, the annual rates of economic growth were 1.2 percentage points lower during the debt-overhang episodes than outside them. Since the average overhang period lasted

23 years, such a difference in annual growth rates translated, when public debt returned to lower ratios, into a real GDP 24 percent below what it would otherwise have been.[24]

If increasing public debt reduces GDP compared to what the extended-baseline and alternative scenarios assume, the federal government will not be able to collect as much in taxes, either to finance current spending or to pay future interest on current borrowing. Consequently, it will have to increase tax rates or borrow more, which will further reduce GDP, and so on in a downward spiral. Downward spirals don't continue forever but, when an equilibrium is reached, taxes or the public debt will be higher than forecasted by either the optimistic or the pessimistic scenarios outlined above. Hence, the pessimistic scenario covered in Chart 5.1 is conservative after all.

None of the envisioned scenarios makes room for exogenous economic shocks and major recessions. An external shock (say, a permanent oil price jump) or a serious recession would cause a major increase in the deficit, which would translate to a new and higher trajectory for the public debt. And none of the scenarios envisions the possibility that growing regulation and intervention would actually kill the free-enterprise goose that laid the American golden eggs; or that the central bank could end up owning so many economic assets that the economy would have been stealthily nationalized. *The Economist*, despite its Keynesian philosophy, fears the nationalization of financial markets and the "rise of the political-financial complex."[25] There is certainly a point where the mixed economy becomes so socialist that the benefits of free markets are crushed by the inefficiencies of regulation and planning.

No wonder that, even in the DC fairyland, the GAO admits that "there is little question that current policies cannot be sustained indefinitely."[26] In mid-2010, the CBO published a brief titled *Federal Debt and the Risk of a Fiscal Crisis*, which stated:

> A growing level of federal debt would also increase the probability of a sudden fiscal crisis, during which investors would lose confidence in the government's ability to manage its budget, and the government would thereby lose its ability to borrow at affordable rates. It is possible that interest rates would rise gradually as investors' confidence declined, giving legislators advance warning of the worsening situation and sufficient time to make policy choices that could avert a crisis. But as other countries' experiences show, it is also possible that investors would lose confidence abruptly and interest rates on government debt would rise sharply... The higher the debt, the greater the risk of such a crisis.[27]

The Fed itself is worried. In its 2011 annual report, the Federal Reserve Bank of St. Louis (one of the regional components of the Federal Reserve System) warned:

> In summary, the U.S. faces difficult fiscal choices. Taxes have to be raised and/or spending must be cut. The pain associated with these actions will fall on different groups, and that leads to political conflict. Political conflict means delay in getting the U.S. fiscal situation on firmer ground. Whether this conflict will scare financial markets and lead to a rollover crisis for the U.S. remains to be seen.[28]

This chapter has reviewed the federal government's fiscal situation, but a concurrent source of problems comes from State and local governments. As we have seen in chapter 2, the gross public debt and unfunded obligations of States and local governments are much lower than the federal government's, yet they add to the problem, not subtract from it. "We are looking at a Ponzi scheme that would make Bernie Madoff look like a Boy Scout," says a public servant in Maryland, where 10 percent of all taxes go to retired public workers and the pension system is grossly underfunded.[29]

The problems of State and local governments will get worse as the federal government has to reduce its subsidies, which make up 20 percent of their budgets. They may even become unable to accomplish their basic functions or to honor the contractual promises to their employees. The city of Central Falls, Maryland, filed for bankruptcy, with the goal of reducing by 50 percent the base pensions of retired policemen and firefighters.[30] Highland Parks, Michigan, is only one of a number of cities so broke that they have had to reduce street lighting.[31] Other cases appear regularly over the radar. There is a smell of Greece floating around.

Is He Really Naked?

In Andersen's classic tale, *The Emperor's New Clothes*, two swindlers claimed they could weave an exquisite cloth that was invisible to anyone who was stupid or not fit for his office. "The whole town," wrote Andersen, "knew about the cloth's peculiar power, and all were impatient to find out how stupid their neighbors were." The emperor, amateur of nice clothes, thought that this special cloth would allow him to discover who among his subordinates were unfit for their office. He paid the fraudulent weavers a large price to make invisible clothes for him. None of his closest official or courtier would admit that they could not see the new clothes, and all reported to the emperor that they were exquisite. The emperor himself, embarrassed that he was the only one not to see anything, confirmed that the clothes were beautiful. He was helped to put them on for a great procession among his people:

> So off went the Emperor in procession under his splendid canopy. Everyone in the streets and the windows said, "Oh, how fine are the Emperor's new clothes! Don't they fit him to perfection? And see his long train!" Nobody would confess that he couldn't see anything, for that would prove him either unfit for his position, or a fool. No costume the Emperor had worn before was ever such a complete success.

" 'But he hasn't got anything on', said a little child."[32] He was not immediately believed:

> "Did you ever hear such innocent prattle?" said its father. And one person whispered to another what the child had said, "He hasn't anything on. A child says he hasn't anything on."
> "But he hasn't got anything on!" the whole town cried out at last.

The emperor is today's sovereign. As Laurence Kotlikoff points out, the state cannot redistribute to everybody more than they earn over their whole lifetimes. The emperor cannot give everybody a negative lifetime tax burden for this would require that everybody consumes more than he produces, which is impossible. The sovereign cannot promise everybody that they will get in public health care and pensions more than they contributed. The sovereign cannot give what he does not have. He can try to have the people consume more than they earn by borrowing abroad for a while, but only as long as the creditors don't realize what is going on. Once somebody admits to himself, and dare to voice, that the emperor has no clothes, everybody will soon realize that he has been naked all along.

Yet, it is widely believed that the emperor is not really naked or, to escape the metaphor, that the state will somehow be able to solve its problems. The bond market testifies to this general confidence: Treasury securities trade at historically high prices, which means that they are highly in demand and—the other side of the same coin—that their holders are satisfied with very low yields, even negative real yields. (The real interest rate or yield is the nominal rate minus the inflation rate.) Garret Jones, an economist at George Mason University, argues that the bond market, which trusts the federal government, must be right.[33] But it is not impossible that the market is wrong, for investors may simply not have yet discovered the magnitude of the problem. Or does the emperor wear clothes that we don't see?

CHAPTER 6

THE EMPEROR'S PRAETORIANS

Is the emperor naked? Is the sovereign really broke? The question may seem preposterous. After all, the sovereign can force its taxpayers to pay. He is well-organized. He has judges and policemen and, if necessary, soldiers to enforce its will. Moreover, in democratic countries, the taxpayers *are* the sovereign; they own the state, they have no emperor but themselves, and they will choose to pay with their own money. But what if they cannot or will not pay?

Force

In the United States, 67 percent of all government revenues (all levels of governments) come from taxes that are effectively called taxes—mainly personal taxes of different sorts. Another 25 percent come from social insurance contributions, of which only a small part consists of voluntary premiums to Medicare, so that most social insurance revenues are nothing but taxes even if called "contributions." Of the 8 percent left, about half is made of interest, and the other half of fines, fees, penalties, and such. This last half of the 8 percent can be thought as representing different kinds of taxes. As for investment income, it comes from assets purchased with past taxes or, through borrowing, with future taxes. Thus, it is fair to say that virtually all government revenues come from taxes. Taxes are how governments get their money. As Willy Sutton would have said, that's where the money is.

Since all of government revenues come from compulsory taxation in one form or another, looking at these revenues as a percentage of GDP gives a good idea of what the state currently extracts in taxes from people's incomes. This average ratio is the effective tax rate (what I have also called the "global tax rate"), the average of all taxes compared to all incomes. Chart 6.1 provides such data for 33 OECD countries: the proportion of domestic income (equivalent to GDP) taken in taxes

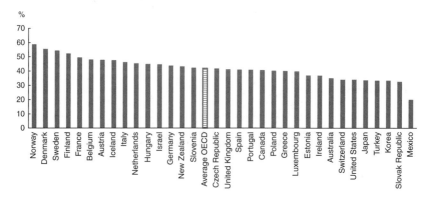

Chart 6.1 Government Revenues as a Proportion of GDP, OECD Countries, 2007

Source: OECD (2011a), p. 59. Contrary to the original OECD chart, Turkey has been included in the calculation of the average as the 2007 figures are available for that country.

by the state.[1] The chart relates to year 2007, so as not to confuse the usual situation with the unusual conditions of the Great Recession. The effective tax ratios have risen since 2007. The OECD average is unweighted, which means that it considers all countries equally; in a sense, the average describes the typical country.

In the typical OECD country, then, the ratio of government revenues to GDP was 42 percent. It means that 42 cents of each dollar (or euro or whatever currency) earned were paid in all sorts of taxes. Another way to say the same thing: the average taxpayer in the typical country faced an average tax rate of 42 percent. The United States stood in the last quintile of OECD countries, with a relatively low ratio of 34 percent, although five countries did enjoy lower tax rates. In more than two dozen countries, the state imposed a higher average tax rate than in America. Canada, a close neighbor, stood at 41 percent, just a whiff below the OECD average. Half the Eurozone countries stand above the OECD average; some notable exceptions with below-average tax rate include Ireland, Greece, Portugal, and Spain. The French faced an average tax rate of 50 percent. And consider the model welfare states of Northern Europe: Finland, Sweden, Denmark, and Norway; their average tax rate ranged from 52 percent to 59 percent. In Norway, the average taxpayer gave the state close to 60 percent of what he earned, or, alternatively, his take-home pay was a paltry 40 percent of his gross earnings. Note that these average rates are not marginal rates: they apply on average to all incomes, and not just to the top income tax brackets (and they include all taxes, not only income taxes). Top marginal income tax rates are often higher than these average rates.

In 2007, Portugal, Greece, and Ireland were, like America, below the OECD tax average. As I mentioned before, Ireland is a special case, as its problem came essentially from a banking crisis and its government bailing out all the banks and their owners: one single mistake of the Irish state—but a big one—crashed the country. Greece and Portugal, which had accumulated high levels of public debt, simply illustrate the danger of financing expenditures by debt as opposed to current taxes. The Spanish state's debt was at the bottom of the OECD ranking before the Great Recession, and its global tax rate just slightly below the OECD average. It appears that the Spanish economy was so regulated and inflexible, especially with regard to its labor market, that it could not absorb the shock of the Great Recession without a catastrophe.[2] As for the later problems of Spanish banks, they were a direct consequence of the sovereign debt crisis. It is useful to recall that all states had become more or less profligate welfare states: it is only a matter of degree.

America appears to be a relatively low-tax country, but this is relative to time and place. In the late nineteenth century, tax rates were much lower in all civilized countries. On the eve of World War I, government expenditures, and thus government revenues at a time of balanced budgets, were about 8 percent in America and 13 percent on average in Western countries.[3] What we now consider normal taxes would have been considered confiscatory not so long ago. Adam Smith's 1762 remark provides a striking illustration:

> No doubt the raising of a very exorbitant tax, as the raising as much in peace as in war, [of] the half or even the fifth of the wealth of the nation, would, as well as any other gross abuse of power, justify resistance in the people.[4]

As of 2007, the average tax rate on GDP was 20 percent only in Mexico. We just saw that it was 34 percent in America, 42 percent in the typical OECD countries, and more than 50 percent in the welfare states of Northern Europe. These rates have increased since, without provoking much "resistance in the people."

The OECD statistics reveal that the tax take in America could be pushed up by 50 percent, from 34 percent to 51 percent, and it would still be comparable to the French tax situation (50 percent in 2007), and remain a healthy ten percentage points below Norway. This suggests that there may be much leeway to increase taxes in all but the Northern-Europe welfare states—and, who knows, perhaps even there.

Are these Northern welfare states the future of mankind? They have financed the growth of their expenditures with current taxes more than with debt (that is, future taxes). At the end of 2007, gross public debt was at 49 percent in Sweden and even lower in Denmark (34%) and Finland (41%). At 57 percent, Norway was still much below the total Eurozone's 72 percent, and roughly at the level of the typical Eurozone country (56 percent, unweighted).[5] That's not bad compared with the US level of 62 percent at the time.

Taxes and debt financing—that is, current and future taxes—appear to be substitutes, that is, alternative ways of raising the same revenue and financing the welfare state. If this were strictly true we would expect countries with the highest taxes to have the lowest debt. This is true in the Northern welfare states, but the hypothesis is not confirmed by data from other countries. There are some countries with high taxes that don't show low public debt—Belgium and France, for example. And among the low tax countries, some have maintained low debts (such as Australia and Switzerland). A closer analysis at the OECD data shows a zero correlation between the tax and debt ratios in OECD countries. We have to look at other reasons than debt avoidance or preference to explain why countries have higher or lower tax rates. These reasons may be related to their political institutions, and the latter's relative capacity to impose current taxes or less visible future taxes. Yet, if taxes were effectively raised to avoid unsustainable debt in Northern Europe, would it not be possible in the United States to raise them *ex post facto* in order to reimburse the accumulated debt?

Modern states can force their subjects or citizens to pay a large part of their incomes in taxes because they hold much coercive power. Bertrand de Jouvenel, the twentieth-century political scientist and philosopher, brought the idea home by comparing contemporary states with the Roman Republic, which had few organized means of coercive power:

> We do not find anywhere in the ancient republic a directing will so armed with its own weapons that it can use force. There were the consuls, I may be told. But to start with there were two of them, and it was an essential feature of the office that they could block one another's activities. On occasions when they wanted to impose their joint will, what means had they to hand? Only a few lictors; right through her republican period Rome never knew the means of public coercion and had for force only the people themselves, who could at need answer the summons of the leaders of society.

De Jouvenel explains that "no absolute monarch ever had at his disposal a police force comparable to those of modern democracies,"[6] a remarkable observation indeed.

We should beware of idealizing too much the ancient world, which knew nothing of the modern conception of liberty and individual rights. Not obeying "the leaders of society," even if they did not exert a continuous authority over free men, was generally not a pleasant option. Yet, the evolution of ancient tyrannies toward modern sovereigns has been accompanied by a formidable growth of police surveillance and effective power. The acceleration of surveillance and regulation, along with the advances of information technology and the events of 9/11, have consolidated and pushed forward an already well-established trend. For a few decades, financial transaction and thus most professional activities have been subject to government regulations that leave a paper or electronic trace. Government tracking numbers (especially the Social Security Number) and ID papers (such as the ubiquitous driver's license) track individuals from the cradle to the grave. In *Les Misérables*, Victor Hugo vividly depicts how, in the early eighteenth century, a convicted felon had, even after being released from his punishment, to carry a "yellow passport" that betrayed him any time he tried to return to a honest life. Today, the yellow passport is even more stringent as it lives in the computers of policemen and other state agents; often, in America, it is accessible online by anybody (such is the plight of sexual delinquents).[7] In the late eighteenth century, it was still thinkable for an individual to escape the system of police surveillance and tracking; today, it is virtually impossible. The mere number of police personnel in today's society is scary. In 2009, American cities of one million inhabitants or more had one police employee (policemen and "civilian" personnel included) for every 232 inhabitants,[8] which is probably not much different from Paris in the last half of the eighteenth century.[9] Add to this the growing militarization of police and the conclusion that police powers have increased manifold since we lived in "less advanced" societies is unmistakable.

The modern state is so incredibly powerful that it seldom needs to resort to overt violence: the mere threat of force suffices. Those who don't immediately fall in line will submit when the subpoena is delivered or when the SWAT team arrives. The threat of violence often appears far removed from daily activities, thanks to a combination of surveillance and a priori control that prevents individuals from disobeying even if they would like to. In many situations, now bordering on most cases, an American cannot receive payment for his work without a form being filed for the tax authorities. One cannot deposit a check without a paper or electronic trace being accessible by the authorities. It requires an extreme system of surveillance and control, an extraordinary spider net, unthinkable by our forebears, for the state to be able to "freeze the assets" of anybody deemed to have broken certain laws.

From 27 BC until the fourth century, Roman emperors were protected by their Praetorian Guard. The praetorians were so powerful that they sometimes murdered emperors and appointed their successors. Times have changed, and coups d'état are less frequent in Western countries; they are thus far unknown in America if we exclude the Civil War. But many of the activities of the police and the armed forces appear to be imposing the will of the sovereign, even if democratic, more than protecting all individuals equally. The minority must submit to the majority, and the armed men of the state enforce this submission. When the majority decides to levy taxes—often on the minority—modern praetorians are there to enforce the decision and make tax collection possible. The modern emperor, with his powerful praetorians, is all but naked. He can make the taxpayers pay taxes, including in order to reimburse his debt.

Some claim that taxes are never morally legitimate, and therefore always coercive. The strongest attack on the idea of a voluntary state imposing legitimate taxes can be traced to Massachusetts anarchist Lysander Spooner (1808–1897). "On general principles of law and reason," Spooner argued, the US Constitution binds nobody because it was never actually signed by the people, and certainly not by those alive today. "The law holds," he explains, "and reason declares, that if a written instrument is not signed, the presumption must be that the party to be bound by it, did not choose to sign it, or to bind himself by it." Thus the state has no legitimacy and can claim the loyalty of no one. The democratic state, argues Spooner, is nothing but "a secret band of robbers and murderers." It is made of agents who claim to represent anonymous principals hiding behind secret votes: "These pretended agents of the people, of everybody, are really the agents of nobody." The Constitution "is, to all moral intent and purposes, as destitute of obligation as the compacts which robbers and thieves and pirates enter into with each other but never sign."[10]

For Spooner, taxes are as illegitimate as the government that pretends to levy them. Compared to the government, the highwayman who shouts "Your money or your life!" is a gentleman, because he does not pretend to rob you for your own good and leaves you alone after his crime is committed. In order to keep their money in their pockets, individuals can resist the state as the band of robbers it is. Public debts, he argues, are no more binding on the people than taxes:

> On general principles of law and reason, debts contracted in the name of "the United States", or of "the people of the United States", are of

no validity. It is utterly absurd to pretend that debts to the amount of twenty-five hundred millions of dollars are binding upon thirty-five or forty millions of people, when there is not a particle of legitimate evidence—such as would be required to prove a private debt—that can be produced against any one of them, that either he, or his properly authorized attorney, ever contracted to pay one cent.

Certainly, neither the whole people of the United States, nor any number of them, ever separately or individually contracted to pay a cent of these debts.

At the time Spooner was writing, the federal debt was under 30 percent of GDP (see Chart 2.2), and had served to finance the Civil War. Spooner believed that the merchants of the North who financed the war were only pursuing Southern markets, "and not any love of liberty and justice." Talking about the federal government and the debt, he writes:

Having no corporate property with which to pay what purports to be their corporate debts, this secret band of robbers and murderers are really bankrupt. They have nothing to pay with. In fact, they do not propose to pay their debts otherwise than from the proceeds of their future robberies and murders.

Spooner's moral argumentation is intriguing, and provides a good antidote to conventional wisdom, but reflection suggests that the argument is built on sand. When Spooner insists on an "open, written, authentic, or voluntary contract," he ignores a pervasive feature of any society—that much of social interaction is made of implicit, not explicit, agreements. A large number of our daily interactions rest on tacit understanding. Many business agreements are sealed with a handshake before being formalized, and sometimes without being formalized at all. Goods and services are often delivered and consumed before being paid, on the tacit promise that payment will follow. At other times, goods and services are prepaid on the promise that they will be delivered at some future date. Even formal contractual agreements rest on a tacit understanding of what words mean, and although some clauses may give rise to court challenges, most of them are honored. Strangers generally come and knock on people's doors without being shot through the door. Men and women can initiate flirt within certain limits. Many other examples could be given. Much of life is tacit and not, as Spooner would have it, ruled by written contracts. And when the anarchist says that he does not want to pay taxes because the benefits are not worth the cost, it may just be cheap talk that does not reveal the talker's real preferences: he may simply want to hold out to pay less, or free ride on the contributions of others.

Consent

Contra Spooner, a system in which the average individual is made to pay one-third or one-half his income in taxes cannot rely only on coercion. Force has its limits. The system does require the consent, at least tacit, of part of the population, for how could one individual keep 232 in leash? Some consent is necessary. One would think that this is true a fortiori under a democratic state. This idea underlies the orthodox approach to political theory and public finance.

According to the orthodox approach (sometimes called "fiscal orthodoxy"), state coercion, at least in a democratic society, does not exist. The state is the product of a social contract among all citizens. The idea received its classic expression in French philosopher Jean-Jacques Rousseau's 1762 book, *The Social Contract*.[11] Individuals agree to form a state because they need it to protect their property and liberty. In today's parlance, we would say that the state is necessary to provide the public goods, such as national defense and public protection, that the market cannot supply. This contractarian explanation of the state does not require that an explicit contract be signed on paper by each and every citizen: the social contract can be implicit, which means that every citizen tacitly accepts the charges of citizenship in order to reap its benefits. The signatories of the social contract naturally grant the state all the power it needs to accomplish its mission, and they decide democratically how these powers will be exercised. The people are the sovereign. We are the state and the state is us. We are the sovereign and the sovereign is us.

If the state results from a unanimous contract, it resembles a voluntary association and taxes are akin to voluntary membership dues. Every individual's immediate interest is that all other members pay their taxes but that he himself evade his, for then he would get all the benefits provided by the state without the cost of supporting it. This sort of situation is typical of what is called a "prisoner's dilemma": it is in the interest of everybody that all do something, but in the interest of every individual to defect. Understanding this problem, the signatories of the social contract grant the state coercive powers to force everyone to do what all think everybody must do. Thus, even when taxes look involuntary—like when a tax evader is put in jail—they are voluntary at a higher level as they have previously, if only tacitly, been consented to. There had been prior consent to the possibility of coercion. It's like observing an individual being forcibly expelled from "his" house, which looks like a coercive aggression until you realize that the culprit has not made his mortgage payments, an omission he had himself contractually agreed would be cause for expulsion.

According to the orthodox approach, we all benefit from the state and, thus, we must all support it. Theodoros Pangalos, a deputy prime minister in the Greek government, said it in different terms when he explained how the Greeks had consumed the deficit-financed manna: "We ate it together."[12] Thus "we" must now agree to pay taxes in order to reimburse what we borrowed. Public debt is no problem because "we owe it to ourselves." It used to be a standard mantra, as James Buchanan and Richard Wagner noted: "It was held to be impossible to implement a transfer of cost or burden through time because government included all members of the community, and, so long as public debt was internally owned, 'we owe it to ourselves.'"[13] Two French intellectuals recently recanted by suggesting that it would make sense for Europe "to lend to itself and reimburse its own people."[14]

Four Reasons Why We Did Not Consent

Something is wrong with the fiscally orthodox idea that the state and all taxes are voluntary. Spooner is not quite right, but neither is the idyllic view of the state and taxes. Perhaps some state activities and some taxes are voluntary for some people, but a blanket statement that everybody ate trillions of debt together and must reimburse it looks problematic. We can summarize the problems under four related headings.

First, we are not really "we"—even if all the public debt were owned domestically. We don't owe the public debt to ourselves. If we did, it would mean that we have borrowed from ourselves. Borrowing from oneself perhaps makes some accounting sense for an individual, or perhaps even for a corporate entity that has assets and debts of its own, although one should not be fooled by the accounting nature of the gimmick. In the case of the state, the gimmick makes no sense, for when we say that "we owe the public debt to ourselves," the we and the ourselves do not refer to the same set of people. The individuals who lend to the government are generally not the same persons who benefit from the public goods produced with that money. Saying that we borrow from ourselves means in fact that some of us borrow from others among us. We don't owe the public debt to ourselves, but some of us owe it to others among us.

In a political context, the very notion of owing something to oneself is absurd. Suppose you don't pay, will you prosecute yourself? Will you force yourself into bankruptcy? If you don't have enough assets to pay yourself, will you fine yourself? This would be an easy fine to pay and to collect: you pay it to yourself, the dollar bills go from your right hand to your left hand, you say "thank you," and each of you is happy! If Europe "lends to itself" and does not reimburse, will Europe put itself in jail? Who will be the jail guard? Once it is realized that we is seldom, if ever, the totality of the population, and that some "we" are not the same as other "we," the logic of whole fiscal orthodoxy starts unraveling.

Second, nonrebellion does not necessarily mean tacit consent. At least from some individuals' viewpoint, all taxes cannot be deemed voluntary. The redistributionist state generates a class of net taxpayers and a class of net tax consumers, and it is difficult to imagine membership in the net taxpayer class as being voluntary. It is true that some net taxpayers may consent to their condition, just as some net tax beneficiaries may disagree with the whole system; but certainly there are some net taxpayers who are coerced. Tacit consent has its limits and is not automatically implied by nonresistance. When people do not revolt against a state that exploits them, their passivity can be explained by something else than consent.

The idea that people may not revolt even if they don't consent to the way they are ruled found its first expression in a book by Estienne de La Boétie, a French philosopher of the sixteenth century. In his *Discourse of Voluntary Servitude*,[15] De La Boétie wondered how tyrants could obtain the continuous obedience of their subjects. Since the subjects are much more numerous than the rulers, they could successfully revolt. Why don't they? The tyrant, De la Boétie observed, "has no other power than the power they give him" and "is able to harm them only to the extent to which they have the willingness to bear with him." He argued that two reasons explain what Bertrand de Jouvenel later called "the mystery of civil obedience."[16] The first reason for the subjects' voluntary servitude is custom and habit: people learn from their birth to obey the tyrant. "The essential reason why men take orders willingly," he explained, "is that they are born serfs and are reared as such." The second reason is that tyrants bribe a portion of the population to support them: "In short," wrote de la Boétie, "when the point is reached, through big favors or little ones, that large profits or small are obtained under a tyrant, there are found almost as many people to whom tyranny seems advantageous as those to whom liberty would seem desirable." We are back to the redistributionist state: tyrants obtain the consent of part of the population because they buy it through redistribution of money, privileges, or other benefits.

There is another, very potent, reason why people don't resist tyranny even when they don't consent to it. De la Boétie could not have clearly explained it, for it was not until the work of contemporary economist Mancur Olson that it was completely understood.[17] Even if all subjects want to fight the tyrant, they face what we now call the problem of collective action: how to organize in order to do it. A certain mass of people is necessary for a successful revolt, if only to protect each other from the tyrant's praetorians. The first person to demonstrate in the street, or to call for a demonstration, is likely to be arrested, perhaps tortured and killed. Being the one hundred thousandth resister is easy. Everybody is ready for that, but nobody wants to be the first one. Hence practical resisters are seldom more than a few eccentrics and heroes, willing to sacrifice themselves with no measurable impact. Obviously, there are ways around the collective action problem, the proof being that tyrants are sometimes toppled. Today's information technologies have made resistance easier—albeit while also facilitating surveillance. But the fact that it takes so much time to topple tyrants illustrates the extent of the collective action problem, and how difficult it is to solve it.

A third reason for entertaining doubts about fiscal orthodoxy is that most people who are part of the collective "we" and are supposed to have borrowed and eaten the money have no clue of what they did. As we saw before, the typical voter in a democracy remains rationally ignorant of the political sphere. He has little incentives to buy information because no information will help him make actual choices that have an impact in his own life. The only choice he can make is whom to applaud (that is, to vote for) in the political arena, and this action has no discernible influence on the choice to come out of the voting process. Moreover, the choice made by voters will be interpreted, and altered, by politicians, bureaucrats, and judges. Hence, the typical voter will not read this book (alas!), nor the complex reports of the GAO, the CBO, the OMB, and the whole alphabet soup of agencies responsible for budgeting, borrowing, and reimbursing. Politicians and bureaucrats thus have an easy job making people believe that everybody benefits from the public debt, and they can get away with this lie. When the next election comes, after tens of thousands of unreadable pages in a plethora of reports from a multitude of bureaus, the voter will be asked to choose from among politicians proposing complex programs with unknowable long-term consequences, which the politicians themselves don't understand and don't really care about anyway except for their electoral prospects.

The fourth reason for denying that all taxes are voluntary lies in the very notion of a social contract, which has been criticized by many economists and political philosophers. It is difficult to imagine the state that we know as the product of a unanimous social contract. The state as we know it is a redistributive machine and, thus, does not produce equal benefits for everybody; it is mainly engaged in redistributing from some of its citizens or subjects to others among them. The state steals from Peter in order to give to Paul. What the state redistributes is not only money, but also what money and power can buy (such as health or education). When the state forbids smoking in restaurants, it renders restaurants more attractive to nonsmokers (or at least to anti-smokers) but makes them less hospitable to smokers. When the state imposes a driver's license or, in the future perhaps, a parenting license,[18] it helps those who otherwise would have been maimed by bad drivers or by rogue offspring from bad parents, but it prevents some from driving or from raising their own children. Whether this or that instance of the redistributive process is good or bad does not matter here; what's important to realize is that the redistributionist state, by design, favors some and harms others. Those benefited will claim that the harmed ones have signed a contract justifying it, but the weight of this claim is low.

An objection to this critique is that everybody is alternatively harmed or helped by the state, that everyone stands alternatively on one side or the other of the redistributive wicket, and that all this cancels out in some way. Economists call this process "churning." The state can also be conceived as a big insurance company making sure that nobody is too unhappy and, in order to achieve this, preventing everybody from being too happy.[19] But for those who don't want this sort of insurance, for the risk-lovers who would rather run the risk of being very unhappy while being free to search for maximum happiness, nothing is gained from state redistribution. Moreover, the more the state tries to redistribute, the more people will want to be on the right side of the wicket, and the fewer will be left to work for the assisted. When the state is responsible for everybody's happiness, some will end up being exploited.

But the main argument against a unanimous social contract is that it cannot apply to a state that intervenes everywhere. The more diversified and numerous the individuals are, the fewer are the ideas, and the narrower the principles, on which they can agree unanimously. Two individuals can certainly agree on the clauses of an extensive social contract if their preferences are similar. Two Puritans will naturally agree on a Puritan social contract prohibiting smoking and alcohol. Two communists will agree on a social contract prohibiting the private ownership of capital. Two communitarians will agree on a social contract forcing each individual to live according to their "community" values. But increase the number of potential signatories within any of these categories, and differences will appear as to whether alcohol consumption or just its manufacturing should be forbidden, whether private ownership of simple capital goods such as taxicabs or restaurants should be allowed, whether the community should intrude in everybody's bedroom, and so forth. Now, put all these categories of people together, and the only social contract they can agree on will be that the state should protect them against violence. They will certainly not agree on creating a coercive organization with the mission of protecting them against all sins and victimless crimes, for the sins of some are the pleasures or even the virtues of others. A social contract may perhaps be presumed to exist if the state is small and has limited functions, but the presumption collapses as the state expands and tries to define and impose the good life.

Public Choice economists have tried to follow the reasoning of rational and diverse individuals trying to agree on a social contract. Fearful of being exploited by the state in the future, they would make sure to include in the contract strict limitations on state power.[20] But this has little to do with the state as we know it, which is essentially a redistributive and interventionist machine, and which has accumulated debts amounting to many years of taxpayers' incomes.

Philosophers have discussed other reasons why a unanimous social contract is difficult to conceive,[21] but enough has been said here to show that unanimous consent is a tall order. Consequently, it cannot be assumed that all people consent to all taxes, especially at a high proportion of their incomes. Much state coercion is then necessary to enforce taxes. But the state has the praetorians to do the job.

Who Ate the Money?

Most people both pay taxes and get money and privileges from the state (what is called churning), and it is often impossible to disentangle who has been a net taxpayer, and who a net tax consumer. Some people have certainly not been net recipients, namely, many high-level, highly remunerated, and heavily taxed entrepreneurs, artists, sport players, and executives: in the net, they paid much more in taxes than they got in public services. Yet some of the rich work for subsidized companies: those ate part of the money borrowed to finance the state. In some countries, artists and performers are heavily subsidized by the state, so they also ate part of the borrowed money. Many had both their hands in the public treasury, including the poor with their welfare payments, Medicaid, and other freebies, as well as students attending subsidized public colleges with subsidized government loans. It gets complicated as some people only ate the money because they had been prevented by regulation from earning a honest living: think of all the people kept out of trades and professions by licensure provisions, or think of the poor who cannot get on the first steps of the employment ladder because nobody is allowed to hire them at less than the minimum wage. Many young Europeans are similarly prevented from working by inflexible market regulation. Despite the appearances, many beneficiaries of the state are thus not really net beneficiaries. It is clear, though, that the politicians and bureaucrats, who are the net tax consumers, were consistently at the table eating the money that *we* are supposed to have eaten together.

The orthodox approach to public finance, which had passed into conventional wisdom, ceased to be invoked the very moment crush time came. Suddenly, it was "they" who had borrowed, and "we" would not reimburse.[22] The state was suddenly not all of us anymore. Consider the mess. The sovereign made people believe that they were borrowing from themselves and eating the money together. Many believed it, and asked for more. Rationally ignorant, they had no idea of what they were clamoring for. The sovereign obliged. Now comes crunch time and people cry: "We did not want that." "Oh! Yes, you did," reply the politicians, "and you will now pay for it." Willy-nilly. The emperor will send his praetorians to collect the money.

Will Americans Pay?

In the last chapter, I wondered if the large tax increases necessary to control the American federal debt would be politically feasible. On the basis of official figures, I estimated that the average federal tax rate in America would have to increase by 50 percent in the very near future. Could the political system, by persuasion or by force or by a mixture of the two, bring Americans to accept such tax increases? Could America become France or Sweden? The answer is not certain, but is likely negative.

Even if a large number of Americans were to consent to the humongous tax increases that are required to maintain current government expenditures, there is still a problem: the present and foreseeable levels of debt might simply not be reimbursable. There might not be enough money around, or raising enough taxes might be impossible without killing the goose that lays the golden eggs. Levying additional taxes equivalent to 8 percent of what people earn is probably impossible without undermining the incentives to work, reducing the tax base, and starting a spiral of impoverishment that would make the government's revenue target impossible to reach. Here we again meet the ghost in the closet and all this is over and above the States' and local governments' debt problems. So there is a real possibility that no amount of repression could squeeze enough money out of the middle class and the poor.

What about making the rich pay? The problem is that they are not many of them around. Consider the super-rich, the 1 percent of the families that occupy the top of the income distribution in America. According to Internal Revenue Service (IRS) data and calculations by Professor Emmanuel Saez of the University of California at Berkeley,[23] these 1.5 million families earned $2 trillion dollars in gross income in 2007. (I use the 2007 figures to avoid distortions due to the recession, which reduced revenues from the super-rich by $300 billion dollars.) The incomes of these super-rich made up 24 percent of all incomes. This percentage has fueled much criticism about income distribution, but note that a family gets into this bracket at an income threshold of $398,909 a year—which many high-salary, double-income couples earn. These super-rich paid $451 billion, or 22 percent of their incomes, in federal income taxes, which provided 40 percent of federal income tax receipts.[24]

Now, suppose that the average federal tax rate of these families had been more than doubled for a new rate of 50 percent. It would have brought some $560 billion of new taxes into the federal Treasury, or 4 percent of GDP. This humongous amount is still dwarfed by the $14 trillion of gross federal debt. It remains much below the amount necessary for closing the fiscal gap, which amounts to 8 percent of GDP; consequently, the public debt would keep expanding in proportion of GDP. Moreover, it could not be a permanent tax increase. There is no way the top 1 percent would see their federal income tax bill double and continue to earn (or to declare) as much as they now do. Consequently, their taxable incomes would decrease. As an example, imagine a wife who earns a second salary of $200,000 and would now bring home only $100,000: she may very well decide to stay at home, fire the nanny, substitute homemade dinners to the previous restaurant outings, and enjoy herself and her children at home. Thus, the tax base of the top 1 percent would shrink, and the doubled tax rate would bring in much less than the assumed increase in tax revenues.

What about the "Buffet rule" promised by Barack Obama? This more modest proposal would establish a tax rate of 30 percent on incomes over $1 million, as opposed to the current 25 percent average tax in that bracket. It can be calculated that the new tax rate would generate very little revenues: over a decade, the supplementary revenues for the Treasury would be less than 1 percent of the budget deficits forecasted by the Obama administration.[25]

Note that any increase of tax rates on the super-rich would generate more active tax evasion or avoidance actions. More wealthy individuals would renounce their American citizenship, a disturbing trend that is apparently growing. It is disturbing because America used to be the land where rich artists, sportsmen, and entrepreneurs wanted to live. The federal government tries to discourage this sort of tax avoidance with "exit taxes" and threats of banning renouncers from visiting the country even as tourists.[26] But, as we saw, force has its limits, and so does a soft Berlin Wall.

The truth is that a tax increase capable of solving the public debt problem would have to hit the middle class hard. The public may simply be unable to cough up the taxes required. There might not be enough money accessible to the emperor.

CHAPTER 7

THE SOVEREIGN'S BANKERS

Banks are only one of the sovereign's lenders, but their holdings of government securities are not insignificant. Consider Europe. At the end of 2010, domestic and European sovereign securities made up about 5 percent of their total assets, to which must be added another 4 percent of straight bank loans to European governments.[1] The amount of sovereign debt often represented a sizeable part of the bank shareholders' equity (and more than total equity in Belgian banks). The BIS notes that "in advanced economies, banks often have sizeable exposures to the home sovereign, and generally have a strong home bias in their sovereign portfolios."[2] In the United States, it is estimated that 2 percent of commercial banks' total assets are made of Treasury securities, but the proportion jumps to 13 percent if we add mortgage securities guaranteed by federal agencies and GSEs.[3] So we can say that banks allocate about 10 percent of their assets to supporting the sovereign (not counting munis).

In countries where the sovereign debt is most subject to default, banks often hold a large proportion of it. At the end of 2010, Greek banks owned 67 percent of their government's sovereign debt! The proportion is of the same order in Portugal and Ireland regarding domestic government securities held by domestic banks.[4] The political class expected that the cheap loans the ECB offered to the banks would lead them to buy even more their own governments' sovereign bonds: French president Nicolas Sarkozy explicitly suggested it. And this is what happened.[5] The *Economist* noted "the circular prospect of governments bailing out their banks that are in turn supposed to bail out the government."[6]

Because banks hold so much public debt, they are generally not deemed more solid than the sovereign under whom they labor. "Banks are generally unable to issue long-term bonds at interest rates lower than those paid by their governments," writes *The Economist*, "because they would be the hardest hit by a default."[7]

"A True Providence for the State"

How could European banks be so imprudent as to hold so much of their assets in securities of their sovereigns? The easy answer, which is not completely false, is that their management sincerely believed, like many other investors, that sovereign debt was safe—like money in the bank, as it were. People were brought up to believe and trust their governments. Who could be stronger and safer than democratic governments that have maintained uninterrupted legal continuity for at least half a century? This motivation is not sufficient, though, for at least two reasons. First, as we have seen, apparently strong democratic governments have defaulted on their debts before. Second, during the actual European crisis, banks continued to hold their own government's securities even after alarms were raised. They were expected to bail out their governments. A related question could be, why do American banks hold so much in domestic government securities? The reason lies in the incestuous symbiosis between banks and their governments.

A bank lends money that it has borrowed from others or that it owns (its capital). Banks borrow either from depositors or by issuing bonds. As deposits can be obtained cheaper, ordinary commercial banks have come to rely mainly on this form of financing. Their financing is typically short-term, as depositors can withdraw their money at short notice (usually on demand). Long-term interest rates are normally higher than short-term ones, so the banks have come to hold much of their assets in long-term loans. A bank can be seen as a financial institution that borrows short and lends long, making its profits from the interest differentials between long and short maturities. The difference between retail banks, also called "commercial banks," and investment banks is that the latter do not necessarily take deposits from the public and that they lend mainly to businesses, to whom they also offer other financial and consulting services. A bank that combines the two types of activity is called a universal bank. Banks used to be free to issue their own banknotes as paper money, but since the nineteenth century this activity has been reserved to central banks, which are the sovereigns' bankers.

Close precursors of banks appeared in the middle ages with "merchant bankers" who purchased bills of exchange from merchants. Bills of exchange were promises from buyers to pay the merchants who had sold goods to them. By purchasing a bill of exchange, at a discount of course, the merchant bank was of course advancing, or lending, the money to the merchant. Commercial banks as we know them, institutions taking deposits and making loans, are a creation of modern times, from the sixteenth century onward. They evolved into issuing warehouse receipts against coins brought for safekeeping, thereby creating the first form of paper money.

Sovereigns soon discovered how banks could be useful lenders. What's better than borrowing the people's money from the institutions they have entrusted it with? The Bank of England was a private bank created by an act of Parliament in 1694 with the main goal of helping the English government wage war against France.[8] "The loan of £1.200.000 linked the Bank from the outset with the State," observed economic historian R. D. Richards. "Moreover," wrote economist Charles P. Kindleberger, "the bank's original charter had been written for a limited period. At the end of each period, it was necessary to renew the charger, usually at the price of lending the government more money on a permanent basis and at an interest rate below the market."[9] One century later, the bank helped the English government finance the Napoleonic wars. As Richards notes, "the bank soon developed into an indispensable organ of public finance."[10] At the end of the eighteenth century, the Bank of England was a primus inter pares among more than 50 banks in London. During the nineteenth century, the government granted the Bank of England a monopoly on paper money, a central bank privilege, but maintained it nominally private until its nationalization in 1946.

Another example is France. Created by John Law, the Banque Générale was chartered in 1716, acquired by the French state two years later, and renamed Banque Royale. It folded four years later after over-issuing paper money, which, in a standard inflationary process, had lost most of its value. In 1776, a Swiss financier created another chartered bank, la Caisse d'Escompte, which was soon obliged to lend a large sum to the king in exchange for an extension of its charter. Many small bank operations also existed, which borrowed from the public and lent to the state at a profit. The Bank of France was created in 1800 with mainly private capital. Its shareholders, included Napoléon Bonaparte, the French consul and future emperor, and members of his family. Although the bank was nominally private, the French government reserved the right to appoint the governor, and exerted much influence on it. The bank rapidly obtained a monopoly of money creation and was often called to lend money to the state. By 1820, it had become, in the words of one historian, "under the King as under the Emperor, a true providence for the state."[11] An important bank bailout occurred in the mid-nineteenth century when the French Comptoir d'Escompte, another large private bank, was saved from bankruptcy by the state.[12] Like the Bank of England, the Bank of France was formally nationalized only in 1946.

The banks that did not morph into central banks have also been close to the political establishment, if not simply creatures of the state. They were monitored and regulated by the state (free banks in nineteenth-century Scotland are the exception). They were also often protected against potential competitors (domestic or foreign). In return, the banks financially supported their benefactor—"a true providence for the state." The symbiosis has continued until present times. It is part of this symbiosis that, at the end of 2010, Greek banks held 67 percent of the Greek public debt, and that some 30 percent of the public debt of the most threatened European states (Greece, Ireland, and Portugal) was owned by European banks.[13]

American history also illustrates the symbiosis between the state and "*its* banks" as we often say. In the early United States, commercial banks (as opposed to existing merchant bankers) had to be chartered by the States or, controversially, by the federal government. Their charters "were seen as a privilege and as a tool of the state (and, possibly, federal) governments to be used to achieve specific, appropriate objectives."[14] The first full-fledge commercial bank, the Bank of North America, was chartered in 1781 to help finance the revolution. In 1791, the Bank of the United States, partly owned by the federal government, was chartered for the specific purpose of financing the government. Banks chartered by State governments—the usual practice then—often had their State as a shareholder. Some were even State-owned. The second bank chartered in Massachusetts was required to lend the State up to $100,000 at 5 percent interest. Especially in the North, the shackles of special legislative charters were broken around the middle of the nineteenth century, but even the new so-called free banks faced many regulatory requirements, often including the obligation to buy government bonds. Some banks continued to be chartered for specific projects including canals, bridges, roads, and railroads. The State governments' defaults of the 1840s were often due to soured investments in banks—this was the case in Arkansas, Louisiana, Mississippi, and Florida—but other States that did not default had made similar moves, either guaranteeing bonds issued by private banks or issuing their own bonds to finance them.[15]

One cannot speak about banking history without mentioning a unique feature of American banks. During a large part of American banking history and over a large part of the country, banks were prohibited from branching, that is, to have more than one branch office. Prior to the Civil War, banks (which were State-incorporated) were prohibited to branch in most States. The American Bankers Association opposed bank consolidation and branching, presumably because established bankers wanted to keep their local monopolies. After the Civil War, the federal government, which got into the business of incorporating banks, also forbade its banks to branch (or to open new branches if they had migrated from the State to the federal incorporation system). At both levels, bank mergers were tightly regulated. All these regulations explain why, on the eve of the Great Depression, some 25,000 banks operated in the country—most of them small, undiversified, and fragile. In turn, the fragility of the system led to calls for deposit insurance, which was tried in a few States and failed, before being established at the national level in 1934. Only from the 1920s on were banks gradually allowed to branch freely, but the legacy of atomized banking persists up to our days.

As Charles Calomiris explains, in return for the privilege of limited-responsibility charters, banks became tools, and source of funds, for the state. Regulation was part of the deal as banks were seen, and saw themselves, as junior partners in public policy. In practice, regulations were often the product of lobbying by interest groups, either bankers fearing competition or local interests (especially large farmers) wanting local savings to be loaned to them alone as opposed to being transferred elsewhere within a large banking organization. "In a world where banks are a tool of the state," writes Calomiris, "it is little wonder that the maximization of depositors' utility was not achieved."[16]

Banks were being granted the right to live in return for loans to government (or taxes) and tight regulation. This system has survived to our days, in America as elsewhere. Heavily regulated banks are under the constant surveillance and control of regulators, to whose goodwill they owe their very existence. In the 1980s, American banks gained the freedom to pay market interest rates to their depositors. In the 1990s, federal banks became free to branch. But this very partial deregulation has often been accompanied by new regulations and more supervision, and the banks remained otherwise tightly monitored and controlled.[17] They still had to support the state, albeit in more sophisticated manners than in former times.

The banks continue to support the state for three broad categories of reasons. First, regulation motivates them to lend money to the state: it's an offer they can't refuse. International regulations, adopted by the states participating in the BIS's Basel Committee on Banking Supervision have been forcing banks to maintain a certain capital ratio, that is, a minimum proportion between their capital (money provided by their shareholders) and their loans. This ratio used to be 6 percent but, with the new Basel III regulations (adopted after the Great Recession), will rise to 8 percent–10 percent over the next few years. The definition of "capital" will also be more restrictive, closer to shareholders' common equity.[18]

To illustrate the general impact of such regulations, suppose a bank lends $100. Regulations forbid it to simply borrow from its depositors or bondholders the $100 that it is lending. Its assets (the loan) must be backed up by capital, so that if the loan is not repaid entirely (or cannot be resold at par on the market, which amounts to the same) the bank won't be technically insolvent. In other words, shareholders must have capital to buffer any drop in the bank's assets. If the compulsory capital ratio is 10 percent, our bank lending $100 must have $10 of capital that backs up this loan. The Basel capital regulations have long established lower risk weights for certain types of loans, including a zero weight for government securities (compared with a 100 percent weight for ordinary loans, and a 50 percent weight for mortgage loans). The securities of a bank's own government don't even need to be top rated by rating agencies (such as Standard and Poor, Moody's, or Fitch).[19] At least, this is how the Basel requirements were implemented in Europe and America, as the BIS seems to shift on national regulators any blame for the detrimental impact the regulation had on bank solvency.[20] Thus, any profit made on a $100 government security, corresponding to the difference between the return on the security and the interest paid to the depositors, goes to the shareholders without them having to invest any capital to earn it. The banks can borrow from depositors, lend all the proceeds to the government at a higher rate, and pocket the difference. The Basel capital regulations thus created a strong incentive for the banks to hold government securities. In short, the debtors have passed laws making it costly for their creditors to stop lending them.

Banks are under heavy pressure to finance their governments in other ways. Since the Great Recession, banks have been urged by their regulators to maintain a "liquidity cushion" of safe assets, which means more government bonds. Hence, we have observed a big expansion of purchase of sovereign bonds by banks, "very handy," adds *The Economist* with typical British humor, "when governments have lots of bonds to sell."[21]

Another way the banks have often been forced to lend money to the state is through mandatory reserve requirements. Reserves are the proportion of their deposits that banks must keep in cash at the central bank in order to (claims the official justification) be able to honor their depositors' withdrawal requests. The mandatory reserve requirements do not really meet this objective, for banks must observe them at all times, over and above whatever the cash they effectively keep on hand to reimburse their depositors in the normal course of business. This supplementary cash can be maintained in excess reserves (reserves over reserve requirements) at the central bank, or obtained through inter-bank loans on the so-called federal funds market. There is nothing "federal" in this private market except for the fact that the short-term rate of interest that it determines is the one which the Fed has tradition-ally tried to influence. Thus, mandatory reserves are really forced loans to the Fed, and ultimately to the state as the Fed can buy Treasurys with the money.

It is true that mandatory reserve requirements have been much reduced by the Fed in October 2008, at the same time as it started paying interest on both compulsory reserves and excess reserves (like many other central banks had been doing). The Fed adopted this new policy in order to better control federal funds rates: these now cannot normally dip below the rate paid on reserves, for if they did the banks would lend short-term only to the central bank, and the reduced supply of loans on private markets would in turn push up short-term interest rates.[22] The state (through its central bank) has eschewed the benefits of no-interest loans in exchange for a better control on short-run inter-est rates.

A second reason why banks support the state is that they must behave if they want to avoid being more hampered by regulation, and harassed by bureaucrats. Banks are regulated by several federal agencies, includ-ing the Comptroller of the Currency, the Federal Deposit Insurance Corporation (FDIC), and the Fed. State-chartered banks, for their part, obey State regulators as their primary regulators. Charters, whether federal or State, are in principle available to any bank, or bank-holding corporation, but the incorporated bank must comply with complex regulatory requirements. Even before the recent regulatory reform, the New York Fed (the Fed is divided into regional units) had hundreds of regulators actually on the premises of large banks.[23] Granted that the situation is much worse in China, where Communist Party apparatchiks similarly operate on-site in all large companies.[24] My point here is that a bank that displeases a regulator is courting legal trouble. Regulations requiring banks to engage in activities claimed to be of public interest in order to obtain certain authorizations are not unknown in our own times. For example, a bank that does not get a good rating under the 1977 Community Reinvestment Act, which mandates special attention to poor neighborhoods and minority clienteles, can be denied an autho-rization to merge, diversify, or open branches.[25] Investment banks are also subject to the SEC and its state counterparts, and all banks must of course abide by general regulations on businesses (in the fields of labor, governance, consumer protection, tax, securities issuance, etc.).

"Social" is a magic word that glorifies good things, and demonizes bad ones. Jamie Dimon, the CEO of investment bank J. P. Morgan, recently had a social attack (like we would say "a Big Mac attack"), and laid bare his altruistic leanings. His bank, he said, had been tempted to pull out from the most troubled Eurozone countries. "But," he added, "we made a decision which was largely social, and partially economic, to stay." He claimed he is defending "the longer term interest of customers, employees and communities." He may be a good man, of course, and have high personal moral standards, but it is unlikely that his company sacrificed making money for altruistic reasons. There is a simple reason to this: shareholders are egoistic, at least as far as their stock investments are concerned. The pension funds, and thus future retirees, who hold J. P. Morgan shares would not be happy if their future returns were sacrificed. Even self-professed altruists often cannot resist half a percentage point more in returns. Before the bursting of the housing bubble, government-employee pension funds such as CalPERS invested heavily in mortgage-based securities, which, although riskier, promised slightly higher returns. Many other public bodies did the same. What Mr. Dimon really meant, besides assuaging his guilt before the large masses, was that he feared pulling out of troubled Eurozone countries would burn his bridges with European regulators on whose goodwill his business on the whole continent depends so much.

The state is no less selfish. Given a chance, the government will tightly regulate banks supposedly for the public interest, and simultaneously exempt them from compliance when its own interest is threatened. Consider the so-called Volker rule, from the name of a former Fed governor, which was incorporated in the Wall Street Reform and Consumer Protection Act of 2011 (a.k.a. Dodd-Frank Act). The Volker rule forbids commercial banks from trading securities for their own account (as opposed to the accounts of their clients, for whom they are still allowed to trade). This means that a bank cannot buy sovereign bonds for speculative purposes. The European Commission, the executive body of the EU, has complained to US Treasury Secretary Timothy Geithner that this regulation may reduce bank demand for European sovereign securities, thereby pushing up their interest rates and making the financing of European sovereigns more difficult. Why would the US government have enacted a regulation that could prevent commercial banks from trading in its own securities? That's the catch: it did not! The US government specifically exempted its own securities, plus those of Fannie Mae and Freddie Mac, from the Volcker rule.[26]

There is a third sort of reason why banks support, and are subservient to, the state: as much as the state can count on them, they want to count on its active support in case of trouble. The quid pro quo is that the banks accept state control in return for state support when they need it. During the recent economic crisis, banks received some $205 billions of dollars under the Troubled Asset Relief Program (TARP) put in place by the Bush administration in the fall of 2008. Nearly half this amount went to four large banks (Bank of America, Citigroup, J. P. Morgan, and Wells Fargo); some 700 smaller banks and other financial firms shared the rest. These bailouts will end up costing "only" a few tens of billions dollars to the taxpayers, as they have been in large part reimbursed with dividends or interest payments, but the bet could have turned worse.[27] The Dodd-Frank Act apparently reduces the probability of future large-scale bailout, but the guarantee is only as strong as Congress's determination not to amend its law when it wants to adopt new emergency programs. Moreover, straight subsidies are not the only way the state helps its banks. During the recent economic crisis, as we learned much later, the Fed lent as much as $1.5 trillion of dollars (in outstanding loans at any one time) to financial institutions.[28] Whether a good argument can or not be made that such temporary loans were necessary to prevent a complete collapse of the financial system, the fact is that, in bad times, the state returns the elevator and helps "its" banks.

Banks, even nominally private, often look more like branches of the state than like private companies. Banks learn to live under their Big-Brother regulators. "We have an excellent working relationship with our regulator,"[29] said the CEO of InterBank, a Savings & Loans institution, after his bank had been twice hit by an order from the Office of Thrift Supervision (OTS). Is this a case of Stockholm syndrome, or something else? Are the banks the state's minions, or is it instead the state that obeys the banks?

It is sometimes difficult to tell. Economists have argued that large firms typically capture their regulators in the service of their own interest. Collective action problems prevent citizens and taxpayers with diffuse interests to organize as efficiently as the bankers' concentrated interests are able to. It is possible that before the recent economic crisis, the banks and other financial institutions had partly captured their regulators.[30] Regulatory capture would explain why regulated companies often speak, nearly fondly, of "our regulator." Ways of saying things often convey underlying realities. "In accordance with guidance from our regulator," mentioned the Federal Home Loan Bank of Des Moines.[31] "In 1972 we received authority from our regulator to offer full trust services," boasts the website of First National Bank of Hartford.[32] As the Dodd-Frank Act was nearing approval, a Wall

Street executive confirmed that regulators are good capture targets: "Frankly," he said, "it's an enormous relief to be dealing with [regulators] again rather than Congress."[33] Yet, at a high level, banks like politicians. The fact that a few CEOs of Goldman Sachs have been Treasury secretaries is well known, as are the large contributions of the financial industry to the two large federal political parties.

It is easy, too easy, to criticize bankers, but they sometimes deserve it. Yet, when the chips are down, whoever controls or influences whomever, the state can prosecute bankers and send them to jail, not the other way around. Another, similar test can be devised to solve the question of who, the banks or the state, have real power; I call it the fear test: who is most scared of the other, the statocrat who is criticized by a banker, or the banker who is criticized by the statocrat? (I borrow the term "statocrat" from Bertrand de Jouvenel to mean politicians and bureaucrats who exercise daily power in the state.)[34] The answer is pretty obvious.

The Real Bankers of the State

Domestic banks represent only one category of bankers of the state, and not the most important one.

Historically, many bankers of the state were foreign entities. In his interesting article on the defaults of American States in the 1840s, William English observes that "a substantial fraction of many states' bonds were held abroad." Most of Pennsylvania bonds were held in England, and even French residents held more of them than the residents of any other American State. In 1846, most of the Illinois canal debt was held in London. In 1843, two-fifths of New York's bonds were held in Europe. Close to one half of Florida and Arkansas bonds were held in Amsterdam and London. The governor of Mississippi claimed that all the State's debt was held by foreigners.[35] Today, at least in developed countries, most public debt is held by the nationals of the issuing government—including, in Europe, by other European nationals.[36] The bankers are thus mainly domestic.

Much American public debt is owned in foreign countries. Because the dollar is a reserve currency and is used in international trade, foreigners often hold dollars. Instead of leaving their cash dollars idle, they often buy US securities, including US government securities. Suppose you live, say, in the UK, and have earned US dollars through exports (including exports of your services). You may choose not to convert your dollars if you expect to import something later. Since the dollar is a reserve currency and enters into 40 percent of foreign exchange transactions, you are likely to be able to pay in dollars. If you own a large amount of US dollars, you may want to invest them in US government securities, and earn interest. When you later need your dollars, you will just sell the securities against dollars. Because there is a wide market for US government securities, and because US debt is thought to be very safe, you are confident that you will not lose money when you sell them. In the meantime, you will have become part of the statistics of foreign holders of US public debt. Of course, a significant number of American residents also hold federal securities (which include both Treasurys, that is, securities issued by the Treasury, and mortgage securities issued by federal agencies and the GSEs).

Chart 7.1 shows the distribution in mid-2011 of the outstanding federal debt (a concept very close, but not identical, to the debt held by the public we analyzed in chapter 2).[37] At that time, the outstanding debt stood at $9.7 trillion. Some 8 percent of the federal debt was held by American residents through their pension funds if we include the retirement funds of all government employees in the country. A large

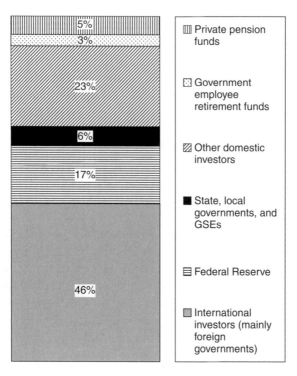

Chart 7.1   Holders of Outstanding Federal Debt, End of Second Quarter, 2011

Source: Hummel (2012a) and Federal Reserve.

chunk (23%) of the federal debt was held by a host of domestic investors, including banks and other financial institutions (a bit more than a fourth of the 23%), as well as money market funds and other mutual funds (slightly more than a third). We don't know exactly which part of this 23 percent is owned under the names of individuals—but, of course, individuals ultimately own everything in the economy. Banks, like other financial firms, are essentially intermediaries. So we can say that nearly a third of the public debt was held by private residents of the United States.

We still need to account for 69 percent of the federal debt. Some 6 percent (of the total debt) is held by State and local governments, and by the GSEs (mainly Fannie Mae and Freddie Mac). Another 17 percent of the outstanding federal debt is held by the Federal Reserve. Here we meet an accounting ghost: components of government hold securities issued by other parts of it. If the Fed's balance sheet were consolidated with that of the federal government, the 17 percent would simply cancel. What happens is that the Federal Reserve has, over its existence, created money to buy 17 percent of outstanding government securities. Another way to understand this bogus debt is to observe what would happen if the federal government repudiated its debt to the Fed. The latter would lose about $1.6 trillion in assets, which would imply a loss of equity (resulting in negative equity in this case) on the liability side of its balance sheet. With negative equity, the Fed would owe more than its assets are worth: it would have become theoretically insolvent. But this insolvency would probably not matter except from an esthetic-accounting view point, for the Fed would still have the power to create money to pay its creditors. Thus, close to a fourth of the outstanding federal debt is owned by other government bodies (the Fed and, as we saw, other levels of government and the GSEs), strangely considered as part of "the public". We are back to the fiction of us owing the money to ourselves.

The rest of the outstanding federal debt, nearly half of it (46%), is held by international investors. That foreign investors are considered part of the public is not shocking per se, and quite consistent with the economic approach, where all individuals count equally. However, the foreign investors category includes two very different types of animals: private investors and government investors. About 30 percent of the foreign-held federal debt (30% of the 46%) is in the hands of private investors, who hold it for the same reasons as American residents would, besides their special need of US dollars for international trade. The other 70 percent of foreign held federal debt (about $3.3 trillion in total), or close to a third of total federal outstanding debt, belongs to foreign governments through their investment funds, state enterprises, or central banks' foreign reserves. Foreign reserves are used to convert currencies as needed, and to manipulate foreign exchange rates. As Alice would say, curiouser and curiouser: foreign governments are part of the public to whom the US federal government owes money. Foreign governments partly finance the US government.

The proportion of foreign-held federal debt has been on the rise since the 1970s. The phenomenon is not difficult to understand. On the supply side, federal borrowing and the supply of federal securities started to balloon. On the demand side, while the domestic savings rate was declining, foreigners—whether private or government investors—had reasons to absorb more US government securities. The persistent trade deficits of the American economy—international imports larger than exports—meant that foreigners had more dollars (including "petrodollars," obtained from the sale of oil) in their hands. Except if their own money is worth nothing and they need actual dollar bills to carry on their daily transactions (like in Zimbabwe after hyperinflation had made the local currency useless), foreigners with dollars normally prefer to buy dollar-denominated securities, a strategy that combines the advantages of earning interest and owning an asset readily convertible in US dollars. The demand for federal government securities was reinforced by the perceived safety of US government securities, and the nature of the dollar as reserve currency. Demand also came from foreigners simply keen to invest in America, an autonomous factor that in return allowed Americans to import more than they exported.

Foreign investors in China account for the largest foreign holdings of US government securities, totaling about $1.1 trillion (as of end of August 2011). This amounts to a bit more than 10 percent of the total federal debt held by the public, or a fourth of foreign holdings. As for other individual foreign countries, we don't know the exact proportions that are held by private and public investors. Given widespread controls on capital and currency transactions in China, it is reasonable to believe that the bulk of US government securities there are held by government or quasi-governmental organizations. Thus, we can assume that about one tenth of the federal debt is owed to the Chinese state. Given the size of its holding of US government securities, the Chinese government has an obvious interest in preventing their price from falling. Consequently, the Chinese state would be leery of dumping them on the market, as an increased supply would bring down their price.

However, political and strategic factors could come into play. The very possibility of selling US government securities does give a bargaining chip to the Chinese government. The possible threat takes the form: behave or else we'll sell your securities (or stop buying more). This would lead to a drop in the price of US government securities and thus to higher returns on them. A general increase of interest rates for federal government financing would follow. All interest rates would be pulled up, for if investors can buy government securities at higher yields, they won't put their money anywhere else until the returns have adjusted throughout the economy. By becoming one of the main bankers of the US government, the Chinese state has gained a potential weighty voice in American foreign and economic policy—if it decides to sacrifice its economic interest to its political goals. As an example, a former international security fellow at Harvard University proposed that the US government strikes a deal with its Chinese counterpart: we stop supporting Taiwan, in return of which you erase part of the federal debt.[38] The American emperor is thus naked in a new way: he is dependent on the good will of another emperor, the one in Peking.

The Limits of Honest Borrowing

Even neglecting foreign policy risks, the US federal government (and other governments in the world) cannot continue to borrow as they have been doing since the 1970s.

The first reason is that borrowing costs will rise as creditors start doubting the solvency of their debtor. Some 6 percent of the federal government's expenditures, and 9 percent of its revenues, went to paying interest on the debt in 2010. The low rate of interest, pushed down by the Fed in the wake of the Great Recession, explains why the interest cost is lower than in the 1990s, when it averaged 16 percent of revenues. Interest rates have also been on a general downward trend in the world since the 1980s. Let them rise to more normal levels, and the interest on the debt may jump to more than a fifth of federal revenues in less than ten years, as our forecasts of chapter 5 suggest. Increased interest costs will become less and less sustainable as they require the federal government to borrow more and more, which will give investors more and more reasons to be nervous. Thus far, investors have maintained their trust in American government securities, but they will likely have second thoughts not too far in the future. They will want higher and higher yields to continue holding government securities. And remember that these investors are your pension fund, your mutual fund, your bank, your insurance company...It is true that investors will want to invest somewhere, and that federal securities may look better than other governments' securities. However, once they realize that the federal government is as bankrupt as the Greek state was, they will consider substitutes, such as highly rated corporate securities or straight cash. The US government might not be able to finance itself but at a prohibitive rate.

More important than the government's financial cost of borrowing is its economic cost. "Economic cost" means the net cost for all individuals. As we saw in the CBO's analysis (chapter 5), government borrowing raises interest rates and evicts private investment. Lower investment causes lower production and incomes. The tax base narrows, requiring even more borrowing if expenditures are not reduced. Higher tax rates would not solve the problem, for they lead individuals to work less and hide incomes, thereby reducing the tax base. Reinhart and Rogoff estimate that when the ratio of government debt to GDP exceed 90 percent, annual growth rates have historically dropped by four percentage points on average; considering whole episodes during which the 90 percent threshold was exceeded, Reinhart, Reinhart, and Rogoff find that the cumulative loss of GDP was 24 percent.[39] The vicious circle between stagnation and debt rapidly leads to a significantly reduced GDP. For the United States, where the ratio is already above 90 percent (we are talking about gross debt, as in Chart 3.2), the CBO's alternative scenario suggests that growing indebtedness will, in 25 years' time, lead to an annual GDP lower than it would have otherwise have been by between 2 percent and 10 percent. And this forecast tells only part of the story as much of GDP would need to be shipped outside America to reimburse foreign creditors: the CBO estimates that annual production and income of American nationals would, in 25 years' time, have been reduced by as much as 7 percent–18 percent.[40] And all this does not incorporate the possibility of serious political disturbances when we hit the brick wall.

As total US public liabilities continue to increase, the sovereign's bankers will want to reduce, not increase, their exposure, worsening the problem further. Commercial banks may not find the regulatory incentives strong enough to maintain their holdings. As they have been doing since the Great Recession started, banks may choose to deposit their money at the Fed, which still amounts to lending money to the government. This works only as long as the banks trust the Fed itself. In the best case, the Fed can influence the economy only as long as people believe that it can do what it commits to do. The state could try different coercive measures, but again force has its limits.

International investors may continue for a while to bankroll the US government, especially foreign governments who are under pressure from their own domestic producers to keep down their currency exchange rate by buying dollars. Take the example of China. When the Chinese yuan exchange rate is low, which means that the dollar is relatively expensive for the Chinese but the yuan relatively cheap for the Americans, Chinese exporters are able to offer great bargains to American importers, whereas American exporters struggle to quote attractive prices in yuans to Chinese importers. (A high dollar means that it is expensive to buy with yuans, and inversely that you can buy many yuans with it.) In order to maintain the yuan low, the Chinese government must, via its central bank, hoard many of the dollars earned by its exporters, for dumping them for yuan i n foreign exchange markets would push the price of the dollar down and the price of the yuan up. It's a simple question of supply and demand: more supply of dollars and more demand for yuan increase the price of the latter and decrease the price of the former (and no pejorative sense is attached to "dumping"). As the Chinese government does not want this result, it keeps its dollars in its coffers—and invests them in US securities, notably Treasury securities.

But this only works up to a certain point. When the Chinese government and other governments holding dollars start doubting that the greenback will remain high, they will want to sell at least some of them, including the securities denominated in them. When they start doubting whether the US government will reimburse its creditors, they will sell more of its securities. At any rate, it is easy to imagine foreign governments refusing to increase their purchase of federal securities. Since all foreign governments own one third of the federal government's debt, and since this debt is continuously increasing, the impact will be severe.

The American state will then reach the limits of honest borrowing, if it has not already passed it. If this stage is not triggered by foreign government lenders, it will be by domestic lenders through the sort of vicious circle described by economists Carmen Reinhart and Kenneth Rogoff: more public debt, higher interest rates, less economic growth, more debt, and so on. Coercive or stealth borrowing will then come into vogue. The state can coerce its domestic lenders through what Reinhart and Rogoff call "financial repression"—the process of creating incentives for lending money to itself, and setting up obstacles to lending to others.[41]

The state has many tools of financial repression in its toolbox. We have already looked into one of the tools, the Basel capital regulations: these capital regulations create incentives for the banks to hold government securities. The BIS explicitly denies that it is facilitating financial repression, shifting the blame on national governments instead, but this reaction confirms the existence of the phenomenon.[42] Another tool of financial repression consists of putting a ceiling on interest rates paid by banks—as regulations mandated for several decades in the United States—which provides banks with cheap deposit money to lend to the state at low interest rates. There is also moral suasion, backed by regulatory threats, overt or tacit. Of course, the availability of bailouts has the same impact: if the banks want to be able to loot the public treasury when needed, they better lend money to the sovereign when he needs it. Observe again the two faces of the banks' relation with the state: obedient to it and well served by it. The ECB's long-term loans to European banks at the end of 2011 have apparently been mainly used to lend money to the state (or to the central bank itself), and earn net interest in the proceeds.[43] Over a two-month period corresponding to the ECB's program, Spanish and Italian banks increased their holdings of sovereign bonds by 13 percent and 29 percent respectively.[44]

Financial repression does not target banks only. Regulatory constraints on holdings of foreign securities lead to more domestic investment, including government securities. Pension funds' portfolios can be limited to well-rated securities, which conveniently include government securities—a good way to force the future retirees to finance the state. Solvency requirements for insurance company can privilege government securities, as shown by the planned regulations that would force insurers to hold safer assets and would conveniently maintain the fictitious risk-free status of government securities. Insurance will cost more, shifting part of the financial repression to consumers.[45] Keeping rates of interest low, or even negative in real terms, through expansionary monetary policy, forces investors who need safe investment to lend to the state at negative interest rates. Inflation can thus be used as a tool of financial repression: savers get little or no remuneration for their savings, while the state creates money to grab resources and goods that would otherwise have been used by individuals. But more later on money creation and inflation.

America has avoided some forms of financial repression, but not all of them. From the New Deal until the early 1980s, federal regulation prohibited the payment of interest on checking accounts and capped interest rates on savings accounts, rendering government securities relatively more attractive. From World War II until the 1980s, inflation often allowed the federal government to pay a negative real interest rate: Reinhart and Rogoff calculate that over one fourth of the period from 1945 to 1980, the average interest rate on the public debt in the United States was lower than the rate of inflation, so that people ended up paying, instead of being paid, to hold government securities. If you lend money to the government at 3 percent and its monetary policy generates a rate of inflation of 5 percent, you lose 2 percent per year, a corresponding gain to your debtor. This trick will only work for a while, for when inflation becomes predictable—rational expectations again—the supply of credit to the government will decrease, pushing up yields. Financial repression was worse in countries where the sovereign had tools like capital controls to prevent his nationals from investing out of the country. In Italy, for example, financial repression reduced the ratio of public debt to GDP by 71 percent during the decade 1945–1955, compared to a 44 percent reduction in America.[46] If laws against fraud and misleading advertising applied to governments, many statocrats would be in jail.

A few measures of liberalization in the 1980s put a temporary end to financial repression, including the freeing of interest rates in the United States and the abolition of foreign exchange controls in Europe. But financial repression could again rear its ugly head as the emperor needs his subjects' money, whether they agree or not. The process has already started, and not just with esoteric means like new regulations for European insurers. In pushing interest rates to historically low levels, the state has reduced its interest payments to the detriment of all savers, including future retirees.

The sovereign's bankers are not only bad, greedy banks, which generally own only a relatively small proportion of public debt. They are not only bad foreigners, although these make up for more than 40 percent of the American public debt. The sovereign's bankers are also, and mainly, individual Americans who have bought government securities through their savings accounts, their pension funds, their mutual funds, or their money market funds. Ultimately, of course, everything is owned or owed by flesh-and-blood individuals, so we can say that more than half of the federal government's debt is actually due to American residents, that is, you and me. We, the people, are the sovereign's main bankers.

CHAPTER 8

REDUCING EXPENDITURES: MISSION IMPOSSIBLE?

From the late 1940s to 2007, total government expenditures in America rose from about 20 percent to more than 30 percent of GDP; total receipts grew from 20 percent to a bit less than 30 percent. Since the recession, expenditures have jumped to 35 percent of GDP. Two economists with the Federal Reserve Bank of St. Louis correctly conclude that "the rise in the federal debt... is entirely a consequence of the federal government's increase of expenditures without an offsetting increase in revenues."[1] Government goodies financed by public expenditures have multiplied like loaves and fishes. Reducing government expenditures thus appears to be the best solution, if not the only one. But it is politically easier said than done.

The Miracle of the Loaves and Fishes

Looking at government expenditures as a proportion of GDP is often useful, but can also be misleading. It is useful because it shows how much of what people produce and earn—GDP—is taken by government and spent on their behalf or, properly speaking, on the behalf of some of them. However, this ratio is also misleading because it is affected as much by its denominator (GDP) as by its numerator (expenditures): when the economy (GDP) is growing fast, for example, the ratio is pushed down even if the numerator (spending) is constant or even on the rise.

Chart 8.1 uses another measure instead: the evolution of government expenditures per capita in constant dollars. Taking actual government expenditures without comparing them to GDP avoids the problem explained above. Calculating them in constant dollars takes away the impact of inflation—the fact that a dollar of expenditure is worth less today than it was in the past. In 2010, for example, a dollar was worth

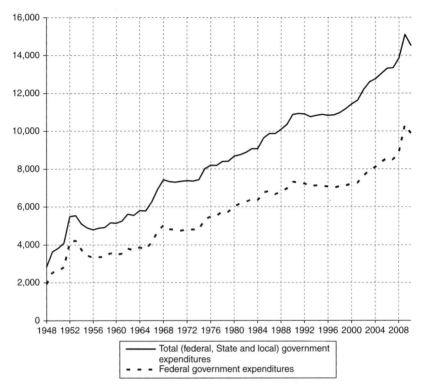

Chart 8.1   Government Expenditures Per Capita, Constant Dollars (2005), United States, 1948–2010

Source: OMB (2011b), and Census Bureau (2012).

about 12 percent less than in 2005, because prices had increased by 13 percent over the period, or roughly 3 percent per year. Worried by the difference between the 12 percent decrease and the 13 percent increase? This happens because the base of the percentage calculation changes: if, for example, 100 (the base) decreases by 12 percent, the result is 88, but 100 is 13 percent higher than 88 (the new base). So if we calculate the 2010 expenditures in 2005 dollars, we want to deflate the actual amount in current dollars by 12 percent. Total government expenditures in 2010 were $5.1 trillion. Taking 12 percent off this figure, that is, multiplying it by 0.88, gives $4.5 trillion, which is thus the 2010 expenditures in 2005 constant dollars. You can double check by adding 13 percent (the price increase over the period) to $4.5 trillion: you get $5.1 trillion. We often say "real expenditures" to describe the figure in constant dollars.

To build Chart 8.1, this calculation is made for every year over the whole period from 1948 to 2010. Moreover, in a second stage, we divide the annual expenditures by the US population (in 2010, it was roughly 310 million) in order to avoid the objection that government expenditures increased just because the population was increasing and required (it is assumed) more services. Note that this assumption is in turn based on the assumption of no increasing returns to scale in government services, that is, the assumption that these services cannot be offered at a lower unit cost if they are produced for a larger number of consumers. This assumption is probably unrealistic, but it allows us to calculate a very conservative measure of government expenditures.

I use 2005 dollars simply because this is what OMB uses. I use expenditures data from 1948 to 2010 because it corresponds to the latest available consistent series at the time of writing.[2]

The bottom, dotted curve of Chart 8.1 follows the federal government's real expenditures per capita (including grants to State and local governments). Real federal government expenditures grew from less than $2,000 per American in 1948 to nearly $10,000 in 2010. The growth is virtually continuous, except during four episodes: a sharp jump during the Korean war in the early 1950s was followed by a temporary decrease; the late 1960s and early 1970s saw a temporary leveling off of federal expenditures per capita; so did the 1990s; and finally 2010 saw a partial retreat from the excesses of the Great Recession. It is especially remarkable that federal expenditures per capita increased by 13 percent during the two terms of Ronald Reagan—but more later on this mystery.

State and local governments added their own expenditures from their own tax sources. As we can see from the difference between the two curves of the chart, they spend from their own sources of revenue about half of what the federal government spends. Adding State and local governments does not change the general shape of the curve. Total real government expenditures per capita in America climbed, continuously for most of the period, from nearly $3,000 to about $15,000. It is a fivefold increase in six decades.

All Expenditures Are Essential

Despite the enormous growth in government expenditures over the past decades, it always seems difficult, if not impossible, to stop or, a fortiori, to reverse the trend. Since 1948 real federal expenditures have grown by 3.9 percent a year, compared to 2.7 percent for real GDP. Not only is this growth differential unsustainable, but also government expenditures become entrenched to the point where most people think they are all essential. Yet, major cuts in real dollars would only bring

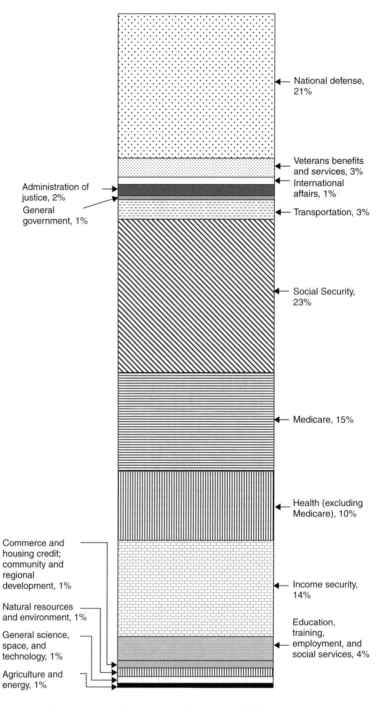

National defense, 21%

Veterans benefits and services, 3%

International affairs, 1%

Administration of justice, 2%

General government, 1%

Transportation, 3%

Social Security, 23%

Medicare, 15%

Health (excluding Medicare), 10%

Commerce and housing credit; community and regional development, 1%

Income security, 14%

Natural resources and environment, 1%

General science, space, and technology, 1%

Education, training, employment, and social services, 4%

Agriculture and energy, 1%

Chart 8.2 Noninterest Outlays by Function, US Federal Government, 2007

Source: OMB (2011b).

us a few years back. Take 2007, when the federal government spent $8,486 trillion in real (2005) dollars for every man, woman, and child in America. Reducing these expenditures by 10 percent would have brought back the level of only five years earlier, 2002. It is not obvious that American were much better off in 2007 than in 2002. It is not obvious either that American were much worse off in 1985, where real federal expenditures per capita were one third lower than in 2007.

Why do government expenditures look so indispensable, so imperative? We can start answering this question with Chart 8.2. The underlying data are the same as in Chart 4.1 (chapter 4), but I have reorganized them to exclude the 9 percent in interest on the public debt, as this expenditure depends on accumulated debt and the rate of interest and is not, barring default, controllable in the short run. In other words, Chart 8.2 represents primary, or noninterest, outlays. I have also detailed some of the "other" outlays of Chart 4.1.[3] The figures relate to FY year 2007, so as to make sure we don't get bogged down in the argument that, during economic crises, some extra spending is justified. Note that, whereas the percentages are rounded up in Chart 8.2, the sections of the bar are not and thus represent slightly more precise proportions. Also, remember from chapter 5 that a reduction of about 33 percent in noninterest spending would be necessary to close the fiscal gap. Now, look at ordinary federal expenditures and ask yourself where to cut:

- National defense? Even if the Pentagon were closed and all US armed forces disbanded (21% of noninterest spending), if all veterans benefits (3%) were stopped, and if the cut included all international affairs (1%, for such things as international aid, participation in international organizations, embassies, etc.), we would still fall short of the required cuts.
- Law and order? The federal government spends only 2 percent of its primary budget on the administration of justice: courts, jails, and other federal law enforcement. Even if we also put in the basket all general government outlays (administration expenditures for the executive and legislative branches, etc.), we only get 3 percent of the federal budget: peanuts!
- Transportation, that is, the road, air, and water transportation infrastructure? Peanuts again, as cutting all these expenditures would only reduce federal noninterest outlays by 3 percent.
- The main welfare-state programs? Now we are talking business because. Add Social Security (23%), Medicare (15%), other health expenditures (10%, including Medicaid), and income security (14%), you get 62 percent of the federal government's noninterest outlays. Do you really want to cut 53 percent (33% over 62%) of these

expenditures in order to plug the fiscal gap? Will the beneficiaries accept such deep cuts in their federal pensions, their Medicare, their Medicaid? Is it desirable to cut so deeply in the assistance programs for the poor, which also include food stamps, housing assistance, and unemployment compensation? It is quite striking that more than one-fourth of the "income security" money goes to the retirement and disability programs of the federal bureaucrats, but do you really want to deprive active and retired federal employees of most of their pensions?

- Education programs and other assistance programs? If you add all education, training, and other social services, you only get 4 percent of federal noninterest spending. It won't get us far in cutting 33 percent.
- All miscellaneous economic interventions of the federal government? Perhaps it would be good riddance but, again, such a radical policy would not get us very far. Expenditures related to these miscellaneous interventions make up for only 4 percent of noninterest spending: 1 percent for the promotion (and regulation) of commerce, housing credit, community, and regional development; 1 percent for natural resources and environment; 1 percent for space, science, and technology; and 1 percent for agriculture (including subsidies to farmers) and energy.

All expenditures go to programs that are important from some point of view, and very important to some individuals, who will resist any cut. Of course, the 33 percent cuts could be shared across categories, but this would just spread the pain in another way. Many beneficiaries and their representatives in government would argue that the cuts cause structural damage to their preferred programs, and that the public welfare is threatened. Indeed, this is why actual cuts—as opposed to cuts in forecasted increases—are virtually never made. It seems impossible to realize the needed cuts without challenging major programs such as national defense, Social Security, Medicare, Medicaid, or income security. All other categories, including "small" intervention areas such as education, add up to only 14 percent of federal expenditures. It could be argued that cost-benefit analyses could be realized to eliminate the least socially beneficial programs, but this argument overrates what this sort of analysis can achieve either in theory or in practice. Ultimately, political choices would have to be made about who would be harmed and who would be favored.

Even if Congress were seriously intent on cutting expenditures, the task would not be easy. It cannot be done by merely voting lower appropriations in annual budgets. Discretionary spending makes up for about 40 percent of the budget. The rest consists of mandatory outlays, fixed by law, which comprise interest on the public debt on the one hand and the so-called programmatic mandatory spending on the other hand. The major mandatory programs are Social Security, Medicare, Medicaid, unemployment insurance, and other means-tested entitlements such as food stamps and the transfers under the Earned Income and Child Tax Credits. When we include interest on the public debt, about 60 percent of federal spending is mandatory and cannot be modified except by amending major and massive pieces of previous legislation, or by an ad hoc capping of future expenditures called "sequestration" (what was attempted by the Budget Control Act of 2011). Of the 40 percent of federal discretionary spending, about half is defense and half nondefense. Making the required 33 percent cuts by targeting only discretionary spending could involve cutting all defense spending (which is 99 percent discretionary) plus most of nondefense discretionary spending. Add to this that the largest part of the increase in federal spending since the 1950s has come from mandatory spending, and you are starting to understand why Congress has so much problems cutting federal expenditures.

The CBO forecasts that the automatic cuts mandated by the Budget Control Act of 2011 will reduce by $1 trillion the projected deficits (that is, the sum of additions to the federal debt) over the 2013–2022 period, which is of the order of $3–$11 trillion depending on the assumptions made.[4] And this relatively small reduction in deficits will happen only if the planned cuts are effectively made, and not cancelled by new legislation or through the exceptions provided for in the 2011 law. To close the fiscal gap, that is, to prevent the federal debt from increasing as a proportion of GDP, about one third of *annual* federal primary expenditures would have to be cut, which would require a reduction of about $1.2 trillion in annual expenditures, which amounts to $12 trillion over ten years, or 12 times what the Budget Control Act of 2011 will (perhaps) achieve.

It is tempting to think that the required cuts can be achieved by efficiency gains, and many people—especially politicians—embrace this illusion. To give an impressionistic view of the opportunities and constraints, suppose that the productivity of federal civilian employees were boosted by 25 percent, which means the same services would be rendered by reducing their number by 20 percent. (If you reduce 100 by 20%, you obtain 80, and 100 is 25% larger than 80.) An estimated $244 billion is spent annually on the wages, salaries, and benefits of the federal government's civilian employees. Reducing this amount by 20 percent would only produce economies of $49 billion, which is about 1.5 percent of total federal expenditures in 2010. It is true that this estimate does not include all the education and health personnel paid through federal subsidies. Suppose then that labor productivity were increased in all subsidized federal health and education so that expenditures in these sectors could be reduced by 20 percent. This would require a tremendous boost of productivity of 25 percent in all health and education activities. Going back to Chart 4.1, we see that these expenditure functions cover about 27 percent of federal expenditures (24% for health and 3% for education). A reduction of 20 percent in those would only reduce primary federal expenditures by 5 percent (27% × 20%), still very far from the 33 percent we are looking for.

Understandably, analysts who try to demonstrate how federal expenditures can be cut are often not convincing. A list established at the Heritage Foundation and rhetorically asking "Nowhere to Cut?" lists mostly small expenditures and would not anyway, and in the best case, produce more than two or three hundred billion dollars of savings, whereas about $1.2 trillion needs to be cut on a budget that, in 2012, reaches $3.6 trillion. Just consider what the author correctly calls "corporate welfare" that is, miscellaneous subsidies to business. He comes up with a total of $92 billion, which indeed should be cut, but would provide less than 8 percent of the cuts needed.[5]

It looks like a mission impossible. Many people have strong incentives in the continuation of the present system: those who live on federal entitlements (pensions, health care, etc.), plus the politicians who give these goodies to their electors, and the government bureaucrats who administer them. It is estimated that 49 percent of Americans live in households receiving some form of government benefits (such as Social Security, Medicaid, or unemployment compensation), including 35 percent who benefit from means-tested programs (food stamps, Medicaid, social welfare, housing assistance,...).[6] Adding the 17 percent of the workforce who are actually in the employment of some level of government,[7] we find that a majority of Americans live off the state and have a direct incentive to continue. Members of this majority often justify their egoism by appealing to fairness, democracy, apple pie, or whatever, but this does not change the fact that they are voting to take other people's money (whether this is their intention or not). Politicians, who want to be elected, will naturally cater to this majority of government-supported electors.

The above estimates exaggerate the number of those who depend on government, for many of them earn private incomes, or benefit from private pensions or savings, that dwarf their government benefits. Total government expenditures in America amounts to "only" a third of GDP, which means that, in a sense, one third of Americans live off the other two-thirds. The theory of collective action teaches us that minorities can often easily exploit majorities, for example by taxing to their own benefits the incomes of the latter. Forms of exploitation other than taxes exist; regulation is a major one. However they do it, minorities can exploit the majority by successfully organizing themselves into special interest groups which, because they represent concentrated interests, can lobby, infiltrate, or capture government more efficiently than the general and disorganized citizenry. Trade unions, which represent only 8 percent of private-sector workers and 40 percent of government employees, are especially efficient at this.

Public-sector unions provide a good illustration of the theory of collective action. Between a government bureaucrat trying to save his $110,000 job (an estimate of the average pay in the federal civil service, including benefits)[8] and an individual taxpayer whose own taxes contribute only $745 per year to federal pay (the cost per capita of the federal public service, excluding the post office), the first one will be very motivated to organize, demonstrate, and lobby, the second one much less. Most people will not go and demonstrate in Washington to save $745 a year. They are much more likely to do it if the possible gain is $110,000 a year—and if their trade union exerts pressures on them to participate. Entrepreneurial union organizers find in their own interests to drive the process. Of course, business interests have their lobbies too: think of the ethanol lobby, or of tire manufacturers demanding and obtaining protection of their domestic market. And these are only examples.

More generally, the political system produces coalitions, whether explicit as when they coalesce into organized interest groups, or implicit as when voters are mobilized by political entrepreneurs called politicians. Economically, an entrepreneur in the broadest sense is anybody who discovers an unsatisfied demand and tries to make a profit by responding to it; in this sense, politicians, like union organizers, are entrepreneurs. Economist Arnold Kling argues that blocking coalitions against change in Social Security and Medicare are easy to assemble. As its name indicates, a blocking coalition is able to stop change even if it cannot agree on, or bring about, an alternative solution. On Social Security, Republicans oppose tax increases while Democrats reject benefit cuts, so both groups form a blocking coalition against a solution to the problems of this program. On Medicare, Republicans oppose rationing while Democrats reject any attempt at privatization.[9] Hence, the result will be no change, and uncontrolled expenditures.

Through the incentives they embody, our political institutions—political technology, as it were—are all geared up to increasing government expenditures. As the experience of the past half-century demonstrates, budget surpluses are virtually impossible to achieve when there is no binding constraints against deficit financing. Whatever revenues the government raises in taxes, somebody will want to get a share of the loot. Politics is a jungle, and the politically stronger becomes the better looter. When perchance, or by the action of a strong leader, a surplus is realized, it gets rapidly dissipated. In a report prepared for Congress's Joint Economic Committee, two economists, Richard Vedder and Lowell Gallaway, present an econometric analysis of the relationship between budget surpluses and increases in federal expenditures in the year that followed. They find that, over the whole history of the United States, an average 37 percent of each surplus was used for increasing federal spending in the following year, and that the proportion reached 60 percent between 1950 and 1998. The spending increases continued for two other years, but these were much smaller. The surpluses of 1957 and of 1969 were quickly dissipated into big spending increases. Moreover, the number of surplus years and the length of surplus situations have decreased dramatically.[10]

If the state naturally grows, whatever "the people" wants, can we really talk about "our" government? Has the state grown into an oppressive organization that imposes its dictates to a large proportion of the people? Has democracy become anything but a facade to justify buying some people's consent? This book is not the place to address these wide and deep questions. But we can see that they are related to the debate between the orthodox approach to budgetary policy, according to which the state is us, and an alternative view of the state as an independent power, as Leviathan. Like Leviathan, the state is all-powerful if not chained. We have seen many instances of this. But how to chain Leviathan?

Reagan's Failure

In recent times, and excluding the forced effects of the sovereign debt crisis in Europe, few politicians have seriously tried to reduce government expenditures. Many people expected Ronald Reagan, who was elected in November 1980 and occupied the White House for two terms, to do just that. A superficial analysis might suggest that he succeeded. In 1981, the year before the first Reagan budget (FY 1982), the ratio of federal outlays to GDP was 22.2 percent; in the last year under a Reagan budget, FY 1989, the ratio had gone down to 21.2 percent.[11] These ratios however are misleading: 1981 was a recession year, which boosted up the ratio, whereas the late 1980s were a period of brisk economic growth, dampening the ratio. If we look instead at total federal expenditures in dollars, we observe that, over the Reagan presidency, they increased by 69 percent, from less than $700 million to more than $1.1 trillion. In constant dollars (excluding inflation), the increase was still 22 percent, and in constant dollars per capita, 13 percent. The tough truth is that President Reagan did not reduce federal expenditures in any meaningful sense; on the contrary, they increased under his watch.

Chart 8.3 shows which federal expenditures increased the most under Ronald Reagan. These official OMB data give outlays in current dollars and cover FY 1981 to FY 1989. Many seem to believe that federal outlays grew because of military expenditures. This is not true. National defense outlays did increase by a brisk 93 percent, but nondefense outlays jumped by 61 percent. Another surprise for those who are not familiar with official statistics is by how much the major welfare-state functions grew: 117 percent for Medicare, 80 percent for other public health expenditures, 67 percent for Social Security, and 37 percent for income security. As these functions make up for much of nondefense spending, it is not surprising that the latter grew so much.

Total federal outlays	**69%**
National defense	*93%*
Non defense	*61%*
International affairs	-27%
Natural resources and environment	19%
Agriculture	50%
Transportation	18%
Education, Training, Employment, and Social Services	7%
Health (excluding Medicare)	80%
Medicare	117%
Income security	37%
Social Security	67%
Veterans Benefits and Services	31%
Administration of justice	96%
General government	-18%
Net interest on public debt	146%
Other	8%

Chart 8.3 Federal Expenditures: Growth during the Ronald Reagan's Two Terms

Source: OMB (2011b).

With only three exceptions, all expenditure functions grew, the smallest increase (7%) being education and related services. One exception is the "general government" function and is explained by lower general-purpose federal aid to State and local governments (this category only contains assistance that cannot be classified in the other functions). The second exception relates to international affairs, where international security assistance and other international financial programs were reduced. The third exception lies in the energy function, which is hidden in "other" category of the chart: energy lost $12 billion of its $15 billion budget over the course of the Reagan presidency. It is notable that all other functions related to government economic intervention (including agriculture, natural resources, and the environment) benefited from increased spending.

In his first State of the Union address, on January 26, 1982, President Reagan voiced some radical intentions: "The budget plan I submit to you on Feb. 8," he said, "will realize major savings by dismantling the Departments of Energy and Education, and by eliminating ineffective subsidies for business." He immediately added, "We will continue to redirect our resources to our two highest budget priorities: a strong national defense to keep America free and at peace, and a reliable safety net of social programs for those who have contributed and those who are in need."[12] We just saw that education expenditures increased, and the Department of Energy was not dismantled. Large cuts were made in the latter, but this was an exception.

On spending cut, Reagan's words were more prudent than his supporters liked to think and his opponents seemed to fear. As the quote above illustrates, he did not promise to dismantle the welfare state. In fact, he immediately added: "Contrary to some of the wild charges you may have heard, this Administration has not and will not turn its back on America's elderly or America's poor. Under the new budget, funding for social insurance programs will more than double the amount spent six years ago." But however prudent he was, he did not live up to his plans. "In our fiscal year 1986 budget," Ronald Reagan declared in his February 6, 1985, State of the Union speech, "overall government program spending will be frozen at the current level. It must not be one dime higher than fiscal year 1985."[13] It turned out that program spending for 1986 was 374,990 million dimes ($37.499 billion) more than the previous year. In his July 17, 1980 acceptance speech of the Republican nomination, Reagan had said: "I will not accept the excuse that the federal government has grown so big and powerful that it is beyond the control of any president, any administration or Congress."[14] History has shown that he had to face a different reality.

It is true that Ronald Reagan had many attenuating circumstances, but I don't think they weaken the hypothesis that the federal government is out of control. Reagan did not control Congress, where the House had a democratic majority during his whole presidency. This just means that Congress is as much part of the problem as the executive branch.

Another excuse for Ronald Reagan's poor performance is that he had not promised to really cut government expenditures. What he had promised was, as he explicitly said in his first State of the Union address, a "reduction of the rate of increase in government spending" or, at most, a "continued reduction of the growth in Federal spending." He thought that it was sufficient to reduce the growth of government spending below the growth of GDP so that their ratio would diminish, without admitting that this could still mean growing expenditures in real dollars. "We must make sure that our economy grows faster than the growth in spending by the Federal government," declared his 1985 State of the Union address. His program was for modest change.

Reagan's policies did not modify the institutions and the incentives in a way to generate self-sustaining reductions in federal expenditures and state power. Despite his frequent libertarian-leaning statements, we find him merely opposing "the intervention and intrusion in our lives that result from unnecessary and excessive growth of government."[15] Only from "unnecessary and excessive growth of government"? He did little, if anything, to check the growth of government power. At other times, he seemed more radical: "It's time," he said in the same speech, "to check and reverse the growth of government." So, not only reduce its growth but reverse it? Who knows? Politicians have a way to make promises that mean different things to different potential electors and to get away with it because of the latter's rational ignorance. Government is quite obviously out of control.

Questioning the State's Missions

Ronald Reagan's failure to tame Leviathan carries lessons. "This is serious surgery," an administration official said of Reagan's plans after he won a reelection in the fall of 1984.[16] It turned out to be more like plastic surgery: Reagan gave a facelift to old Leviathan. William Niskanen, one of his former economic advisers, put his finger on the immediate cause of the president's failure: he tried to control expenditures by "eliminating fraud, waste, and abuse," as the 1986 budget stated.[17] "He did not even suggest that the termination of some programs would be necessary," explained Niskanen, and he "put off limits some of the most important elements of the welfare state."[18] The lesson is clear: cutting expenditures while keeping all major government programs revealed to be an impossible mission.

Reducing waste is popular among statocrats for it allows them to share the illusion that they are doing something about out-of-control government expenditures while in fact doing nothing that threatens their empire. And they get paid while giving the impression of doing something. Barack Obama's February 2012 budget used expressions strangely reminiscent of Reagan's intention of "eliminating fraud, waste, and abuse." Obama's budget proposed to "detect and prevent fraud, waste, and abuse,"[19] to "reduce fraud, waste, and abuse,"[20] to "cut waste, fraud, and abuse,"[21] etc. Note the different rhetorical permutations of the same vacuous mantra. There is certainly some waste, fraud, and abuse in the big machinery of the federal government, but bringing it under control requires addressing a deeper dimension of the problem, that is, waste in the very existence of programs that cater to organized interests and popular minorities, fraud in the way politicians sell programs they can't finance, and abuse by civil servants of their monopoly power. Productivity gains can't solve any of these problems. Questioning Leviathan's scope of intervention would be required.

Although the real money is in welfare-state expenditures, the attack cannot be confined to this front. In a sense, expenditures are overrated as a way for the state to grow and control society. Other ways are often more efficient: individual mandates, regimentation in public programs, criminal prosecution, surveillance. Of course, spending money and bossing around are correlated: the latter requires money, and the more money is available to spend, the more bossing around becomes possible. But one cannot keep state power intact while reducing its expenditures. And any success on the expenditure front requires a parallel reduction of state power. One cannot hope to chain and humble the state while giving its enforcers the power necessary to, say, control money laundering, wage a war on drugs, or raise outrageous taxes. Richard Rahn, a former chief economist of the Chamber of Commerce of the United States and advisor to Ronald Reagan and to George H. W. Bush, reports that a Senator is pushing for a federal government's power to refuse passports to those who owe more than $50,000 in unpaid taxes to the IRS—another pursuit of the soft Berlin Wall.[22] There is no way to finance the actual welfare state that is not wildly coercive. The welfare state as we know it cannot be maintained without granting government powers that are repugnant to individual liberty and the rule of law. Bertrand de Jouvenel, who often defined himself as a man of the Left, understood the dynamics of state power: "The more one considers the matter, the clearer it becomes that redistribution is in effect far less a redistribution of free income from the richer to the poorer, as we imagined, than a redistribution of power from the individual to the State."[23] In short, the debt problem cannot be solved without reducing state power.

Anybody on a mission to cut 33 percent of federal expenditures and the power that comes with the money is facing tough enemies. Although some are hurt by the Big State, others are favored and will fight tooth and nail to keep their privileges and entitlements. Cutting welfare programs will hurt their beneficiaries, who are not just the poor. Participants in the poverty industry have the largest monetary interests to defend. The poverty industry is made of individuals who make money by representing and helping the poor with the taxpayers' money: employees of welfare-state bureaucracies, employees of subsidized associations working in the field, trade union do-gooders, and apparatchiks in international organizations. These individuals will fight hard to maintain the status quo. So will those who generally benefit from the power of the state—the whole police-corporate complex, from TSA bureaucrats and IRS agents to firms who provide surveillance equipment to the state: they will not want their employer or customer to relinquish power. If we want to solve the public debt problem, we are up against all these interests. Forcing Leviathan to act against the incentives of its most influential actors and supporters is a difficult mission.

CHAPTER 9

INFLATING THE DEBT AWAY

In a way, everything is more complicated than it appears, for we always find new mysteries and new questions in what we think we knew. In another way, everything is simpler than it looks like, for the general features of any complex phenomenon are usually explainable with a simplified representation of reality, called a "model." Monetary theory and policy are complex topics, which are approached by economic theories based on such models. We won't dwell deep into these models for we need to understand only two relatively simple points: increasing the money supply creates inflation and inflation reduces debt obligations. We'll then be in a position to look at what the US government can do in this regard.

The Cause of Inflation

Inflation is an increase in the general level of prices, that is, in all prices, compared to what they would otherwise have been. The prices we are interested in are mainly the prices of produced goods and services that are part of GDP or, more specifically, the prices of consumer goods and services (that is, excluding capital goods, the goods used to produce other goods). Since relative prices—prices relative to other prices—always change, inflation will show up in practice as a set of unequal price increases; perhaps some prices will even drop as the generally climbing level of prices does not compensate their falling *relative to other prices*. Think of a rough sea: even if the tide is rising, the trough of waves can be lower than the average tide level some time before. From December 2010 to December 2011, for example, the level of consumer prices (measured by the CPI, or consumer price index) increased by 3.0 percent in the United States. Some prices climbed more, such as the prices of hospital and related services, which showed a 5.3 percent increase; some less, such as footwear, by 1.3 percent;

and a few other prices even dropped, by 12.5 percent in the case of personal computers and peripheral equipment.[1] The CPI averages all these price changes. Since 1913 in America, inflation has averaged 4.3 percent per year.

As it reduces the value of money, inflation lightens the burden of debts. Look at this with round numbers. If you borrowed $1,000 one year ago and inflation has been 100 percent (equivalent to a price increase factor of 2), what you owe now is equivalent to $500 in constant dollars of last year. This is because what now costs $1,000 cost $500 then (1,000 is 100% more than 500), which is the same as saying that the dollar has lost 50 percent of its value. Arithmetically, the dollar is worth the inverse (1/2) of what the price increase factor has been (2). If inflation had been 4 percent instead, the price increase factor would have been 1.04, and the dollar would now be worth $0.962 (the inverse of 1.04), which means that it would have lost 3.8 percent. You can now reimburse your debt with dollars that are worth 3.8 percent less than when you borrowed the money, and your creditor will get 3.8 percent less in real terms.

The same is true for public debt. Suppose that inflation over the next five years will be 10 percent per year. With compounding, prices at the end of the period will have increased by 61 percent, or a factor of 1.61. Alternatively, the value of the dollar will then be 1/161, or 62 percent, of today, which means that its value will have fallen by 38 percent. Suppose the debt owned by the public today is $10 trillion (in fact, it is estimated to be $11.6 trillion at the end of FY 2012,[2] but it will be easier to do our calculations with round numbers) and will be reimbursed at the end of the five years. The $10 trillion that will then be paid to creditors, will be worth only 62 percent of what it is worth today, for it will buy only $6.2 trillion; creditors will lose 38 percent of the value of their securities in real dollars. Moreover, raising $10 trillion in five years may be easier for the government since nominal incomes will have followed prices (wage rates are just a price like any other, which rises along with inflation), and tax revenues will have increased at least as fast as inflation. Add to this some real economic growth, and the government will take more in taxes. In real dollars, the creditors will receive less, and the government will pay less with money easier to raise.

Inflation has to do with money. Money is what is used as a medium of exchange. A medium of exchange is a generally trusted means of paying for what you buy, and of being paid for what you sell. Being generally accepted by definition, a medium of exchange makes commercial exchanges much easier. If you have produced tomatoes and you want a haircut, you don't have to find a barber who happens to want tomatoes; you just have to sell your tomatoes for dollars, pay your haircut with dollars, which the barber uses to buy whatever he wants. Money is by definition liquid, that is, it can be used easily to buy something because everybody accepts it as payment. Dollar bills are money (in the United States and in many other countries too), but most money is now scriptural money, that is, accounting balances in your bank account or retail money market fund (very similar to a bank deposit), which can be transferred by check, debit card, electronic transfer, and other such means. This measure of money is called "M2"—the total of currency, demand and other checkable deposits, savings deposits (including money market deposit accounts), time deposits in amounts of less than $100,000, and balances in retail money market mutual funds. Other measures of money exist depending on the degree of liquidity incorporated in the concept. In early 2012, the total stock of US money (measured with M2) was worth about $10 trillion, of which only less than $1 trillion was made of actual dollar bills (and coins).

Like everything in economic life (and in social life in general), the stock of money and its additions or subtractions are determined by supply and demand. People demand money as opposed to other assets because they need a readily accessible medium of exchange for their current or future purchases. One individual's (or corporate body's) demand for money corresponds to the money he wants to keep in the bank (or in actual currency) instead of buying bonds, shares of stocks, mutual fund shares, or other assets. Add all these demands and you get the total demand for money in the economy. Demand for money is a function of (depends upon) the total value of transactions (goods and services times their prices) individuals engage in during a certain period of time and thus, directly or indirectly, of GDP. It is also a function of interest rates, for one will keep less money in bank accounts (or currency) if yields are higher in other investments.

The supply of money is determined by the central bank (the Federal Reserve System, or Fed, in the United States) and by commercial banks to the extent that the later can piggyback on the money created by the central bank and lend more. The reason why banks can further increase the money supply after the central bank has had its pass is that all the money created ends up in some bank accounts, which allows the banks to lend more, which creates further deposits, and so forth. The process is called the money multiplier. In a fractional banking system (a system where banks lend part of their depositors' money), banks generate a multiple of the money created by the central bank. Similarly, when the central bank reduces the money supply, banks will magnify the reduction. At least, this is what old, standard, simple monetary theory claims.

The price of money can be measured in terms of other goods (and services), that is, in terms of its purchasing power. This makes obvious sense on the demand side of money: the higher the price of goods—the higher the price level—the less money is worth in terms of these other goods; in other words, the lower is the purchasing power of money, the lower its price. Since prices of goods and services are calculated in terms of money, the price of money is calculated in terms of other goods and services. The lower the price of money thus defined, the more of it will be demanded in order to carry ordinary transactions. If the prices of all goods and services doubled, you would want (if possible) to hold double the amount of money you keep in the bank or in actual dollar bills in order to have enough for your daily transactions—as opposed to investing your money. How the quantity of money supplied would react to this price of money depends on motivations and decisions of the central bank (and potentially of other creators of money).

The insight that money and the price level of goods and services are related has been central to economics since the eighteenth century. The interest rate is not the price of money, but the price of credit and savings. It does influence the demand of money, though, as it represents an opportunity cost of holding money (instead of savings instruments). The concept of "opportunity cost" is crucial in economics: it refers to the best alternative that somebody foregoes in doing something, like purchasing a given good or, in the present case, in holding cash. The higher the interest rate, the less money people will want to hold because they can get higher returns by investing it.

Imagine that the supply of money doubles, ceteris paribus. We maintain other factors constant (as conveyed by the ceteris paribus) in order to see the consequences of an increase in the money supply without confounding these consequences with those that would flow from other, simultaneous causal factors. What will happen to prices? The easiest way to follow the story is to consider a situation where, like during a large part of mankind's history, money is made of gold coins. Everybody suddenly finds himself with double the quantity of gold coins he had before. Everybody will double his demand for goods and services, or will lend his gold coins to somebody who will spend them. The demand for everything will double. If demand for everything doubles, all prices will more or less double, including of course the price of labor since everybody will also want to hire twice as much labor in order to produce twice as many goods to satisfy the new demand. Assuming that all resources were previously employed (that there was no recession), nothing else than this increase of all prices and wages will happen. When more money chases the same number of goods and services, an equilibrium—a situation where everybody is satisfied with the money he holds—will be attained only when prices have increased more or less proportionately to the new money in circulation. Over the period considered, the rate of inflation will have been 100 percent. Inflation will stop, at the higher price level, if the money injection stops; prices will continue to rise if more money is pushed through the system.

Some economists—especially those belonging to the so-called Austrian school of economics—have argued that this theory of money supply growth translating into proportionate price increases is not totally correct. Newly created money generates new bank deposits. With more deposits, the banks will want to lend more money, and competition will push interest rates down. The reduction in interest rates generated by the new money will make long-term production processes especially attractive, for these are the ones that cost more to finance as more time is needed between the investment and when the good reaches the consumer. Financing the production of steel, from ore extraction to the construction of the high furnace, costs more in investment and interest than financing the production of an equivalent value of, say, wheat. Because a lower interest rate attracts more investment in some production processes and industries than in others, a misallocation of resources will ensue: too many resources will flow in certain industries, too little in other—compared to the unchanged structure of consumer demand. The misallocation of resources becomes evident when the money infusion stops and the rate of interest goes back to its normal level. Then, a correction is necessary to reinstate the previous allocation of capital. This correction is called a recession. The Great Recession can be thought of as the latest illustration of this approach: low rates of interest lead to overinvestment and to a price bubble in residential housing; the inevitable correction generated the recession. In this perspective, it is still true that a growth in the money supply brings inflation, albeit at possibly different rates for different goods or assets.

Who is able to increase or decrease the money supply? As implied above, central banks are the main actor in this field; indeed, manipulating the money supply was one of the main justifications (with lending money to the state) for their creation. But how does the central bank change the money supply?

The central bank, which is both the banker of commercial banks and one of their regulators, manipulates the money supply by changing the amount of reserves that the banks have on deposit with itself, sometimes under legal requirement. These reserves together with the paper currency are called "base money" or "high-powered money," because they generate still more money when they are lent by banks and redeposited in other banks. The central bank has a number of tools to change the banks' reserves and thereby starts a cascade of increasing or decreasing money in the economy. One of the major tools lies in open-market operations, which are the buying or selling of (usually short-term) Treasury securities on the market. When the Fed buys Treasury securities from banks, it credits the latter with a corresponding deposit, which they will normally use to make loans, starting the chain of increasing money in the public's hands. Inversely, if the Fed sells Treasury securities to banks, the transaction reduces the latter's deposits in the former's coffers, which leads to a reduction of bank loans, thereby diminishing the money supply. Of course, the Fed can only buy securities by bidding up their price, which amounts to reducing interest rates; similarly, it can only sell securities by offering them at a lower price, which means offering a higher yield. Market operations thus affect interest rates, even if the power of central banks in this respect may be overestimated. Except perhaps in a centrally planned economy, the central bank cannot simply decree what interest rates will be.

Other policy instruments are available to the central bank. It can increase the reserve requirements that the banks must maintain, thereby reducing lending and the money supply; lowering reserve requirements has the opposite effect. Now that the Fed pays interest on reserves, it can also increase the interest rate on these reserves, thereby pulling money out of the economy and reducing the money supply; it can reduce the interest rate on reserves if it wants to have the opposite effect.

The central bank can also increase the money supply by purchasing securities with newly created money (as opposed to money it already holds on its balance sheet), a process called "quantitative easing" or QE. When it purchases government securities with newly created money, it is said to be monetizing the debt, which is essentially financing the government with printed money.[3] When the central bank purchases securities from banks, it pays for them by increasing the latter's reserves. In case of QE, the accounting operation is simple: the central bank's balance sheet will show new assets corresponding to the securities it acquired and new liabilities corresponding to the banks' higher deposits. Only a central bank can acquire new assets by simply telling the seller "I am crediting your account" without transferring other assets to complete the operation. As we have seen, 17 percent of the federal debt owed to the public (and this excludes GSE securities) is held by the Fed, which suggests that a significant part of the federal debt has been monetized through money creation. The proportion of the UK government debt held, and monetized, by the Bank of England reaches more than 30 percent.[4] It is estimated that in 2011, the Fed bought the equivalent of 77 percent of new federal debt.[5]

A central bank is a very powerful institution. In many ways, as Jeff Hummel claims, it is the new central planner.[6] Yet, its power must not be exaggerated. Central banks remain only one actor in financial markets. They can significantly increase the money supply only if the banks choose to lend the new money they obtain from selling other assets to the central bank—as opposed to returning it as deposits to the central bank itself. The standard money multiplier explained above works only if banks do the multiplying. The current crisis has shown that, despite all efforts by central banks to manipulate interest rates monetary policy is not necessarily a very potent tool to pull the economy out of recession. They succeeded pushing short-term rates close to zero, but not long-term rates: nobody can get a mortgage at 0.5 percent. Even as regulated as they are, commercial banks now have many ways to independently increase or decrease the money supply in response to consumer demand: money market funds, for instance, supply something very similar to money, and will contract or expand depending on people's preference for liquidity. The money supply has, in some sense, become endogenous. The central bank is also limited in its capacity to finance the public debt, for people could cancel part of any such attempt by losing confidence in, and reducing their purchases of, government securities. Because of such rational expectations, public policy is not as potent as it looks at first sight. The freer the society, the truer this is.

One crucial point on which most economists agree is that, as suggested above and except in exceptional circumstances, an increase in the money supply will, ceteris paribus, result in a more or less proportionate increase in the general level of prices. At least this should be obvious when the growth in the money supply exceeds GDP growth, for some money supply growth may not be inflationary if it responds to an increase in production and transactions, which would normally translate into an increased demand for money. If money supply grows more than money demand, inflation will follow. The empirical evidence confirms that inflation results from money creation.

Consider Chart 9.1, borrowed from an econometric study by Professor John Frain of Trinity College Dublin. Every dot, or point, on the chart represents one country's combination of average annual growth in the money stock (read on the horizontal axis) and average

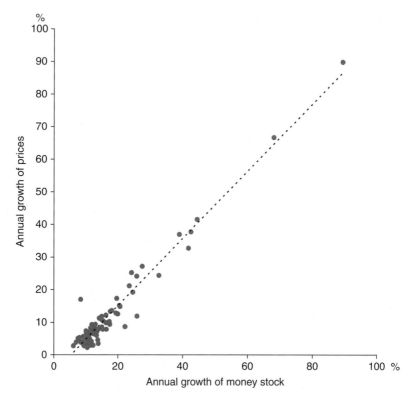

Chart 9.1   Average Money Growth and Inflation in 87 Countries, Second Half of the Twentieth Century

Source: Frain (2004).

annual growth in the country's CPI (vertical axis). The money stock in each country is an estimated value of M2. The 87 countries for which enough data were available from 1948 to the early 2000s produce the scatter of points on the chart. Visual inspection reveals a quite obvious correlation between money stock and inflation among countries: the more the stock of money grew over the period, the higher the inflation was; in fact, the inflation rate is nearly proportional to the growth in money stock. The very high-inflation countries (the four dots on the upper part of the best-fit line) are, from the highest annual inflation rate to the lowest—Nicaragua, Argentina, Peru, and Bolivia. Switzerland and the United States show the lowest growth in the money supply, and also stand among the countries with the lowest inflation.[7] The best-fit straight line shows a close fit, the deviations being easily explained by random factors. Evaluating the significance of these deviations is what statistical analysis tries to do. Technically, for the whole set of countries, the correlation between money growth and inflation is 0.95,[8] meaning that 95 percent of the variation in inflation is explained by the growth in the money supply. A perfect correlation would be indicated by a coefficient of 1. The correlation is statistically significant at a 1 percent threshold, which means that the probability of accepting it if false is less than 1 percent. Other empirical studies have reached similar conclusions.[9]

It is true that correlation does not imply causation. A standard example of spurious correlation is that ice cream sales and the number of drownings are correlated. This correlation does not imply that either eating ice cream causes drowning or that drownings lead people (presumably the nondrowned) to eat ice cream. In this case, the causal factor is a third variable, nice weather, which causes both more demand for ice cream and more swimming, and thus more drowning. Even when causation is present, a statistical correlation does not indicate in which direction it runs. If the number of firemen at fires and the size of fires are correlated, it is not correct to conclude that firemen cause larger fires: the causation goes in the other direction. This last example illustrates an important point. We know that the causation runs from the size of the fire to the number of firemen (and not the other way around) because we have a theory that explains why: when a fire is large, more firemen are dispatched to fight it. However, we don't have any credible theory claiming that, in general, firemen fuel fires. Thus, although a correlation does not imply causation one way or another, it can serve to confirm (or, more technically, to not disprove) a theory that logically establishes a causation. Economists George McCandless and Warren Weber are thus able to argue convincingly that the sort of correlation between money and inflation shown here does say something about causation because it supports standard economic theory to the effect that more money chasing the same number of goods will generate inflation.[10]

We are as sure as one can be that, in ordinary times, an increase or a decrease in the money supply initiated by the central bank will lead to inflation in the first case, to deflation (the contrary of inflation) in the second case. During a recession, which is not ordinary times, economists are not so sure. John Maynard Keynes, the famous, or infamous, inventor of macroeconomic stimulus, suggested an exception: the possibility of a liquidity trap, when the interest rate is so low or uncertainty is so high that people prefer holding money to buying other assets, and when banks will not lend their increased reserves: "But whilst this limiting case might become practically important in the future," Keynes wrote, "I know of no example of it hitherto."[11] Many analysts think that this is what happened during, and following, the Great Recession, when the Fed increased money supply by purchasing securities from the banks, but the latter, instead of lending the money to private parties, preferred to keep it in their accounts at the Fed—which amounts to lending it back to the Fed.

One of the reasons banks preferred lending to the Fed—and thus to the state—than to businesses and individuals is what economic historian Robert Higgs called "regime uncertainty":[12] with mounting regulations and the possibility of sovereign debt crises, the banks wanted to play it safe. Regime uncertainty describes the situation where nobody knows what future government interventions and disruptions will be. In such circumstances, what can be safer than to deposit money at the very place where bankruptcy is prevented by the power of creating money? The phenomenon was very visible in Europe. Between December 31, 2010, and the same date in 2011, European large banks increased their deposits with the ECB and other central banks (including the Fed) by 50 percent.[13]

When (or if?) the economic horizon clears and interest rates start rising again, the banks will want to lend the money they have been accumulating, and inflation will shoot up. The Fed might prevent that with measures to reduce the money supply. But the Fed may also be pressured by the government to let inflation run its course.

Default by Inflation

A central bank is a powerful organization. It can be constitutionally limited, as the ECB is, but these limits are paper barriers. It is a vital component of the sovereign. With the central bank's powers, it appears relatively simple and tempting for the state to inflate its debt away. The Fed could reduce the public debt by creating money and generating inflation. It is true that the Fed is independent, or "independent within the government" as it itself puts it, and that financing the federal government is not within its mandate.[14] Yet, it does finance the government, and it is not immune to political pressures. Its independence could be reduced by Congress if it did not behave. Congress can change the Federal Reserve Act and other laws governing the Fed any time it wants, as it has done numerous times since 1913. Theoretically, Congress could even abolish the Fed and transfer its powers to politicians or to other parts of the federal bureaucracy. If the powers that define the central bank were transferred to somebody else, the locus of monetary power would simply have shifted. The new wielders of monetary power could then decide to inflate in order to reduce the public debt.

There is a long history of rulers inflating the money supply in order to finance their expenditures. The process was more straightforward before fiat money, when all money was metallic. The trend may have been started by Dionysius, the Greek tyrant of Syracuse, in the fourth century BC. Unable to reimburse money he had borrowed from his subjects, Dionysius decreed that all coins should be brought to him under penalty of death. He then changed the marks on the coins from one drachma to two drachmas, used half of them to return the coins tendered, and the rest to pay off his debts.[15] We have no data on inflation at that time, but if economic theory is right, prices must have more or less doubled, so that the creditors got only half what they had lent to the ruler. In early modern Europe, the technique used to debase money was to reduce the precious metal content of coins, either by shaving the coins or by mixing cheaper metals into them. For about a decade in the middle of the sixteenth century, Henry VIII and the Regency Council that ruled after his death removed 83 percent of the silver content of the pound. This was not an isolated phenomenon. Between 1258 and 1799, economists Carmen Reinhart and Kenneth Rogoff find a large number of episodes in several countries where the national currency was debased in this way, often by 10 percent or more in one year, sometimes by more than 50 percent (France in 1303). In 1798, in order to finance the war effort, the Russian czarist regime debased the ruble by 14 percent. Between the fourteenth century and the middle of the nineteenth century, the average silver content of European currencies was reduced by nearly 90 percent.[16]

Paper money based on gold, and then fiat money more or less divorced from gold, evolved over a few hundred years culminating in the twentieth century.[17] As money stopped being convertible into gold, central banks only had to issue more paper money in order to fuel inflation and reduce its value. In fact, the printing of actual paper money is unnecessary: the central bank simply writes accounting entries creating new deposits to the credit of whomever it has paid. On all continents, and especially in Europe, high inflation became more common. States often used this method to get out of debt. Since World War II, we observe a high correlation over time between the percentage of countries experiencing high inflation crises (inflation above 20% per year) and states in default on their public debt—for example, Greece, Italy, and Norway in the 1920s; Japan during World War II; and several South American countries in the 1980s and 1990s.[18] This is no coincidence.

More money creation leads to higher inflation. Here again, historical evidence is overwhelming, as shown on Chart 9.1. Interesting episodes include hyperinflation in France after the 1789 revolution, inflation in the South during the Civil War, German hyperinflation after World War I, Brazilian hyperinflation of the 1950s, United States inflation during the 1970s, and the recent hyperinflation in Zimbabwe. The experience of the two world wars and their immediate aftermath (1914–1920 and 1939–1948) is illuminating: in each case, the US money supply more than doubled and prices also more than doubled. Indeed, inflation is how the government succeeded bidding up and diverting to war uses the resources that would otherwise have been allocated to producing consumer goods.

Inflation is a means of financial repression, that is, of forcing people to lend to government more than they want, for it reduces what the latter has to reimburse. Inflation also serves financial repression by reducing the real interest government pays. In the early 1970s, the government of India capped bank interest at 5 percent while engineering an annual inflation rate of more than 20 percent, so that people received a negative real rate of interest on the money they lent to the state.[19] This kinder and gentler sort of financial repression does not occur only in underdeveloped countries: we saw that for over one fourth of the period from 1945 to 1980, the average interest rate on the public debt in the United States was lower than the rate of inflation, so that people ended up paying, instead of being paid, to hold government securities.

It is true that once inflation becomes anticipated, it loses much of its power for financial repression, as people build their anticipations into their choices. As we saw, economists call this rational expectations. If people expect inflation to be 4 percent per year, they will not have much incentive to save at any rate of return below this. The dearth of savings will tend to push interest rates and other returns over 4 percent. However, this protective stance works only if there is competition between financial intermediaries and if people have savings alternatives. If the state controls strategic interest rates (by capping interest on bank accounts, for example), the only alternative becomes foreign banks and financial institutions. This option can be closed with foreign exchange and capital controls, which have long been a favorite policy of states intent on exerting financial repression. Moreover, savings immobilized in long-term instruments (life insurance policies, pension funds, etc.) are not as easily cashable and will be depleted by bouts of inflation. And by waging hyperinflation (usually defined as inflation of more than 50% a month), the state can, for a time, frustrate anticipations and get its hand on resources before prices have risen to new levels.

The state's tools of financial repression are not perfect, especially in an open economy with an advanced financial system and an independent central bank, but some stealth default by inflation may be doable. Some would say that, by showing the danger of currency manipulations by the state, history has provided an antidote to the temptation, but history has a way of repeating itself, and the state has often proven not to be a faithful servant.

Could the US Government Pull the Trick?

Could the US government pull the trick of defaulting by inflation? At first sight, it has the means to do so. It would suffice for the Fed to increase the money supply enough by purchasing government securities or other assets with new money. The ensuing inflation would reduce the real value of the government's debt, which could be serviced with devalued dollars. This would require that the monetary authority abandon their goal of fighting inflation, but the developing public debt problem will require *some* agencies to change their goals, so why not the Fed?

The trick, however, may not work that simply. Inflation would also affect government spending, and indirectly increase the deficit and the debt. It can be argued that this would reduce, perhaps eliminate, any advantage the government would derive from a lower debt in real terms. The reason is that a large part of federal expenditures are, formally or informally, indexed to inflation, and would rise with it. As the CBO notes, Social Security, federal employees' retirement programs, disability compensation for veterans, Supplementary Security Income, Supplementary Nutrition Assistance (the food stamps), child nutrition programs, many of Medicare's payment rates, and some other programs are formally indexed to the CPI or to one of its components. And other programs, such as Medicaid, that are not formally indexed periodically get adjusted to inflation in the budget process.[20] Explicitly or implicitly indexed programs account for at least half of federal expenditures.

At one time, the CBO suggested that inflation could fail to reduce the real value of the public debt. In its 2010 *Budget and Economic Outlook*, the agency estimated that every percentage point of inflation above the 1 percent–2 percent embedded in its baseline scenario would increase noninterest federal outlays by $1.9 trillion over a ten-year period. Moreover—back to rational expectations—inflation would rapidly be added to interest rates on government securities, because investors would not otherwise continue lending. The effect would be immediate for the 7 percent of the federal debt that is financed by Treasury inflation-protected securities (the so-called TIPS), on which both the principal and interest are indexed to inflation. As the debt is rolled-over, the federal government would have to pay higher interest on other securities too. The CBO estimated that higher interest on the debt would add $1.3 trillion in outlays over a decade. However, inflation would increase federal receipts as personal taxes are not perfectly indexed, and corporate taxes are not at all. This would bring $2.5 trillion more in revenues over the same horizon. The net consequence forecasted by the CBO was that the deficit, and thus the debt, would increase by $0.7 trillion ($700 billion) during the decade.[21] This may not be sufficient to cancel all the gains from depreciating the debt in real dollars—about $100 billion per year per percentage point of inflation for a $10-trillion federal debt—but it would greatly reduce the government's benefits of inflating.

This sort of forecast is very sensitive to the assumptions underlying future expenditures and revenues. In its January 2012 outlook, the CBO forecasts had changed its tune: for every supplementary percentage point of inflation, it now forecasts lower increases in expenditures—assuming that the caps imposed by the 2011 Budget Control Act hold—and higher increases in revenues, with the consequence that the deficit is reduced by about $0.2 trillion over the next ten years.[22] In this scenario, inflation would be beneficial for the federal government, as it leads to a concomitant drop in the real value of both its existing debt and the continuing deficits. But these forecasts are necessarily very uncertain, if only—but not only—because taxpayers may refuse tax hikes. So the possibility remains that an increase in expenditures brought about by inflation could reduce, or even eliminate, the reduction in the real value of the debt. Moreover, when inflation becomes anticipated, the yield required by investors on government debt would increase, leading to higher government spending.

The worst impact of inflation is neither on the government's budget nor on the public debt, but on the economy in general, that is, on you and me. For one thing, it changes the distribution of income and wealth. Debtors win, creditors lose. Most people are both debtors and creditors: debtors as they owe money through their mortgages, their car loans, their credit cards, and so on; creditors as they are owed money by their pension funds, their life insurance companies, their banks (through their deposits), and so on. Properly speaking, inflation hits those who are net creditors, and favors net debtors. Moreover, individuals who are paid in more sticky wages will be hurt more.

The higher the inflation rate, the worse these distributive problems. In the United States, inflation has recently hovered around 2 percent or 3 percent. The highest rates of inflation over the past 100 years have been 18 percent during World War I and between 10 percent and

15 percent at the turn of the 1970s and 1980s. These high rates could easily return if enough inflation were generated to significantly pare down the federal debt. For example, reducing the value of the federal debt by 50 percent over a 5 year period would require an annual inflation rate of 15 percent—for this is the rate required to double the price level over the period, and thus cut the real value of the debt by 50 percent. In fact, inflation higher than 15 percent per year might be necessary if it becomes anticipated and leads to higher interest rates and higher government spending.

One danger of inflation is that it easily leads to hyperinflation, as the state is tempted to issue ever more money in order to run faster than rational expectations. Hyperinflation multiplies the bad consequences of inflation. Note that, by virtue of compounded growth, a hyperinflation of 50 percent a month means a total increase of 125 percent after two months (the original 50% increase plus the new 75% increase, which includes the increase on the first increase), 337 percent after three months, and so forth, until a total increase of 12,875 percent after twelve months; a monthly inflation of 50 percent translates into a 12,875 percent annual inflation. At the hyperinflation stage, people rush to bring their wheelbarrows of paper money to the grocery store before prices increase again. When the Reserve Bank of Zimbabwe was issuing single notes worth 100 trillion Zimbabwe dollars in mid-2008, the monthly inflation rate was 3,740 percent and soon to reach 79,600 million percent. A loaf of bread was priced at several million Zimbabwe dollars.[23] In late 2009, the 100-trillion dollar bill from the Reserve Bank of Zimbabwe could be purchased on eBay for $3.35, which gives an indication of what it could buy. In such situations, the ones who suffer most are ordinary people who are paid with lagging wages, have no reserves of hard and stable foreign currency, and cannot move out of the country.

Inflation also creates allocative problems. A purely *distributive* phenomenon has two sides that cancel: what one loses (the creditor in case of inflation), the other (the debtor) gains. Distribution is a zero-sum game. *Allocative* phenomena are different: in the case of inflation, they are negative-sum gains, where everybody loses or, at least, the losers lose more than the winners gain. In other words, allocative phenomena raise issues of efficiency. Saying that a situation is economically inefficient means precisely the existence of a net loss, something that is wasted for everybody. Inflation is inefficient in this sense: it creates allocative problems. It distorts the signals that prices convey about the state of the economy. Higher prices convey the fleeting impression of brisk demand while it is merely a monetary phenomenon. The rod of money, so essential to exchange and civilization, becomes unreliable. The additional money that people don't need for their daily exchanges will be spent on assets, such as stocks or houses, and generate bubbles of apparently ever increasing prices. It becomes impossible to distinguish real opportunities from mere bubbles. Real interest rates go down—until the market incorporates inflation expectations. Individuals and businesses increase their borrowing to levels that would otherwise be unsustainable—and which are in fact unsustainable since the credit bubble will not last. Businesses increase investments, including in longer-term, riskier projects.

When people realize that they have overextended themselves into bad investments, and try to correct their mistakes by deleveraging (reducing their debt), the bubble bursts. Some people are left with worthless investments—they default on their loans, their lenders default on theirs, and the contagion spreads to the whole economy. People reduce their exchanges (their buying and selling), which is what a recession is all about. In this perspective, it is not a coincidence that inflation was unusually high in the 1970s, before the recessions of 1980–1982—although it was not especially high in the few years preceding the Great Recession. During a recession, production (GDP) is reduced and the vast majority of the people in the economy lose. Consequently, there would be a high net economic cost in the federal government inflating in order to default on its debt.

The US government could try to inflate its debt away. I have argued that it would be very risky, costly, and difficult.

CHAPTER 10

CONTAGION: WHEN THE EMPEROR COUGHS

We think we know an economic crisis when we see one: it typically includes bankruptcies, unemployment, lower incomes, lower consumption, lower investment, uncertainty, and fear. Sometimes, it is accompanied by deflation (drop in the price level), or even by inflation like in the early 1980s. But what exactly is an economic crisis?

Contagion Fuels Recessions

An economic crisis is essentially a crisis of production, a reduction of GDP. The reason why lower production is deemed a crisis is that it imposes lower consumption: it means fewer cars, fewer new houses, fewer restaurant meals, and so forth. There is thus less to consume for most people. Production should not be a fetish. It is only useful because it allows more consumption—including more consumption of leisure for those who choose that. Consumption, not production, is the goal of economic life. Employment is not the goal of economic life either, but only a means to produce in order to consume. If economic crises resulted in unemployment only and no reduction at all in production and income, most people would welcome them, for they could do what they want with their free time, even working for fun if they enjoy some types of work. In reality, "working for fun" is an oxymoron: even if some aspects of work are pleasurable, and give many people a sense of purpose and usefulness, most work is a cost for virtually all people, a cost they have to incur in order to earn money and to consume.

Many people confuse "economic crisis" and "financial crisis." Although there are relations between the two concepts, they are not identical. "Financial" and "economic" don't mean the same thing. Economic refers to the real side of the economy: the real goods and services that people produce, exchange, and consume. Financial refers to the mere claims on goods, services, or resources that accompany acts of exchange. The simplest of all claims is a bank note such as a dollar bill. When you give me a dollar for my apple, the dollar represents a claim on some real good worth one dollar. Similarly, but at a higher level of financial sophistication, if I build a factory or an office building and sell you a bond to help me finance it, your bond is a claim on part of the real goods or services that my investment will produce: your bond is like dollar bills in the future. An economic crisis is a disturbance in production and exchange of real goods and services; a financial crisis is a problem in the flow of claims that accompany all acts of exchange. To illustrate, consider this analogy: a mechanical break in the assembly line in a plant could be considered an economic crisis; if the owners of the plant can't find investor to help them build or repair the plant, we have a financial crisis instead.

A related question is whether financial crises provoke economic crises, or if the causality runs the other way. No doubt that it can run both ways, but we should expect more often to find real factors at the root of financial problems, for finance is only a means to do real things. Think about a currency crisis—when a currency depreciates so that importers have to pay more for their foreign goods, and those who have borrowed in foreign currencies suddenly see the value of their obligations rise. A currency crisis is financial in the sense that it hits a monetary claim (the currency), yet the value of this claim transcribes market participants' opinions on the future real production of the region using the currency. People don't want pesos if they know that they will soon be worth only a fraction of their current value in terms of the real goods and services they can buy in the country where they are accepted in trades. Similarly, a sovereign debt crisis shows up in the value of the securities issued by a sovereign power, yet this value is traceable to the sovereign having borrowed more than he can reimburse, that is, having used up real resources (whatever was used to produce the capital or consumption goods he got with the borrowed money) that did not produce enough to reimburse the creditors who have, through the sovereign bonds, a claim to these resources. There is always something real, or something that some people think is real, behind finance. It can of course happen that financial markets are defective and thus create a truly financial crisis: for example, if firms cannot borrow or sell equity because financial markets are inefficient or inexistent, production will drop. But we must not imagine that all economic problems stem from financial causes; until proof of the contrary, it's the other way around.

Hyperinflations, currency devaluations, bank runs, and other disorders have a claim to be called economic (or financial) crises. However, all these disturbances are thought of as crises in large part because they are, sooner or later, followed or accompanied by recessions. Characterized by declining production, unemployment, and lower consumption, recessions (and a fortiori depressions, which are long and deep recessions) are the paragon of economic crisis. From the nineteenth century to our days, generations of economists have debated the nature and causes of recessions and depressions and, more generally, of what is called the "business cycle." Why is it that, from time to time, economic growth, sometimes accompanied by inflation, slows down and is followed by a recession? Although the intellectual adventure of economics has yielded many insights, the answer is far from making unanimity. We must approach the topic with some humility.

Recessions are a temporary phenomenon and must be distinguished from secular stagnation if we want different expressions for these two different phenomena. We can define a recession as a general, unwanted, self-perpetuating but temporary, mutual reduction in exchange. If less is produced, less can be exchanged and consumed. Some economists—like those who follow John Maynard Keynes—stress demand factors, that is, the reduction in consumption, instead of problems on the production side. This debate may be overrated. Whether it is demand or production that drops first does not matter as they are intimately related: people come to the market with incomes obtained from what they have produced, and they produce because others express a demand for their production. We can see a recession as a situation where the level of exchange in the economy is reduced: consumers exchange less with producers; workers exchange less with employers. Stressing the exchange aspect of recessions has the advantage of downplaying the hiatus between demand and production interpretations.

The mystery is why people reduce their level of exchange when everybody wants everybody to keep it up. Imagine a simplified economy: you produce bread and you exchange part of it for beer with your neighbor who, conversely, produces beer part of which he exchanges against bread from you. A recession is a situation where you want more beer and your neighbor wants more bread, but neither of you produces more because one does not trust the other to live up to his part of the bargain. In a simple economy like this, a conversation between the two might signal the problem and solve it, but it gets more messy in a complex economy where one doesn't personally know who buys what he produces, and has no way of knowing if these buyers will continue to buy. When a recession hits a complex economy, the signaling process does not work. The question which has occupied, and continues to occupy, so many economists is, why and how?

Why is it that most of society is locked into a situation where lots of people don't produce enough because others don't consume enough whereas all would want to produce more in order to consume more? If a large number of workers want to work more, a large number of companies would like to sell and hire more, and everybody wants to buy more, why is it that the economy cannot get it done? Part of the answer must be that recessions (and other forms of economic crises) get going when localized problems in one part of the system spill over to other parts. This spillover process is often called "contagion." The biological analogy is risky as is any such analogy in economics, but it will do for our present purposes. Of course, only naming the culprit does not solve the problem, for the question remains, why is there contagion? Why is it that one individual exchanging less leads to many others also reducing the quantity of goods and services they exchange with others?

Economists have recently done much theoretical and empirical research on contagion, but we need here to grasp only a few simple ideas. Contagion is a necessary ingredient of recessions, and contagion requires many people. There would be no scope for recessions in autarky—where each individual produces everything he consumes—although other sorts of economic crises could occur. Imagine Robinson Crusoe alone on his island. He produces everything he consumes, and can consume only what he produces. Even fruits falling from the trees have to be harvested and perhaps stored, which are all parts of the production process. In economic parlance, production covers all activities that transform resources (land, labor, equipment) into something that the consumer can put his hands on and his teeth in, here and now. (Economists even include advertising in production.) If Crusoe is ill and stops producing, he faces a personal economic crisis. But the economic crisis ends as soon as he can resume production. Recessions, which seem to be happening even though everybody is able-bodied and no one wants to produce and consume less, belong to social life.

Can we blame exchange among individuals as the cause of contagion and recessions? No, for it would be like saying that health is the cause of disease. Health is not the cause of disease, but what disease unfortunately undermines; similarly, exchange is not the cause of contagion, but what contagion compromises. If individuals in one country stop exchanging with individuals in another—if "a country" stops exchanging with another, as we commonly say—both groups will be worse off. People exchange with one another because it is in all parties' benefit (compared to a situation without exchange); otherwise, they would not. From that baseline of no exchange, there can be no exploitation in exchange, except if people are stupid. Exchange also allows everyone to specialize in what he is most efficient at producing. Economic exchange in the narrow sense is just a special case of social exchange where people interact with each other in their own interest. If exchange were a curse, recessions would be felt as a blessing.

In analyzing contagion, many economists have focused on the international variety,[1] but domestic contagion works basically the same way. The main difference is that, in domestic contagion (or in a monetary union like the Eurozone), exchange rates are replaced by other forms of adjustments to people's or regions' future prospects. For what is a currency exchange rate if not the market participants' evaluation of a country's prospects? People choose not to hold, or they get rid of, the currency of a country with poor economic prospects, because it will not be useful for future purchases there. Their actions push down the targeted country's exchange rate. Now imagine that this country is instead a region within a single-currency area. If this region's economic prospects are poor, people would move out, stop investing there, perhaps refrain from establishing long-term contracts with businesses there, and so on. Mississippi is poor, because it has poor future prospects, and people know it. If the State of Mississippi suddenly obtained its own currency, its exchange rate in terms of dollars would depreciate to a level consistent with the same lower investments, lower immigration, and so on. Foreign exchange rates are the transcription of the market's evaluation of different countries' prospects. The currency adjusts to bring the situation that would otherwise be visible only in the change of real variables. The adjustment may be more or less efficient with or without a different currency, but my point here is only to stress that adjustments within and between currency areas are of the same nature.

International crises thus help understand domestic crises. In every international economic crisis between 1980 and 2000, financial intermediaries played a major role in the contagion process: American banks who retrenched from emerging markets after the 1982 external defaults of the Mexican state; hedge funds that traded in European currencies in 1992; mutual funds that lost confidence in South American countries after the 1994 devaluation of the Mexican peso and depositors who ran from Argentine banks at the same time; Japanese and European banks retrenching from Asia after the Thai baht depreciated in 1997; brokers' making margin calls to their customers (calls to bring more money as the value of the customers' securities dropped), and hedge funds selling off securities in emerging markets and, concurrently with mutual funds, in high-yield markets after the domestic default of the Russian state and the bankruptcy of Long Term Capital Management in 1998.[2]

Similarly, the 2007–2009 recession, which originated in the American residential housing market, spread when financial intermediaries questioned the assets-based securities tied to the mortgage market.

The common denominator in these contagion episodes is credit granted and then pulled back by some financial institutions (banks, mutual funds, hedge funds, etc.). Under different forms, this idea has been recognized by economists ever since economic crises and recessions have been analyzed. Take Irving Fisher, a famous economist and Yale professor who lived through, and was ruined by, the Great Depression. On theoretical explanations, he sided more with pre-Keynesian economists; on policy proposals, he was more of a Keynesian interventionist. Fisher stressed overindebtedness and deflation as the "two dominant factors" in "the great booms and depressions." He believed that "easy money is the great cause of over-borrowing," thus generating a boom that will end in a bust. Overindebtedness means that a localized disturbance will be transmitted by cascading defaults throughout the economy: credit and money supply will drop, and deflation will set in.[3]

Just as international contagion, domestic contagion spreads in large part through credit relations. When a debtor defaults, his own creditors will themselves default or, at any rate, be forced to cut credit to other debtors. These creditors and other debtors have to reduce their own levels of exchange. Since people are less able to exchange, everybody produces less. Less production leads to less exchange, which in turn leads to less production, and so on. Perhaps the process can be seen more easily through its extreme form, a cascade of defaults: the first debtor defaults, his creditors default, the latter's creditors too, and so forth. Moreover, as credit diminishes, the money supply (money in bank accounts) shrinks, which sets a deflationary process into motion: lower prices, lower consumption as people wait for prices to drop more before buying, lower production, and so forth. The process continues, until no more losses can occur, and the remaining lenders feel they can start again lending to the economic survivors.

If there were no credit in the economy, one individual reducing his level of production and exchange would only affect himself and the individuals who are in contractual relations with him—and who would continue exchanging with others. If you stop exchanging your oranges for my apples, I will continue exchanging the rest of my apples with the other people who wanted them before. By and large, only you and I will be poorer. Credit raises a special problem because it ties the fortunes of everybody with everybody. It is a transmission belt for both prosperity and depression. Indeed, credit plays such a large role in contagion that the latter term is generally used as meaning financial contagion.

Can we then say that credit is the cause of contagion and thus of recessions? Perhaps, but again only in the rather crooked sense that health is the cause of disease, for credit is essential to a prosperous economy. Imagine that I order a good (tomatoes) from you, and that you find the terms attractive but you don't have the equipment and inputs to fill the order. Fortunately, there is a third party (who can also be myself, the buyer) who has money that, if he gets interest, he would prefer to spend next year instead of right now. He lends you the money, you produce what I want, and you eventually reimburse the loan with interest. Everybody is happy and thus more prosperous. Happiness ("utility" as economists call it) is ultimately the real measure of prosperity, and other measures like GDP are only pale and often misleading approximations of what we are after: understanding this idea is crucial for understanding the economy.[4] What does this mean for tomatoes and financial services? Production has increased (by a dozen tomatoes), the three of us have exchanged more (including the exchange of financial services—the loan), and we are all better off. If we were not, we would not have engaged in these acts of exchange. Credit, like everything people voluntary engage in, is beneficial, but it does carry the risk that it may disappear through contagion, killing the benefits it was previously generating.

Contagion can also spread by people losing confidence in future economic prospects. Businesses reduce their production when they believe that consumers will reduce their expenditures, consumers reduce their expenditures when they think they might lose their jobs, and so on. General pessimism, like general optimism, is up to a certain point self-sustaining. They generate herd behavior. Credit failures only make matters worse. Perhaps lack of confidence is the ultimate cause of contagion.

A recession can be ignited by an external shock—such as a bad harvest, a hurricane, or an increase in the price of oil. Instead of rapidly self-correcting, the recession may persist, or even deepen into a depression, because the economy is not flexible enough to absorb the initial shock and its repercussions. Economic rigidities are a major issue. Think of a business that has seen its demand dry up and cannot fire workers, or hire workers who charge less, or consider other solutions. On inflexible European labor markets, a firm is often restricted in its adaptive responses and is thus more likely to go bankrupt or to lose credit facilities, creating a new cascade of problems. If firms cannot easily fire, they will think twice before hiring. If an individual put out of work cannot start a taxi service or an interior designer business because of quotas or licensure regulations, he is not going to absorb the shock smoothly and will reduce his level of exchange more.

In the Greek sovereign debt crisis, a big problem was the need for the government to reduce its expenditures and the concomitant impossibility of individuals hit by loss of government jobs or subsidies to find other employment in the very constrained and regulated labor market. Greece, notes *The Economist*, is "one of Europe's most regulated economies." In France, where lots of new regulations hamper businesses with 50 workers or more, an economic study found a steep fall in firms with precisely 50 workers, suggesting that some firms deliberately try not to pass the threshold. It is true that small businesses create jobs, but, as another study suggests, it is the ones that are growing and trying to get bigger that do this, not the perpetually small ones.[5] The economies of Greece, Portugal, Spain, and Italy are all biased towards small businesses through regulation. Small is not beautiful per se, especially if it comes from bigness and efficiency being regulated out of the economy.

Sovereign Default Fuels Contagion

A default from one of the major states in the Western world would create a shock capable of unleashing much contagion that would likely plunge the world into recession. This is because sovereign securities have come to occupy a central place in our economy. Recall that when investors are said to be holding cash, the pile is in large part made of government securities, which are—or were—considered the best substitute for cash, besides earning a small return. Many investors, and the ordinary people whose savings they invest, would thus be affected. Total government debt amounts to a big share of credit markets: 18 percent for the federal Treasuries alone in the United States (excluding mortgage debt guaranteed by federal agencies and the GSEs). Treasuries serve as collateral in a large number of loans, so many creditors would be harmed by government default, starting another credit contagion thread. Since banks hold much of their cash in government securities, a government default could provoke a bank crisis, which would reverberate through the economy. In the Eurozone, about 5 percent of bank assets are invested in domestic sovereign debt.[6] The proportion of Treasuries held by commercial banks in America is lower (about 2%), but the proportion jumps to 13 percent when government-guaranteed mortgage securities are added.[7] Two economists affiliated with international government organizations, Eduardo Borensztein and Ugo Panizza, calculate that a government default multiplies the probability of a banking crisis by about 3.5.[8]

The recent and still evolving European experience confirms these fears. The fear of a Greek default first pulled down the price of Greek government securities or, which is the same, pushed their yields up. Investors then realized that other European governments could default, leading to higher yields on the latter's securities and to a higher budget cost of financing their debt. States had to cut expenditures. In the meantime, investors started doubting the solvency of European banks, which held sizable amounts of government securities—a typical credit contagion. It is widely believed that if large states such as Spain, Italy, or France, were to default, bank runs might ensue and banks might fail. If banks fail, credit is reduced elsewhere in the economy, as well as the money supply. Some of the banks' losses are insured through CDSs, and will be passed on to third parties, but these issuers of CDSs are often other banks or, at any rate, other financial institutions. Contagion would also spread through this channel. These fears led Europe's political leaders to try hard to contain sovereign defaults.

The European contagion has not spread to American banks because the latter's holdings of European sovereign debt is low compared to their capital (and because no large European state has yet defaulted).[9] Another reason is that, in times of international disturbance, investors retreat into US securities, especially US government securities. They figure out that the situation will be at least not as bad in America. This outlook will change once the market realizes that a default on US government securities is also possible.

The fear of contagion is generally framed in the context of banks because banking crises easily turn disturbances into recessions or depressions. The link between banking crises and recessions becomes especially important when it is realized how the state and the banks are in such a symbiosis that the bankruptcy of the former could, even in America, lead to banking failures. Banks do not even need to be literally insolvent for contagious fears to fall them: bank runs and bank panics (which are generalized bank runs) suffice. If many people fear that their bank may fail and rush to withdraw their deposits, the banks will hurry to sell assets, such as long-term bonds or loans, in order to raise cash. They may have to sell their assets at fire-sale prices, turning them from illiquid into insolvent banks. The Great Depression witnessed such a phenomenon in America: nearly half the banks failed. It is true that deposit insurance now shelters depositors from bank defaults, concentrating the loss on bondholders and shareholders. But the shelter is only as solid as the government that finances it.

Banking crises are not unicorns, even in the contemporary world. If we adopt Reinhart and Rogoff's definition of banking crises as events characterized by bank runs or large-scale government assistance to at least one major financial institution, there have been many banking crises in the world since 1800. The most recent include Spain in 1977, Venezuela in 1993, Argentina in 2001, the Savings and Loans Association crisis in America in 1987, Norway in 1987, Sweden in 1991, Japan in 1992, as well the United States and many other countries during the Great Recession. We can count about 100 such crises worldwide since 1945.[10]

When a banking crisis hits, government can guarantee all banks' liabilities, like the Irish state did at the beginning of the Great Recession, but then all losses are born by the taxpayers. The consequences in Ireland have been a prolonged recession, a worsening of the public debt, and an international bailout. Now, if the banking crisis is created by default of the state itself, which is what we are considering now, the government may be incapable of bailing out everybody, perhaps not even the banks' depositors. What the sovereign debt problem points to is a situation where everybody calls on the sovereign to bail them out, but the great savior is impotent because he is the cause of the problem and would himself need a bailout.

Many believe that, ultimately, the central bank can solve a sovereign debt crisis and a banking crisis. *The Economist* was among those arguing for the ECB to buy the threatened states' sovereign bonds in order to reassure the market. The ECB officially resisted this suggestion, but partly heeded it by offering European banks three-year loans that have been partly used to buy sovereign bonds. In other words, the ECB engaged in indirect quantitative easing and monetization of the public debt. We have seen the risk of inflation that this implies. Moreover, these medium-term ECB loans carry such a low interest that the banks may use them as a substitute to private financing. *Financial Times* writer Steve Johnson argued that the government has in fact replaced private bondholders in the banks' financing, with unforeseen consequences when the three-year loans mature.[11] What will the ECB then do? Continue financing the banks? Will the banks become state corporations, de jure as well as de facto? People may not always believe in the central bank's omnipotence. As Thomas Sargent and Neil Wallace have argued, a central bank eventually runs out of ammunition if the government can't manage its debt.[12] When investors realize that, even disguised as a central banker, the emperor is naked, their fears will not be calmed by the central bank announcing that it will create more money to solve the problem.

That many people, in America or Europe, are now trusting central banks to prevent contagion from spreading shows how we have become dependent on the state. The sovereign has assumed debts that he cannot repay, and we count on his central bank to solve the problem. What is more likely to happen, in Europe and probably in America later, is that contagion will spread, banks will fail, people will lose their jobs, and their life savings. People will call for help, and nobody will answer.

CHAPTER 11

THE LEAST BAD OF ALL POSSIBLE WORLDS

Pangloss most cruelly deceived me when he said that everything in the world is for the best.

—Voltaire, *Candide*[1]

Avoiding the looming debt crisis in America would require the federal government to increase taxes by 50 percent or reduce its expenditures by 33 percent, like right now (see chapter 5). If this is not feasible, the federal government has three options: (1) repudiating or otherwise defaulting formally on its debt; (2) defaulting stealthily through inflation; or (3) doing nothing. Famous eighteenth-century philosopher Voltaire mocked the idea that everything in the world was for the best. His admonition applies to the present debt predicament, for there is no good option, only bad ones. Mind you, if there are only bad options, the least bad becomes the good one, just as a cost reduction is equivalent to a benefit. But what is the least bad option?

Repudiation or Open Default

The most radical alternative would be for the federal government to simply repudiate its debt: stop paying the interest and announce that it will not reimburse the capital. Short of this, it could default and force its creditors to accept a restructuring. Repudiation is simply a permanent default. What would be the consequences of a federal repudiation?

Most analysts agree that the cost would be high: government default is seen as problematic because it tarnishes the reputation of the defaulting state, shuts off its access to financial markets, and may bring other states' sanctions (such as trade sanctions) against its population. I'll come back to the issue of access to the financial markets. As for sanctions from other states, we may accept the observation of two experts writing in an IMF scholarly publication that "there is no evidence that defaults ever led to sanctions."[2] Other costs of a government default, though, can be heavy. The closer to repudiation a default is, the higher the cost.

What is a cost? It is important to distinguish costs from transfers, and especially a net cost from a pure transfer. A *pure transfer* is a cost that gives rise to an equivalent benefit for others; it is a distributive, or redistributive, operation, and carries no net cost. If you lose a $10 bill and the wind blows it to me 1000 miles away, you support a cost of $10 and I enjoy a benefit of $10: there has been no net cost, but a pure transfer of $10 from you to me. In the current debt situation (just like in the recent housing market turmoil), imprudent loans have been made to (government) debtors who cannot reimburse. Somebody has to support the cost—if not the borrowers, then the creditors who took the risk, or some other third party. Whoever pays will transfer money to somebody: the former will lose, the latter will gain. Now, if a transfer ends up generating a lower benefit to the payees than the cost supported by the payers, we have a *net cost*, sometime called a "real" or "social" cost; stated otherwise, the transfer is not a pure transfer; in still other words, we have an efficiency issue besides a distributive one. A standard example is progressive income taxes, which incorporate both a transfer, from those who pay taxes to those who benefit from the corresponding government spending, and a net cost, in terms of the GDP that will not be produced because some incentives to work will have been dampened. Whether progressive taxes are good or not is not our topic here: we just need to understand the difference between a pure transfer and net cost (which may be accompanied by a nonpure transfer).

Suppose the federal government reneges on its debt. An obvious transfer would follow: holders of government debt would lose, taxpayers would gain as they would not have to reimburse. Since holdings of the defaulted securities are widespread, many taxpayers would in fact lose too: for example, the value of their pension funds (which amounts to 5% of the federal debt for private pensions only) would drop. Similarly, State and local governments (which hold 6% of federal debt) would lose. Saying that State and local governments would lose implies that the average taxpayer, who pays more tax to the federal government, would gain in the net. The exact impact is complicated, and impossible to know in details: some taxpayers would lose, some would gain; and some creditors would lose more than others, including those who would be the last ones to get rid of their federal securities. A massive transfer from foreigners to American residents amounting to 46 percent of the federal debt—that part owned outside the United States—would occur.

Would taxpayers have to wait decades before cashing the benefits of default in reduced future taxes? And would investors lose all the value of the defaulted government bonds? Not necessarily. Because of Ricardian equivalence, taxpayers might reap benefits as rapidly as if current taxes had been reduced, and investors would be at least partly compensated, as Jeffrey Hummel explains.[3] After a government default, private assets such as bonds and shares of stock would support lower future taxes; they would thus become more valuable. The increase in the present value of private assets would push up their price and at least partly compensate for their holders' wealth loss from government default. Thus, taxpayers holding private assets in their portfolios would cash the beneficial impact of default now. And that's not all. Wage earners would expect higher after-tax incomes in the future and could, if they wish, borrow against part of these higher incomes. To summarize, investors would lose less than it appears at first sight, and taxpayers and wage earners would be able to cash rapidly part of their future benefits.

Would these transfers be pure transfers, or would they leave a net cost in their wake? The answer is that a net cost will ensue if the process provokes a recession, which is nearly certain. In a recession, everybody (or nearly everybody) is harmed. We have good reasons to believe that a federal government default would, through contagion, generate a recession. Economists estimate that, during the past few decades, defaults by governments have been accompanied by an average 1 percent drop of GDP for purely external defaults and by 8 percent for domestic defaults (although the direction of the causation is not always clear).[4] A US default would be half domestic as roughly half the debt (54%) is held in the country. Immediately after the default of the Argentine state in 2001, GDP dropped by 11 percent.[5] Greece is suffering a very serious recession. To give some perspective, recall that during the Great Recession the American GDP dropped by 5 percent. A recession provoked by a default of the US government, which rules over the world's largest economy, would precipitate a world recession that would feedback on the American outlook.[6] And since investors would stop lending to the federal government, the problems could not be alleviated by deficit-financed government subsidies, as it was attempted during the recent recession.

Statistics should not hide the grim reality. Let me give just two examples. In Greece, the unemployment rate reached 24 percent in the spring of 2012, and the percentage of unemployed youths (aged 15–24) had grown to more than 50 percent.[7] Suicides have apparently jumped. One man, a former pharmacist, shot himself in a public square, leaving a suicide note: "I have no other way to react apart from finding a dignified end before I start sifting through garbage for food."[8]

Bank failures and a banking crisis would only make things worse. On the basis of 111 banking crises in 148 countries between 1975 and 2000, it has been estimated that a government default multiplies the probability of having a banking crisis by 5 (the probability goes from 3% to 14%).[9] Besides fuelling contagion, a banking crisis could lead to a reduction of the money supply and to deflation. Deflation—a drop in the price level—can worsen a recession as consumers wait to get back into the exchange circuit, hoping they can buy at cheaper prices later. It is true that the monetary authorities could try to boost the money supply, but people might hoard cash (the Keynesian liquidity trap) thus negating the expansionary monetary policy. Central banks could also, as often happened in history, choose the wrong sort of monetary policy, worsening the crisis. Like economists and a fortiori laymen, central bankers often don't have a clue. At any rate, a banking crisis would push up the ultimate cost of default.

The larger the scope of the default (up to outright repudiation), the darker the outlook would be. Yet, the cost must not be exaggerated. As Jeffrey Hummel notes, total repudiation by the federal government would cost private domestic holders of Treasury securities about $4 trillion, which is approximately equal to the fall in the value of US real estate between 2007 and 2009 and less than the $10 trillion fall in the US stock market between 2007 and 2008.[10] If the mortgage-backed securities guaranteed by the federal government were to crash though, the loss could be larger than the stock market crash during the Great Recession. It remains that the American economy is more flexible than many other economies in the world and would likely come back to growth within a few years. The cost of the default would also be a function of the other policies adopted to deal with the fallouts. For example, protectionism or heavier regulations or higher taxes would exacerbate the recession. So we may venture to say that the cost of an open government default in America would be serious, but not necessarily catastrophic.

Stealth Default

The second option for the federal government is stealth default through inflation. For many reasons, it is not a better alternative than open default or repudiation.

Attempts at stealth default might not really work, except at the cost of dangerous inflation. As we saw in chapter 9, part of the decline in the real value of the debt could be cancelled by increased federal expenditures, which in turn would push up the deficit and the debt. The pace of inflation has to be unexpected in order to drive a time wedge between the reduction in the real value of the debt and the increase in the interest rates payable on it. Only unanticipated inflation would be effective, but it would not stay unanticipated for long. Trying to reduce the real value of the federal debt by 50 percent with a 15 percent annual inflation over a five-year period, as hypothesized in chapter 9, would rapidly generate inflationary expectations that would be incorporated into the interest rates charged to the government as its debt is rolled-over or new debt is added. It has happened before: from the mid-1970s to the early 1980s, the yield on Treasury securities followed CPI increases, both rising from around 6 percent to over 14 percent.[11] The average loan to the US government has a maturity of about five years, and 15 percent of the Treasurys held by the general public have a maturity of less than one year, so any inflation would rapidly hit new financing.[12] If the government chose to accelerate the money supply growth, the race against the lag could lead to hyperinflation, which carries a very high cost.

As we saw, the cost of inflation lies in the misallocation of resources and the bubbles that the false price signals generate. This cost becomes obvious, and is actually paid, when the inevitable correction, that is, the recession, follows the artificial growth generated by inflation. Stealth default through inflation would impose the same cost as straight default, plus possibly more. The higher the inflation generated, the higher would be the following recession and, thus, the cost of the default.

The costs of hyperinflation are especially devastating. Recall that a monthly rate of inflation of 50 percent translates into an annual inflation of 12,875 percent, which means that prices are multiplied by 129.75 over a year. Something that costs $1 will cost $129.75 after one year. Whatever remained of Zimbabwe's prosperity was destroyed by hyperinflation. Between 1998 and 2008, Zimbabwe's GDP has been halved.[13] The cost of hyperinflation also includes the efforts that people make to protect themselves by transferring their money to other countries and, on a daily basis, by trying to spend their rapidly melting currency. A depression is a likely follow up to hyperinflation.

Hyperinflation and depression can destroy not only the economy but also the institutions that make peace and prosperity possible. In its economic-sociological sense, the term "institution" does not refer to specific organizations, like "financial institutions," but to accepted

ways of doing things, whether they are imbricated in actual organizations (organized exchanges or chambers of commerce, insurance, pensions, elections, for example) or not (honest rules of conduct, civility in
competition, family relations, etc.). Money is only one of the important institutions that are undermined by inflation. Many years, if not
decades, may be necessary to repair betrayed trust and recreate broken
institutions. Hyperinflation can also lead to disastrous political consequence, as people desperately look for a strong leader to put an end
to economic disorder. The German inflation, which reached 29,500
percent per month in October 1923, helped the rise of the Nazis. Even
if significant inflation in the United States did not have such dire consequences, it could lead to calls for more government intervention in
the economy and seriously undermine traditional American liberty.

The distributive effects of stealth default would differ from those of
an open default. Besides helping taxpayers to the detriment of government creditors, inflation would benefit all private debtors by diminishing the real value of all debts, and it would harm all creditors. It would
also hurt people on fixed incomes and those whose income lags on
prices but benefit individuals at the beginning of the chain of newly
created money. If you are the first to get the newly created dollar, you
have a chance to spend it before prices have risen. Relative to foreign
currencies, the dollar would fall more in the inflation scenario than in
the open default case: not only would foreigners get rid of their dollars
because they would not want them to buy US government securities,
but they would also demand to be paid in other currencies for their
exports. A flight from the dollar would hit foreign exchange markets.
If people want fewer dollars, the exchange rate of the dollar will fall.
Americans would have to produce more in order to import the same
amount of foreign goods or would get a lower amount of foreign goods
for what they produce. Any American resident who does business with
foreign countries—whether by importing foreign-made goods, buying good with foreign-made components, or just traveling there to see
friends or family—would be harmed.

From a distributive as well as an efficiency viewpoint, the impact
of stealth default through inflation would be massive. It would add
another layer to the cost of open default or repudiation. Given the risk
of high inflation, it is the most costly way to default.

The Cost of Doing Nothing

The third alternative for the federal government is to do nothing, that
is, to take no serious action to resolve the debt problem and instead

continue its unenthusiastic quest for ad hoc tax increases or spending cuts. From a distributive viewpoint, this alternative would have the inverse impact of a default—assuming that a default is avoidable. If default is unavoidable, doing nothing would only postpone the day of reckoning and ultimately would have a similar distributive impact, and it would also end up imposing the same sort of net costs as default—or probably higher, as the default would come after more debt accumulation and would be more disorganized.

Given what we have seen, it appears quite obvious that, at some point, the federal government will be unable to reimburse its debt and meet its other future obligations. Defaulting one way or another seems inescapable. Economist Peter Wallison provides one possible scenario of what would follow the discovery of this reality by investors "next year, 10 years from now, or even later."[14] The yield on government securities (and other securities) would gradually increase, or perhaps the rise would be sudden as financial markets catch up with reality. Interest on new government securities would jump, worsening the budget deficit and the debt outlook. Wallison assumes that the federal government would not stage an open default but would increase the money supply and monetize the debt. The ensuing inflation would push the dollar down relative to other currencies, preventing Americans from buying the formerly cheap foreign commodities and lowering their standard of living. The price of tangible assets (land, gold, etc.) would rise as individuals and businesses try to hedge against inflation by exchanging their dollars for nondepreciating assets. Government expenditures tied to inflation would increase. Perhaps tax revenues would increase too, as inflation pushes more and more people into the AMT. At that point, we would, like in the late 1970s and early 1980s, face a mix of GDP drop, unemployment, and price increases—simultaneous stagnation and inflation, a mix called "stagflation." Either the government tries to increase the money supply at an increasing rate, generating accelerating inflation (what Wallison thinks will happen), or it resigns itself to a deepening recession. At any rate, a recession, or perhaps a depression, would not wait long. Especially in case of high inflation, the exchange rate of the dollar would fall more, until foreigners refuse to accept dollars in international transactions. The dollar would lose its status as an international currency, possibly to be replaced by the yuan. By that time, the economic dislocation would have led to unemployment levels not seen since the 1930s and to a world-wide drop in the standard of living.

One of the real costs of doing nothing is the influence that the Chinese state will gain. This is a cost if the Chinese state remains tyrannical and is in a position to exert a negative influence on our liberty and prosperity (or what is left of them). At least, it is a cost for those who value the Western ideals, principles, and institutions that have produced what used to be called the free world. If, on the contrary, the Chinese state were to become less liberticidal than our own, then its influence would carry no cost, at least for those who value our ideals, principles, and institutions. The first scenario is probably more likely to prevail.

As the Chinese state holds 10 percent of the federal debt, any move to sell a significant part of these holdings would have a visible downward impact on the price of federal securities, increasing the latter's yield. The dollar would drop as demand for it decreases. The threat of these consequences will give the Chinese government much bargaining power. When Chinese financial support for European sovereigns was being discussed, a spokesman for the Chinese government was paraphrased as saying: "Beijing might [in return] ask European leaders to refrain from criticizing China's currency policy" (its attempts at keeping the yuan overvalued). The spokesman added, "if we see protest and chaos all the time, then China won't have confidence in Europe's political ability."[15] The demands of foreign state creditors might be very detrimental to America's independence. Who pays the piper calls the tune.

One may argue that instead of doing nothing, the US government should default only on its foreign debt, leaving American holders more or less unaffected (except indirectly by the reduction in trade with China as that country is hit by a recession). But such a selective external default is impossible because all US government securities are denominated in an international currency, the dollar. The federal government cannot discriminate against foreign borrowers by defaulting only on its securities denominated in foreign currencies, because it does not issue any. If the federal government decided to continue servicing and reimbursing only the securities held by American residents, then any of them could make money by buying federal securities held by foreigners at any positive price higher than what foreigners could get, that is, higher than zero, but lower than the par value that residents would be entitled to. The consequence of this arbitrage would be that all foreigners would get rid of their securities by selling them to US residents, and that all federal securities would have to be serviced. When a state issues securities to both domestic and foreign buyers in an international currency, which is naturally the case when this international currency corresponds to the money of the country in question, there is no way (at least in a free society) to stage a selective default against foreigners.

Doing nothing amounts to accepting an eventual disorganized default. The political consequences can be much worse than those of an open default. A fall into violence and authoritarianism cannot be excluded. In the worst case, long-term impoverishment and tyranny could be the ultimate outcome. Even if these extremes are avoided, doing nothing, like stealth default and hyperinflation, would bring deep changes in American society. America would soon be unrecognizable.

An overt default appears to be the least bad solution, since its cost is not augmented by the possibility of inflation, the risk of hyperinflation, and the political consequences that can follow from devastating disturbances. Tough economic times accompany all alternatives, but an overt default limits the downside and allows for some advanced planning. It is true that as soon as investors learn that a default is on the drawing board, they will immediately start dumping securities and pushing up their yields, accelerating the process. Yet, a deliberate decision to default could better avoid desperate measures such as inflation, trade restrictions, or capital controls, which would otherwise further increase the cost of a default that looks inevitable anyway. A deliberate default is a means of containing the cost of the inevitable.

The Benefits of Open Default

Not only is default of the federal government probably the least bad solution, but it also carries a big direct benefit: it can approximate a balanced-budget amendment, that is, it would force the government to balance its budget. Jeffrey Hummel has made a convincing case about the benefits that would stem from open default on the federal debt, both in the sense of reducing the cost of the inevitable default (reducing a cost is a benefit) and in the sense of providing the positive benefit of controlling government expenditures in the future.[16] The term "default" can have two different but related meanings: a default followed by restructuring or the repudiation of the debt. And there are the intermediate positions: default with restructuring of part of the debt and repudiation of the remainder. All this is a question of degree. Professor Hummel seems to argue for repudiation of the whole debt, but a partial repudiation would provide some of the benefits of the more radical alternative.

Default and a fortiori a repudiation would close access of financial markets to the federal government and, quite probably also, to State and local governments. A federal deficit would become impossible, and the government would have to live within its means—that is, within the taxpayers' means. Assuming that American taxpayers would not accept to pay European-style tax rates, the federal government would be forced to reduce its expenditures, and so would State and local governments, who would probably lose a large part of their federal manna. As the largest part of the fiscal gap is made of promises for Social Security, Medicare, and Medicaid, these programs, or large parts of them, would collapse or have to be very radically restructured. Solving the debt and fiscal gap problem cannot be done without a radical rethinking of the missions of the state. If one believes that the state is out of control, this would be a benefit, not a cost.

Hummel illustrates the feasibility and the benefits of default with the case of the 1840s State defaults in America. In an episode prefiguring in some ways the current European debt crisis, the deflation of 1839–1843 led to a deep debt crisis among many American States. They had borrowed heavily, especially to finance canals in the North and banks in the South. Unable to reimburse, eight States and one territory defaulted. Four of them—Illinois, Indiana, Maryland, and Pennsylvania—defaulted temporarily but later repaid virtually all that they owed. Three others—Louisiana, Arkansas, and Michigan—repudiated part of their debts, and only the first one ended up repaying everything; Arkansas and Michigan never settled some of their defaulted bonds. Finally, Mississippi and the Territory of Florida, which had borrowed mainly to invest in banks or had guaranteed private banks' bonds, repudiated their debt completely and never repaid.[17]

The experience of State defaults in the 1840s suggests that the cost of default should not be overestimated. The deflation of 1839–1843, which precipitated the States' defaults, provoked neither a drop of GDP nor high unemployment, and sustained economic growth restarted after the episode. Jeff Hummel contrasts the relative mildness of the recession with the devastation caused by the Great Depression three quarters of a century later. Note that the American economy was much freer and flexible than now, which points to the policies that would be needed to minimize the damage of a contemporary default.

In the wake of the 1840s crisis, foreign investors became cautious about buying American public debt, including federal government's debt. The States that had not defaulted were able to access the international capital market again in the 1840s and 1850s. Florida and Mississippi, who had totally repudiated their debts, were only able to come back to capital markets after the revolutionary institutional changes brought by the Civil War. The other States, those that had defaulted but restructured in some way, had varying experiences; some of them were able to access the capital markets relatively rapidly, albeit by paying higher interest rates.[18] Not only did the defaulting States had trouble accessing the capital markets but also, as a result of this experience, two-thirds of the States amended their constitutions to restrict State investments in private corporations and their own capacity to issue debt. Moreover, writes Jeffrey Hummel, "the period after the fiscal crisis was when the states finally threw out their mercantilist heritage and, for the first time, moved toward a regime of *laissez faire*."[19] As Hummel admits, default is not a fail-proof balanced-budget amendment, but history suggests that it can be partly effective in forcing the sovereign to put his house in order.

At this stage, we may open a parenthesis and ask whether it is morally defensible for a state to default on its debt obligations. Ethics is more complicated than economics, at least if we judge by the level of consensus developed in each discipline—over the past 300 years for economics and the past 2,500 for ethics. A practical constraint circumscribes our moral interrogation: the American federal government will not be able to honor all its obligations—to its creditors, to its retired employees, to the contributors to Social Security and Medicare—a point made by economist Arnold Kling[20] and which is amply documented in this book. The federal government will have no choice but to renege on *some* promises. The question is: Which ones? What is impossible to avoid cannot be immoral. Is it more immoral to renege on promises to citizens or on promises to lenders?

Somebody will have to be expropriated: either the taxpayers will be expropriated to repay the lenders or the lenders by not being paid their due. Which group is it more morally justifiable, or less morally condemnable, to expropriate? Given that the taxpayer-citizens have had little real say in the issue (see chapter 6), it might be more immoral to force them to pay for what was mainly an enterprise of self-aggrandizement of the state. "We" only "ate it together" because it was fraudulently sold to us. Moreover, some of us ate much less than others. The we is not all of us. The big eaters comprise those who were part of the machinery of the state: the politicians and the bureaucrats. For sure, bureaucrats include little people with whom it is difficult not to sympathize, but taxpayers also include innocent little people.

Moreover, the lenders must have been more conscious of the risk they were taking, if only through their financial intermediaries. Either you are in the lending business, and you consciously took a risk, or you assumed the risk, directly or indirectly, under the advice of your pension fund or bank, but it is still your risk. Having the cost fall on the lenders appears more moral not because they are bad capitalists, but because they have simply taken a risk and lost. As Lord Palmerston, the British Foreign Secretary, said circa 1841: "British subjects who buy foreign securities do so at their own risk and must abide by the consequences."[21] Why would this moral evaluation change when it is Americans who have, directly or indirectly, bought securities from their own government? The fact that most Americans are both taxpayers and, indirectly, lenders to their governments messes up the transfer picture and its moral dimension. The situation is a mess—thanks to the state and its bards—but a minimum conclusion seems to be that having the lenders bear the cost is not immoral.

Wishes and Reality

We can summarize, qualify, and extend the different arguments on the least bad alternative with three broad points: (1) In theory, an open default or repudiation is the least bad alternative. (2) It would be a useful tool, but not a panacea, for controlling Leviathan. (3) It will not be easy to achieve in practice.

The first point lies in the arguments I have already reviewed: an open default of the federal government, and even a repudiation of the federal debt, would be less costly than the other alternatives (inflating or doing nothing). Moreover, the open-default alternative carries political benefits in terms of an implicit balanced-budget amendment. The larger the default, the larger the benefits. An outright repudiation would certainly close access to financial markets for a longer time period. And it is probably preferable for the government to repudiate its public debt than to renege on promises it has made to its citizens.

The second point is that, although useful, default on the public debt is not a panacea for controlling Leviathan. As Hummel admits, a government default does not automatically equate to a durable balance-budget amendment. In a research paper published by the IMF, economists Eduardo Borensztein and Lugo Panizza review the econometric literature on the consequences of state defaults during the past three or four decades, as well as providing their own estimates. States that have defaulted on their debts have regained access to international markets after successfully restructuring—that is, after persuading bondholders to "voluntarily" accept a haircut. Four to eight years after default, they had regained partial or total access. "Once the restructuring process is fully concluded," Borensztein and Panizza observe, "financial markets don't discriminate, in terms of access, between defaulters and nondefaulters."[22] The two economists also find that borrowing costs increase immediately after a default, but that the risk premium probably doesn't last long either.

Another example is the Argentine state, which defaulted at the end of 2001, later restructured its debt and, as we saw, is still facing investor holdouts. Yet, it has been able to increase government expenditures by increasing taxes and using other means of stealth taxation and financial repression. Primary government expenditures in proportion of GDP (including state corporations) dropped by 14 percent in the year following the default, but had gone back to their former level by 2005, and then increased by a further 14 percent by 2007.[23] The Argentine government has also created inflation, long dissimulated by false government statistics, up to the point where economists criticizing government figures were subject to fines. One reason for lying about the inflation rate was to cheat domestic holders of government securities indexed on inflation, a tool of financial repression among others. A general decline in the rule of law as well as mounting corruption have been observed.[24] We should still be weary of a naked emperor.

A third broad point to keep in mind is that open default, and a fortiori outright repudiation, would not be easy to achieve. In this chapter, I have mainly considered what government *should* do given that it would be able to keep all its promises. What *will* happen in fact is another question. It will depend not on what you or I think should happen, but on the outcomes of the political, bureaucratic, and judicial subsystems that make up the sovereign. Depending on what the courts would decide, there may be legal constraints on whether the federal government can avoid reimbursing its creditors. Like in the Argentine case, there would be holdouts, and vulture funds would try to make money by purchasing devalued securities and suing the government in the hope of getting more. Repudiation may morph into restructuring, or aggressive restructuring into a milder form. But what if the taxpayers cannot or will not pay? The real crash would then just be postponed, and perhaps only radical political change could handle the problem. The theoretically least bad solution is not necessarily attainable.

Whichever of the three alternatives (open default, stealth default, or doing nothing) ends up being followed, some people will gain and others will lose, and the gainers and the losers are not the same in all cases. This is where organized interest groups—whether unions, corporations or other interests—enter the game: they will lobby for the alternative that least harms their members and their apparatchiks. What will in fact happen depends in large part on the efficiency of organized interest in the competition for privileges (what economists call "rent seeking").

Garret Jones, an economist at George Mason University, argues that any form of open default will be strongly resisted by powerful creditors' interests, and that, therefore, this alternative will not be the outcome of the political process.[25] Banks and financial firm shareholders would lose at least part of their equity; many would be wiped out depending on the extent of the default. State and local governments would also stand to lose a significant proportion of their financial assets if the federal government defaulted. These powerful interests would lobby the federal government not to default, and it is likely that they would win against the general, nonorganized taxpayers.

Openly defaulting may be so difficult that the federal government would resort to a variant of doing nothing: doing more or less nothing. This is what Professor Jones thinks will happen. He argues that, like other states in the world, the American state will try to avoid default because maintaining continuous access to financial markets is a must from its viewpoint. He also points out that planning a future default is virtually impossible, for the rumor would spread in financial markets like wildfire. A default is by necessity disorganized; how much disorganized is only a matter of degree. Moreover, rationally ignorant and nationalist voters will not accept the default alternative, because they don't want the United States to lose its clout in the world. Jones forecasts a "scenario of fiscal contrition" where a series of ad hoc spending cuts but mostly tax increases are enacted to pare off succeeding crises. Jones duly notes that America differs from the rest of the world because of its strong antitax movement, but he suggests that higher taxes are unavoidable.

If Garret Jones underestimates American resistance to taxes, a policy of doing more or less nothing would lead to default, hopefully without too much inflation. Some default may be not only the least bad solution, but also the only feasible one. And note that even if this chapter has dealt mainly with the federal situation and if the situation of State and local governments is not as dramatic, the main arguments also apply to them. Especially if they lose the 20 percent of their revenues that come from the federal government, many States may have no choice but to default too. The best of all worlds is challenging.

CHAPTER 12

OPPORTUNITIES

If this is the best of possible worlds, what then are the others?
—Voltaire, *Candide*[1]

As I am writing these words, the Social Security trustees report that their two trust funds (for retirees and for disability benefit recipients) will be depleted in 21 years, 3 years earlier than previously estimated.[2] By the time this book hits actual and virtual bookstores many other events will have happened. The future takes no time off. Debt problems will likely have surfaced in new countries, or crises will have deepened in countries previously hit. Depending on the depth of these problems, the world economy will be plunging in recession again or will be riding some fragile or illusory recovery. Precise forecasts are impossible, but the main fault lines are easy to imagine. The earthquake will come in due time. The Damocles sword of the federal budget will still be hanging over America. The CBO will have published new long-term forecasts, marginally different from the previous ones, but still predicting an unsustainable growth of the public debt and implying a crash sometime in the future. As usual, the CBO's optimistic forecast (as opposed to their more realistic "alternative" one) will involve humongous tax increases in order to cover forecasted growth in primary expenditures. At the time of writing and on the basis of available official estimates, an immediate 50 percent increase in all federal tax rates would be required, not counting the adverse impact that such taxes would have on economic growth and the tax base. The CBO's alternative scenario, which maintains the overall tax rate (federal revenues over GDP) constant, will probably show a debt-to-GDP ratio of close to 200 percent in 25 years' time and exploding over the following half century.[3] The future course of the country, as the politicians have set it, will still show either unsupportable taxes or unsustainable debt. State and local government budgets will have worsened and added to the dire outlook.

Perhaps the incapacity of a deadlocked Congress to raise the debt ceiling will soon bring again the threat of technical default, fuel investors' fears, push up federal securities yields, and start the avalanche of a sovereign debt crisis in America.

Tough Times Ahead

Whether you live in Europe or America, tough times lie ahead. Governments will have to reduce their debts; if they don't want to, sovereign debt crises will force their hands, one way or another. A sovereign debt crisis starts with the refusal of investors to continue lending to the state except at higher interest rates. As rates go up, servicing the debt becomes more costly. More investors become conscious of the risk, which further compounds the problem and increases the probability of default. Banks and other financial institutions, which hold significant quantities of government securities, suffer liquidity or even solvency problems. A bank panic, where depositors rush to withdraw their deposits, would precipitate the crisis. Once a certain point is reached, depositors will not believe that deposit insurance can save their money, except with devaluated money. History shows that the emperor—a metaphor for the sovereign who rules the state—is tempted to solve the problem by printing money, which creates inflation. We can then only hope that he will stop the printing press before hyperinflation develops. Raising taxes seems to be a natural solution for Leviathan, but the taxpayers may refuse to pay, or they may be incapable to pay a tax rate sufficient to feed the emperor. To force the taxpayer to pay, the sovereign will try to exert more surveillance and more control over private transactions and private life. The Greek government wants a database of personal data from financial institutions and utility bills to check against tax returns.[4] You better have nothing in your life to hide, for the emperor likes transparent and naked subjects. Leviathan has become ravenous. Alternatively, the sovereign may try to reduce expenditures, which may mean reneging on health care or pensions he has promised to his subjects, some of whom have built their lives around these promises. Since half of Americans receive some transfers from government, lots of people will be directly hurt. One way or another, a recession, or perhaps a depression will follow, compared to which the Great Recession, and perhaps even the Great Depression, will look like little bear.

Such are the consequences of the emperor having borrowed money he cannot reimburse. The consequences will be ugly and will make most people's lives difficult for a number of years. It may be the poorest who will face the most difficult times, or perhaps those not poor enough to get public or private charity but not rich enough to have accumulated important savings hidden from the state. As they have been accustomed to, people in trouble will beg for help, but the state won't be able to answer effectively. The banks will cry for help from a state that will simultaneously ask them for help.

The worse may still be to come if the people call for an authoritarian power to help them out. The famous nineteenth century political theorist Alexis de Tocqueville noted how, after major disturbances, "the taste for public tranquillity then becomes a blind passion, and citizens are subject to becoming enamored with a very disordered love of order."[5] The statocrats will be most happy to oblige. If only to save their own skins, they will try to boost their power to control more aspects of life. History is replete with examples of ordinary people turning toward the state to deliver them from disorders created by the state itself, who is the main beneficiary of the process.

The emperor is not totally naked. He still enjoys the support of a majority of the public. Indeed, he financially bribes half the population. Some of his subjects are net tax consumers: they get more from the emperor than they give him in taxes. Of course, net taxpayers labor to pay these transfers, but this does not change the fact that those on the good side of the wicket are natural supporters, tacit or overt, of the emperor. Just look at public demonstrations: many assemble people asking for more, not less, power to the state, and usually power that will benefit themselves. People make their ideology fit their interest more often than the other way around. They use the threat of withdrawing their support as a weapon to blackmail the emperor. And it is not just a question of money (even if most benefits are translatable in terms of money, as there is in most cases a price at which one would accept to leave others alone or pay to be left alone). The emperor imposes bans and controls on some people in order to satisfy the preferences of his supporters. Regulation is the paradigmatic way to force some people to adapt their lifestyles to what others consider the good life, *their* good life. The conservative crowd wants the state to grab more power in order to impose its own conception of law and order, its own version of the surveillance state. The liberal crowd asks the state to impose its own ideal of social justice. The state sometimes favors one crowd and sometimes the other, hence the continuous growth of its power, irrespective of who sits on the throne.

Who is able to challenge the emperor today? He has armies of inspectors, investigators, policemen, judges, and supporting bureaucrats. He may be broke, but he still enjoys the support of many, especially those who won't pay much to reimburse the debt. He can still marshal his power into forcing obedience on dissidents. He still has a credit card. The emperor is only nearly naked. Many believe that he is sumptuously dressed, and his courtiers repeat it all the time: "Mr. President, Your Majesty, you can do it!"

Moreover, it is easy for the emperor to bluff and lie. In early 2012, the Greek finance minister assured the states who had bailed out his own state that the latter's promises would be kept: "Signatures are signatures. Commitments are commitments," he said. Even elections, he claimed, could not change the state's commitments: "Elections are not a problem," he explained. "People will choose how they will be governed, but the country will be governed with respect to the commitments it has made to its partners."[6] In fact, a democratic sovereign can break its promises just as easily as ancient sovereigns, if not more easily: it suffices that the majority change, or that it be inconsistent as majorities often are.[7]

I hope my reader is now persuaded that the emperor metaphor is not as exaggerated as it may look at first sight in describing our democratic states. The emperor, the sovereign, is not one person, but neither is he the totality of a big undifferentiated blob that would be called the people. Even in a democratic society, only some individuals rule. Besides fleeting majorities who are allowed to occasionally express themselves, the rulers are the statocrats (politicians and bureaucrats), and those close to them, such as special-interest lobbyists and politically correct elites. Democratic statocrats rely more formally than rulers in other regimes on the support of a large proportion of the public, but they still impose the preferences and values of some—theirs and their supporters'—on others. The more the state intervenes, the more it discriminates among preferences and values to impose to larger minorities—as opposed to a night-watchman state, which only has to impose basic peace requirements to violent individuals. What Bertrand de Jouvenel called "totalitarian democracy,"[8] a democratic regime that grants the majority the right to intervene in anything, constantly negates some individuals' preferences and values in favor of some other individuals. Indeed, we have seen democratic emperors buying the support of a rationally ignorant majority with borrowed money to be reimbursed by somebody sometime in the future. The "somebody" can be a different majority or some minorities. Technically, *the* majority does not exist, there is only *a* majority that can change if only a small number within it switches places with previous minority members. In the meantime, the statocrats have consolidated their power and perks, and they knew they would never *personally* have to pay back but a tiny fraction of the public deb.

Even if one rejects this analysis in favor of a mystic conception of democracy, even if one thinks that the emperor is us and we are all the emperor, the debt accumulation still cannot continue. Just to stabilize it in proportion of GDP would, as we saw, immediately require a 50 percent increase in the global tax rate or cuts in noninterest expenditures by a third. These estimates are for America, but they must not differ much in the typical European country. The emperor can probably neither force such a large tax increase on the public, nor can he maintain his needed popular support by slashing expenditures on which so many of his wards have come to rely. And the emperor is leery of defaulting on his debt because it would displease not only some of his supporters in the financial world but also ordinary people who indirectly hold a large number of his securities. It remains to be seen how the emperor will save himself. One way or another, the current situation is unsustainable.

What cannot continue will not. The problem is to know exactly how it will stop, and what will be the consequences.

"Governments used to worry about their banks," wrote *The Economist* at the end of 2011. "Now the reverse is also true."[9] The problem is worse than a literal reading of this observation would suggest. Ever since the Great Depression, policy analysts and a large number of economists, not to speak of the general public, have come to believe that some institutions and types of behavior threaten the whole economic system, that they constitute "systemic risks" against which an overall regulator must protect us. The state was to be the overall regulator controlling systemic risk. Keynesian theory of macroeconomic policy justified fine tuning the economy to control these risks: add a little public expenditure now, subtract a bit of money later, and get GDP at its potential level with no inflation or unemployment. The Employment Act of 1946 declared that "it is the continuing policy and responsibility of the Federal Government...to promote maximum employment, production, and purchasing power."[10] To the state's toolkit were added numerous regulatory controls that, from Franklin D. Roosevelt to Barack Obama, were imposed on finance. The Dodd-Frank Act of 2010 was only the latest salvo in this fight of the sovereign against systemic risk.

One crucial fact was forgotten in the process, which should have been obvious to anybody with open eyes: the regulator himself became a large systemic risk. As Latin poet Juvenal asked in another context, *Quis custodiet ipsos custodies?* ("Who will protect us against our protector?"). Inflationary monetary policies created bubbles that could only be deflated by recessions. Sometimes, like during the Great Depression, the omniscient regulator—the Fed in this case—adopted the wrong economic policy and deepened the problem. Eight decades later, the regulating state actively and systematically encouraged the housing bubble and the securitization of risky mortgages that led to the Great Recession.[11] The systemic danger of a powerful state is also true in the broadest political sense: consider the two world wars that marred the twentieth century, not to talk of the continuous growth of Big Brother. When government is powerful enough to intervene in any interstice of social and economic life, it is also capable of wreaking havoc in the whole system. The developing sovereign debt crisis provides another demonstration. We must not forget that the sovereign debt crisis is the debt crisis of the sovereign, not the result of some bad capitalist conspiracy. The state is the worst systemic danger around.

Another Possible World

Is the best of all possible worlds a miserable one? Are we condemned to live in a Brave New World where voting citizens smile while legally elected or hired statocrats bury them under debts, regulations, and controls? Is there another possible world where we could escape the corner into which the sovereign debt has painted us? Complex questions. When facing an apparently insuperable problem, it is useful to think out of the box. The problem with thinking out of the box is that we first have to find where the box is. We cannot hope to review and discuss here all the economic and philosophical issues related to the nature of the sovereign state, but our explorations thus far in this book should provide some indications on the general direction where to go.

Markets are not perfect, they are not always right. Witness how much time they took to take notice of the dire financial situation of many European sovereigns, and how they still trust other heavily indebted ones in both Europe and America. When the euro was introduced, investors naively assumed that, because supranational politicians and bureaucrats were in charge, there was no risk of default from state members. As the crisis developed, investors went through waves of deep pessimism to wild optimism each time European leaders opened their mouths to say they were in charge, only to fall in prostration again when the latest political panacea failed. As the old Latin saying goes, *errare humanum est*—"to err is human." Yet, actors on the market face incentives to be rational, in the sense of discovering problems and correcting errors, because their financial survival or at least their usual standard of living depends on it. Contrarians can coexist with crowd followers and act on their unconventional ideas: this is how the market eventually changes course; this is how it will increasingly question the capacity of Western states to reimburse their debt. Private actors learn from their mistakes. When the Great Recession started, investors reviewed their mistaken optimism and started questioning the convergence of European sovereign bonds, which lead to pricing bonds as a function of each issuer's risk. Markets marshal all the information of the participants. They cannot remain in error forever and usually self-correct rapidly.

However imperfect markets are, the state is worse. This is not because of any special wickedness in politicians, bureaucrats, or voters, but simply because they are not generally given the right incentives to correct their errors. The individual politician wins perks and power if he offers immediate benefits to his constituents, even if the complex and entangled consequences of his actions will be detrimental in an uncertain future when he will probably be out of office anyway. The individual bureaucrat will not be personally affected by his own policy errors, provided that he works within the rules and doesn't undermine state power. He will be rewarded with career opportunities and perks the more problems the public wants him to solve, even if he has contributed creating the problems in the first place, and the more power he will be given to do so. The individual voter, whose own vote is not going to change anything from the viewpoint of his own interest, remains rationally ignorant: he doesn't have a clue on who does what with his taxes and with the debt. Moreover, the margin of action of a contrarian is very limited in the state. For sure, a democratic system allows him to criticize and dissent with words. But if a citizen, like a contrarian speculator who buys when others sell, *acts* according to his contrarian beliefs by, say, buying a forbidden product, offering a security not approved by the authorities, or opening a smoking restaurant, he will be punished with fine, jail, or worse. It is much more costly to be a political dissident than a hedge fund contrarian.

It follows that state processes—that is, political and bureaucratic processes—make more errors than markets, and these errors have heavier systemic consequences. When the state errs, the consequences are much more catastrophic than when economic actors mess up. Hitler or Stalin would have done relatively little damage as Wall Street financiers. Interestingly, even John Maynard Keynes admitted that much: "It is better that a man should tyrannise over his bank balance than over his fellow-citizens," he wrote.[12]

The box, then, is the monopolistic, centralized state, which makes decisions for everybody. This is what we have to think out of if we want to solve the debt crisis (and a host of other problems).

Imagine the lack of diversity and the potential mistakes to be made if the state (a bit like in centrally planned economies) were to decide, even in a fair referendum, which single brand, make, and color of car will be available to buy. Everybody would drive an identical car, a situation that would be both fair and conducive to economies of scale. Granted that recognizing one's car in a parking lot or along the sidewalk would be more difficult, but the state would certainly be nice enough to allow people to paint their initials on their cars. At any rate, there already exist door lock remote controls and smartphone apps to help one find one's car. In a democratic society, everybody would have had an equal (and insignificant) voice in the democratic process in the choice of the common car. "We" would democratically choose "our" car. But what about individuals who have different tastes? What about the lack of experimentation that uniformity implies? What if the electorate makes a mistake and "buys" a car that is badly adapted to the weather, or consumes too much gas, or is not durable enough, and so on?

The car referendum analogy illustrates the typical uniformity imposed by state intervention, including in financial regulations and in decisions to borrow. But there is an alternative world. To the extent possible, each individual should decide how he will himself mortgage his future, contrary to the state imposing an equal public debt burden on all taxpayers. Our effort to think out of the box requires favoring individual choices over collective choices whenever feasible. The state could, for example, allow individuals to hold and trade in any currency they wish, so that they could protect themselves against inflation and financial repression by contracting in currencies they think are less likely to be inflated and depreciated. This idea, proposed by Friedrich Hayek, a 1974 Nobel laureate,[13] would impose budget discipline to the state.

Another implication of thinking in terms of individual, as opposed to collective, choices lies in the advantages of decentralized federalism based on free trade and free mobility as opposed to central harmonization and standardization. In this perspective, the EU should probably not have imposed a central currency. Participation was voluntary, but only at the state level; the decision was still coerced at the individual's level. The EU should remain as decentralized a federation as possible. Similarly, in America, the power of the federal government should be better checked, and States' constitutional rights be better respected (except when they interfere directly with free trade or other fundamental rights). If public borrowing is required, it should be done at the level closer to the individual: at the local level rather the State level and at the State level rather than in Washington DC. Public debt should be incurred and managed at the level closest to the individual. This way, individuals can escape debt-ridden polities by moving with their feet, which imposes the right incentives to governments. Competition makes governments more accountable.

The Fourth Alternative

Thinking out of the box has more immediate implications for the solution of the current public debt problem. We may not be condemned to the three bad alternatives reviewed in the last chapter: open default, stealth default through inflation, or doing nothing. If a default appears unavoidable, we should be prepared to experience it as an opportunity, not a catastrophe. In other words, there may be a forgotten option, a fourth alternative, which we have perhaps neglected too cavalierly: cutting expenditures. At least, let's hope so.

We can imagine a set of concurrent circumstances where the fourth alternative would be the only one available: taxpayers refuse to pay, powerful financial lobbies prevent an open default, other lobbies such as exporters successfully oppose inflation, and the courts try to enforce government debt contracts. We have seen that, in order to keep the federal debt held by the public at its current proportion of GDP (62% at the end of 2010), noninterest federal spending has to be cut by one third. Unrealistic? Perhaps, but cutting one third of federal spending from its current (2010) level would merely mean going back—or is it not forward?—to its level of 2000 in constant dollars. This is worth repeating: the level of federal spending in constant dollars was, in year 2000, one third less than in 2010. Were Americans so unhappy a decade ago?

Many people seem to think that the increase of federal expenditures in the first decade of the twenty-first century was due to national defense, but this belief is mistaken. Only 27 percent of the growth of federal expenditures in constant dollars from 2000 to 2010 came from national defense. The rest (73%) of the increase came from nondefense expenditures.

It may be also objected that the constant-dollar comparison is deficient because Social Security expenditures were bound to increase. The truth, however, is that nearly all categories of real federal expenditures per capita have increased during the past 25 years, and that Social Security was barely above the average increase. It is mainly health expenditures, including Medicare and even more with Medicaid, that have gone through the roof. Income security programs came next as spending in that area nearly doubled. Over this quarter of a century, national defense expenditures have increased much less in constant dollars than social expenditures. We may admit that Social Security and health care expenditures will normally increase more from now on, but the point is that there is room for cuts in other areas. Many expensive but useless, if not harmful, areas of federal intervention could be simply abandoned. Moreover, Social Security itself could be gradually phased out and replaced by private alternatives. It would be difficult to avoid deep cuts in Medicare and Medicaid, but a gradual recourse to private insurance substitutes and to paring down the welfare rolls could be envisioned. In the long run, many things can be done gradually; the challenge is to start now. The whole process should be viewed as an opportunity to build a better world of more self-reliant and free individuals.

For reasons reviewed in this book, the fourth alternative, even if desirable, may be impossible to implement deliberately. Growing government expenditures have created new, dependent constituencies that will fight tooth and nail to preserve their privileges. Most of these constituencies have been assembled before 2000 but at least three are recent: users of the Medicare drug coverage plan created by George W. Bush, holders of private health insurance who have started benefiting from rules imposed to insurers by Barack Obama, and employees and suppliers of the wide security apparatus created by antiterrorist laws. The TSA, which is barely more than ten years old but employs some 50,000 persons, is just one example of constituency building that lead to results that many citizens, if not most, find unacceptable.

The fourth alternative may anyway be forced on the federal government by financial markets, just like several European states are now being forced to control their expenditures. If powerful financial lobbies succeed in preventing a default, especially of the open sort, if the courts try to enforce the government's debt contracts, if inflation is resisted, and if taxpayers will not or cannot cough more, the federal government will have no choice but to drastically reduce its expenditures. The fourth alternative could become a welcome default option.

Whether out of a deliberate decision to choose the fourth alternative or as the consequence of default, the federal government would have to establish strict priorities and would be led, as by an invisible hand, to abandon whole fields of intervention that have been detrimental to prosperity and have negated America's heritage of liberty. Let's reconsider what I presented, in chapter 8, as the impossibility of eliminating one third of federal expenditures because they are all considered essential. The truth is that most of these expenditures are useless, if not positively harmful, for one of two reasons: they don't correspond to an essential mission of the state, that is, to a need that can't be satisfied by voluntary market relations; or they should fall under the responsibility of lower levels of government, because governments closer to the people are usually better placed to cater to their needs, and because intergovernmental competition is a good thing.

Standard economic interventions and regulations in agriculture, transportation, science, space and technology, energy, commerce and housing credit, and community and regional development fit into one of these two bins. Eliminating them would save 7 percent of federal noninterest expenditures (see Chart 8.2). Education, which makes up for another 4 percent of federal expenditures, should also be left either to the market or to lower levels of government. Even in traditional government functions, much could be saved. The federal government spends 2 percent of its budget on law and order, and this category has increased by 79 percent in constant dollars per capita since 2001 and by 233 percent since 1985. It is not the amount of real crimes (murder, assaults, theft) that have jumped but the continuous manufacturing of new crimes, the federalization of much law enforcement, the savage enforcement of laws against victimless crimes, the militarization of the police up to drone surveillance against citizens, and in general the growth of the surveillance state. If the federal government were forced to reduce its budget, it would be discovered that half its law enforcement mainly helps to undermine American ideals. Thinking that another 1 percent of expenditure cut would be found in that area is not unrealistic. Last but not least, the national defense budget is overgrown. In 2001, it was 16 percent of federal spending, 5 percentage points lower than in 2010, which translates into a growth of 83 percent in real dollars during a decade. Moreover, national defense spending in 2010 is 10 percent higher in constant dollars than 25 years ago under Reagan. Surely another 5 percent of federal budget cuts can be found there (and more might have to come later as the government already plans to cut that much by 2016). Adding up these cuts would produce a 16 percent reduction in federal spending, half of our objective. A similar amount of cuts would have to be found in the "social" programs—Social Security, health, and income security—that make up 62 percent of total spending and a bit more if we add education. These cuts are still massive and would not be easy to achieve, but aren't we seeing some light at the end of the tunnel?

Cuts of that order will anyway have to be made if America is to survive as America, with its liberty and prosperity. They would define a new world, for sure, but the alternative may well be poverty and tyranny. The back-of-envelope calculations above are meant to show that deep cuts are not totally unrealistic. Reduced by one third in real dollars (from 2010), federal government expenditures would still equal their level of 2000. Once it is realized that one third of federal spending has to be cut, priorities will have to be established so that only the most important federal functions are maintained. We have a great opportunity to bring the federal government to a level consistent with liberty and prosperity.

We already see the beginning of the realization that priorities have to be set because the government cannot do everything for everybody. Budget cuts are forcing local governments to make tough choices. Reduced police departments have, like in Baltimore, to focus on the most violent offenders—a good idea in a context of a proliferation of laws criminalizing wide areas of human endeavor. The city of Stockton, California, on the verge of bankruptcy, had to cut its police personnel. As a result, the police cannot always enforce petty, harassing laws, such as drinking in public.[14] In Europe, people drink in public without compromising social order (with the possible exception of the Brits during soccer games!). The opportunity of the federal debt crisis is to do the same at that level of government, which is even more in need of serious priorities than State and local governments. We can then hope that the TSA will be disbanded, that the Justice Department will stop prosecuting the likes of Google and Apple, and that the purchase and maintenance of drones to spy on citizens will be halted. And so on and so forth. Hope becomes possible.

I have argued that federal taxes cannot be raised anywhere near the levels that would be necessary to close the fiscal gap. I would also argue that tax increases should not be part of the solution at all. A global tax rate (government revenues or taxes over GDP) lower than in most other countries is both an essential feature and a powerful symbol of American liberty. Low taxes are a weighty condition for vibrant economic growth. Moreover, there is no guarantee that higher taxes would be used to control the deficit or reimburse the debt instead of fuelling expenditures, maintaining the cruising speed of regulation and control, and buying more time for Leviathan. In chapter 8, I have mentioned Richard Vedder and Lowell Gallaway's econometric analysis indicating that, over the whole history of the United States, 37 percent of each federal surplus on average has been used to increase spending in the following year, and that this figure increased to 60 percent in the years between World War II and the end of the twentieth century.

One danger must be guarded against: it is in the bureaucrats' interest, and perhaps even in the politicians' interest, to operate the cuts where it hurts the public the most in order to persuade it to accept tax increases or, more generally, to grant still more power to the state. Instead of establishing true priorities and focusing on the most important missions of government, the statocrats will be tempted to reduce the most popular public services. The bureaucrats, on whose data and information the politicians depend, have little to lose and everything to gain, in using this tactic. Instead of reducing enforcement of laws against victimless crimes, the police will be tempted to stop responding to nonurgent burglary calls. Instead of reducing regulations, bureaucrats will be tempted to increase delays in issuing the numerous permits and licenses that these very regulations require. Instead of reducing transfer payments to corporations and the rich, bureaucrats will be tempted to drag their feet in assisting publicly sensitive motherhood welfare cases. Instead of reducing their harassment of taxpayers, IRS bureaucrats may delay reimbursements, take more time to answer the phone, and drag problem resolution. The most difficult policy problem in the upcoming turmoil is to find and implement rules that will prevent this hijacking of the reform agenda.

Even in the most favorable case, cutting government expenditures will be difficult. In many cases, we don't really know where it is best to cut, and we cannot know until forced to do it. Government missions have been creeping up, and sometimes exploding, for more than a century. Give Leviathan an inch, and he will take a mile. Some of these expenditures may be irreplaceable, many are impeding private efforts to solve the same problems, most are probably impediments to prosperity and liberty. But where can spending be cut when all beneficiaries think that their own perks are part of the most crucial mission of the state and when everything the government does seems to be tied to everything else? What are the really indispensable government programs and at which level? The best way to find out is to actually force Leviathan to establish priorities, and this is done by cutting its resources. Liberty is a process more than a fully known end state. Confronting the monstrous contemporary state with broad requirements of budget cuts will help discover which of its missions are absolutely indispensable to liberty, property, and the pursuit of happiness and which ones are secondary, useless, or positively damageable.

The idea of limiting the state by "starving the beast" has been controversial, because it is not sure that cutting tax rates can effectively prevent the state from exploiting the citizens in other ways, like borrowing and regulating. The opportunities offered by the growing debt crisis are that spending cuts may be unavoidable (either before or after default) and that Leviathan will not be able to continue borrowing to feed its addictions.

Some will repeat that it is unrealistic to cut one third of federal spending, and chapter 8 provides them with some good arguments. But, two questions must be asked. First, is it that unrealistic to go back to 2000, when federal expenditures were in real dollars two-thirds of what they are today (data for 2010)? Second, what are the alternatives? The complete list is now easy to decline: (1) openly defaulting, (2) engineering inflation and a multifaceted crisis, (3) waiting for the crisis to come, or (4) operating deep cuts in overgrown federal spending. I don't mention the alternative of increasing taxes toward the European level: although this seems a solution more easily available to America than to most European countries, it may reduce economic growth to the point where the deficit and the debt would get out of control anyway, not to mention the deep impact on the nature of American society. Is any of the alternatives more realistic than the fourth one? The least bad alternative is default, if feasible *and* if spending cannot be deliberately reduced. The first best solution remains to cut spending before being left with only the least bad alternative by uncontrolled and unpredictable crises.

I have focused on the federal government because it is likely to become the mother of all sovereign debt crises. But the US government is not the only naked emperor around. Europe is full of them. Moreover, many American States and local governments are in dire financial straits too and some may have to default or operate dramatic cuts in their budgets. Their outlook will become darker as the federal government reduces its grants, which make up one fifth of their budgets. It is in the whole Western world that the sovereign debt crisis provides an opportunity to chain Leviathan.

One happy circumstance may help the difficult process of cutting government spending. In general, government expenditures dampen economic growth, because they have to be financed by either incentive-reducing taxes or by public debt that evicts private investment. As we saw in chapter 5, official forecast scenarios do not incorporate this factor, which is difficult to quantify. (Mind you, no guess about the future is ever easy to quantify.) Separate estimates by the CBO suggest that solving the debt problem with higher taxes, which is what its baseline scenario assumes, would reduce annual GDP by 2 percent–10 percent in 75 years. Historical estimates by economists Carmen Reinhart, Vincent Reinhart, and Kenneth Rogoff suggest a ratio of gross debt to GDP exceeding 90 percent leads on average to a cumulative 24 percent loss of GDP. America is now over the fatidic threshold. The impact could be much harder if the debt problem leads to hyperinflation, economic crash, or more authoritarian government. But the inverse is also true. Solving the debt problem by reducing government spending could generate higher economic growth that would, by itself, help taxpayers eliminate the public debt. If lower government spending means less regulation, or less enforcement of detrimental regulations, economic growth would get another boost.

The dilemma is the following. We can refuse to recognize that the emperor has failed us and sail toward the public debt crisis oblivious to its possible consequences in higher taxes, financial repression, economic stagnation, and extended systems of surveillance and control to which no free society may survive. Or else we can seize the opportunity of the looming crisis to starve Leviathan and force the state to reset its priorities. Despite its many dangers, the sovereign debt crisis thus offers a great opportunity to restore liberty and prosperity. The future will tell which road was taken.

NOTES

Chapter 1 The Genie Out of the Bottle

1. The Argentine story is told in "Gauchos and Gadflies," *The Economist*, October 22, 2011, at http://www.economist.com/node/21533453 (accessed November 9, 2011).
2. "Swap Offer Is Final: Greek Finance Minister to Bondholders," *CNBC*, March 5, 2012, at http://www.cnbc.com/id/46628729/Swap_Offer_Is_Final_Greek_Finance_Minister_to_Bondholders (accessed June 11, 2012).
3. "Deferring to Leviathan," *The Economist*, April 28, 2012, at http://www.economist.com/node/21553502 (accessed April 28, 2012).
4. See Lemieux (2004).
5. "Insurance Pays Off in Greece," *Wall Street Journal*, March 19, 2012, at http://online.wsj.com/article/SB10001424052702304636404577291281319135996.html (accessed March 26, 2012).
6. "Charting the Year," *The Economist*, December 31, 2011, at http://www.economist.com/node/21542191 (accessed March 25, 2012).
7. Barley (2012).
8. "The Safety-Net Frays," *The Economist,* February 11, 2011, at http://www.economist.com/node/15498231 (accessed March 25, 2012).
9. "51% Predict U.S. Government Will Go Bankrupt Before Budget is Balanced," *Rasmussen Reports*, May 21, 2012, at http://www.rasmussen-reports.com/public_content/business/federal_budget/may_2012/51_predict_u_s_government_will_go_bankrupt_before_budget_is_balanced (accessed June 20, 2012).

Chapter 2 Understanding the Public Debt

1. Attributed to former congressional leader Everett Dirksen, but probably apocryphal.
2. I am grateful to Pierre-Anthony Lemieux for helping with these estimates.
3. See, among other documents, CBO (2011a) and GAO (2011a).
4. CBO (2012), p. 2.
5. Compare GAO (2010), p. vi, with OMB (2011b), p. 203.
6. See http://www.gao.gov/special.pubs/longterm/debt/debtbasics.html (accessed June 22, 2012).
7. GAO (2010), p. 3.
8. Ibid., p. 10.

9. Ibid., p. 42.

10. London: Macmillan, 1936.

11. Davis (1971), p. 149. I am grateful to Jeff Hummel for pointing out this book to me.

12. Ibid., pp. 143 and 153.

13. Huxley (1932), pp. 41–42.

14. See Lemieux (2011a), notably pp. 41–43 and pp. 48–49.

15. See Lemieux (2004).

16. Buchanan and Wagner (1977), p. 50.

17. GAO (2010), p. 10.

18. Quoted in Vock (2009).

19. Miron (2011).

20. "Calpers May Cut Target Return," *Wall Street Journal*, March 13, 2012, at http://online.wsj.com/article/SB10001424052702304537904577279572284 025222.html (accessed March 14, 2012).

21. "Michigan's Pension Changes Serve as Model," *Bloomberg News*, October 11, 2011, at http://www.bloomberg.com/news/print/2011–10–11/michigan-s-embrace-of-401-k-may-show-remedy-for-ailing-state-pensions.html (accessed November 2, 2011).

22. "Shares and Shibbloleths," *The Economist*, March 17, 2012, at http://www.economist.com/node/21550273 (accessed March 17, 2012).

23. Tett (2012).

24. Miron (2011), pp. 6 and 21.

25. De Rugy (2011).

26. Tanner (2012). See also Kotlikoff and Burns (2012).

27. OECD (2011a), Table 13.2, and database doi: 10.1787/gov_glance-2011–19-en.

28. Fed (2011).

29. "Rushing for the Exits," *The Economist*, November 12, 2011, at http://www.economist.com/node/21538195 (accessed April 11, 2012).

Chapter 3 Lessons from Europe (and Elsewhere)

1. "The Safety-Net Frays," *The Economist,* February 11, 2011, at http://www.economist.com/node/15498231 (accessed March 25, 2012).

2. English (1996), p. 260.

3. "Greek Bond Deal Makes German Banker See Red," *Wall Street Journal*, February 24, 2012, at http://online.wsj.com/article/SB10001424052970203 960804577240570332762612.html (accessed February 24, 2012).

4. "Fingers on the Trigger," *The Economist*, June 2, 2011, at http://www.economist.com/node/18775351 (accessed March 19, 2012) and "The Wait is Over," *The Economist*, March 17, 2012, at http://www.economist.com/node/21550271 (accessed March 19, 2012).

5. Reinhart and Rogoff (2009), p. 87.

6. See English (1996) and Mysak (2010).

7. "Largest Municipal Bankruptcy Filed," *Wall Street Journal*, November 10, 2011, at http://online.wsj.com/article/SB1000142405297020422460457702 8491526654090.html (accessed April 27, 2012) and "The Sewers of Jefferson County," *The Economist*, December 3, 2011, at http://www.economist.com/node/21541053 (accessed March 30, 2012);

8. Lemieux (2011a). See also Cochran (2012).
9. Data from Fed (2011).
10. "Islandic Court Rules to Repay British and Dutch," *Financial Times*, October 28, 2011, at http://www.ft.com/intl/cms/s/0/18152320–018d–11e1–8e59–00144feabdc0.html#axzz1tD2cuuJN (accessed April 27, 2012).
11. See "The Big Fat Greek Gravy Train: A Special Investigation Into The EU-Funded Culture Of Greed, Tax Evasion And Scandalous Waste," *Daily Mail Online*, June 24, 2011, at http://www.dailymail.co.uk/news/article-2007949/The-Big-Fat-Greek-Gravy-Train-A-special-investigation-EU-funded-culture-greed-tax-evasion-scandalous-waste.html (accessed December 1, 2011) and "For Ordinary Greeks, Big Bailout Adds Up to Years of Hardship," *Wall Street Journal*, October 9, 2011, at http://online.wsj.com/article/SB10001424052970203554104577003892831820960.html (accessed April 1, 2012).
12. OECD (2011d), p. 35.
13. Ibid., pp. 37–38.
14. I have discussed the evolution of the public debt before the Great Recession in Lemieux (2011b). Chart 4 incorporates data that were very slightly revised by the OECD after my *Regulation* article had gone to press.
15. Tanzi and Schuknecht (2000), p. 6 and OECD (2011a), p. 65 (and related database).
16. Reinhart (2010), p. 53.
17. Reinhart and Rogoff (2009), pp. 96 and 99.
18. Quoted in Lemieux (2008b).
19. "U.K. Financial Sector Fears Europe Fallout," *Wall Street Journal*, December 13, 2011, at http://online.wsj.com/article/SB100014240529702034304045770094222074837342.html (accessed September 4, 2012).
20. "Norway Wealth Fund to Cut European Exposure," *Financial Times*, March 30, 2012, at http://www.ft.com/intl/cms/s/0/81286ed4–7a51–11e1–839f-00144feab49a.html (accessed April 2, 2012).
21. "Will Slovakia Take a Bullet for the Euro?" *The Economist*, October 7, 2011.
22. Reinhart and Rogoff (2011).

Chapter 4 The Hidden Welfare State

1. Quoted in Alber (2010), p. 103.
2. The figures that follow are taken from OMB (2011b), Table 3.2.
3. This section relies on Lemieux (2012a).
4. Called NIPA, or "National Products and Income Accounts," in the United States.
5. See UN (2004), pp. 61ff.
6. OECD (2011b). These averages are averages among countries, and are thus unweighted.
7. CBO (2011a), p. 36–37.
8. Alber (2010), p. 109.
9. CBO (2011a), p. 39.
10. See Bartlett (2012) and, for an elaboration of my argument, Lemieux (2012b).
11. Baldwin (2009), pp. 71 and 35.
12. Baldwin (2009).

13. De Rugy (2012).
14. See http://www.medhealthinsurance.com/vermont.htm and http://www.maine.gov/pfr/insurance/consumer/indhlth.htm (accessed December 23, 2011).
15. See http://healthvermont.gov/family/insurance/index.aspx (accessed December 23, 2011).
16. See http://www.massresources.org/health-reform.html (accessed December 23, 2011).
17. Alber (2010), p. 107.
18. Ibid., p. 104. Evidence to the same effect is presented in Alber and Gilbert (2010) and in Castles (2007).
19. Howard (1997).
20. Vatter (1979), p. 298.
21. Ibid., p. 307.
22. Quoted at many places, including http://millercenter.org/president/policy/economic and http://www.answers.com/topic/employment-act-of-1946 (accessed December 20, 2011).
23. Quoted in Snowdon and Vane (2005), p. 146.
24. Kliesen and Thornton (2011), p. 2.
25. Lemieux (2008a), pp. 350–351.

Chapter 5 Federal Outlook: The Naked Emperor

1. Gokhale and Smetters (2003, 2006).
2. Kotlikoff (2006). See also Kotlikoff (2004) and Kotlikoff (2012).
3. Kotlikoff (2006), p. 235.
4. Ibid., p. 248.
5. Kotlikoff (2011).
6. Hummel (2009).
7. "Could the American Government Default?" *The Economist*, February 20, 2012, at http://www.economist.com/blogs/buttonwood/2012/02/fiscal-crisis (accessed March 8, 2012).
8. The last issue at the time of writing is CBO (2011b), which dates from June 2011.
9. GAO (2012).
10. CBO (2011b), p. 2.
11. Ibid., p. 14.
12. Ibid., "Notes" section.
13. CBO (2011b), Supplementary data online, Figure B-4. The CBO's 2012 *Long-Term Budget Outlook*, published in June 2012 after this book was written, shows forecasts similar to the 2011 edition.
14. CBO (2010c). Private correspondence with accountant Les Antman, January 26, 2012.
15. CBO (2011b), pp. 8, 15, and 22; GAO (2011b), p. 7; and GAO (2012), p. 7.
16. The CBO's 2012 *Long-Term Budget Outlook*, published in June 2012 and not incorporated in the research for this book, has increased its fiscal gap estimate to 9%.
17. GAO (2012), p. 7.
18. CBO (2011b), p. 15.
19. I am grateful to an anonymous reviewer for stressing this point.

20. CBO (2011b), p. xi.
21. Fed (2011), Table L.1. As we saw in chapter 2, the proportion is 23% when we add State and local governments.
22. CBO (2011b), p. 28.
23. Reinhart and Rogoff (2011).
24. Reinhart, Reinhart, and Rogoff (2012).
25. "The Nationalisation of Markets," *The Economist*, May 26, 2012, at http://www.economist.com/node/21555936 (accessed June 25, 2012).
26. GAO (2011a), p. xiii.
27. CBO (2010b), pp. 1 and 4.
28. St. Louis Fed (2011), p. 17.
29. "The Little State With a Big Mess," *New York Times*, October 22, 2011, at http://www.nytimes.com/2011/10/23/business/for-rhode-island-the-pension-crisis-is-now.html?pagewanted=1&_r=1&hpw (accessed January 1, 2012).
30. Ibid.
31. "Darker Nights as Some Cities Turn Off the Lights," *New York Times*, December 29, 2011, at http://www.nytimes.com/2011/12/30/us/cities-cost-cuttings-leave-residents-in-the-dark.html?_r=2&pagewanted=1&hp (accessed December 29, 2011).
32. Andersen (1837).
33. Jones (2012).

Chapter 6 The Emperor's Praetorians

1. A technical point: OECD (2011a), p. 59, provides a similar graph that excludes Turkey and Chile from the computation of the averages because data for these countries were missing in some of the years. I reinclude Turkey in the average because the 2007 figure for this country is available. My average thus covers 33 OECD countries instead of the 32 in the original graph of OECD (2011a).
2. See OECD (2010).
3. Tanzi and Schuknecht (2000), p. 6.
4. Smith (1762). There is obviously a typo in this book as Smith must have meant "of the half," not "or the half."
5. OECD, dataset of *Economic Outlook No 90*, data extracted December 2, 2011.
6. De Jouvenel (1945), pp. 23 and 101.
7. On the problem of sexual delinquents, see "Unjust and Ineffective," *The Economist*, August 6, 2009, at http://www.economist.com/node/14164614 (accessed June 17, 2012).
8. See http://www2.fbi.gov/ucr/cius2009/data/table_74.html (accessed January 9, 2011).
9. See Chassaigne (1906).
10. Spooner (1870).
11. Rousseau (1762).
12. Friedman (2011) and "Greece's Agony: What Have We Become?" *The Economist*, June 30, 2011, at http://www.economist.com/node/21550421 (accessed April 8, 2012).
13. Buchanan and Wagner (1977), p. 33.

14. Neiertz and Cronk (2012).
15. De la Boétie (1577).
16. De Jouvenel (1945), p. 21.
17. Olson (1971).
18. On the parenting license, see Lemieux (2001).
19. See Rawls (1971).
20. Buchanan (1975) and Brennan and Buchanan (1980).
21. See De Jasay (1996).
22. See Lancaster (2011).
23. See http://elsa.berkeley.edu/~saez/TabFig2007.xls (accessed January 13, 2011).
24. Tax Foundation (2009, 2011).
25. "Obama to Visit Swing State to Push His Millionnaire Tax," *Wall Street Journal*, April 9, 2012, at http://online.wsj.com/article/SB1000 1424052702304587704577334130244925226.html?mod=WSJ_hp_ MIDDLENexttoWhatsNewsTop (accessed April 9, 2012).
26. "Facebook Co-Founder Saverin Gives Up U.S. Citizenship before IPO," *Bloomberg*, May 11, 2012, at http://www.bloomberg.com/news/2012– 05–11/facebook-co-founder-saverin-gives-up-u-s-citizenship-before-ipo. html (accessed June 14, 2012).

Chapter 7 The Sovereign's Bankers

1. ECB (2012), p. S10.
2. BIS (2011), p. 14.
3. Hummel (2011b), p. 8.
4. EBA (2011), p. 28 and "Finance: A Union to Bank On," *Financial Times*, June 18, 2012, at http://www.ft.com/intl/cms/s/0/2dca4dce-b936–11e1- b4d6–00144feabdc0.html#axzz1yBpF707P (accessed June 18, 2012).
5. "CDS on Spanish Debt at Record High," *Financial Times*, June 18, 2012, at http://www.ft.com/intl/cms/s/0/47d9a47a-b955–11e1-a470–00144feabdc0. html?ftcamp=published_links%2Frss%2Fmarkets_capital-markets%2Ffeed %2F%2Fproduct#axzz1yBpF707P (accessed June 18, 2012).
6. "Staggering to the Rescue," *The Economist*, December 17, 2011, at http:// www.economist.com/node/21541858 (accessed April 10, 2012).
7. "Rushing for the Exits," *The Economist*, November 12, 2011, at http://www. economist.com/node/21538195 (accessed April 11, 2012).
8. Kindleberger (1993), pp. 77ff.
9. Ibid., p. 77.
10. Richards (1934), p. 271.
11. Marion (1934), p. 318.
12. Kindleberger (1993), pp. 97–117.
13. Storbeck (2011) and EBA (2011), Chart 28.
14. Calomiris (2000), p. 44. My summary of American banking relies heavily on this book.
15. See English (1996). I am grateful to Professor George A. Selgin (University of Georgia) for emphasizing the limited freedom of "free" banks in the North (correspondence of January 24, 2012).
16. Calomiris (2000), p. 58.
17. Lemieux (2011a), pp. 91–94.

18. Quignon (2010); Jenkins (2010); and "New Bank Capital Rules," *Financial Times*, September 13, 2012, at http://www.ft.com/intl/cms/s/3/35537d22-bf14-11df-a789-00144feab49a.html#axzz1nXZqinp4 (accessed February 29, 2012).

19. Milne (2011). See also http://www.fitchratings.com/web/en/dynamic/articles/Solvency-II-Sovereign-Risk-Charges-Unlikely-In-Near-Term.jsp (accessed January 27, 2012).

20. See the speech given by the deputy general manager of the BIS: Hannoun (2011).

21. "Oat Cuisine," *The Economist*, February 11, 2012, at http://www.economist.com/node/21547245 (accessed April 10, 2012).

22. See "The Fed Moves Again—and Here's What It Means," *Wall Street Journal*, October 6, 2011, at http://blogs.wsj.com/economics/2008/10/06/the-fed-moves-again/ (accessed January 27, 2012) and the Fed's press release of October 6, 2008, at http://www.federalreserve.gov/newsevents/press/monetary/20081006a.htm (accessed January 27, 2012).

23. Taylor (2010).

24. "Themes and Variations," *The Economist*, January 21, 2012, at http://www.economist.com/node/21542924 (accessed April 10, 2012).

25. For more information and sources on bank regulation, see Lemieux (2011a), especially Chapter 5.

26. "EU Red-Flags 'Volcker,'" *Wall Street Journal*, January 27, 2012 and "The Volker Diversion," *Wall Street Journal*, February 17, 2012, at http://online.wsj.com/article/SB10001424052970204795304577223343757678760.html (accessed April 11, 2012).

27. SIGTARP (2011). See also "TARP: Billions in Loans in Doubt," *Wall Street Journal*, April 24, 2012, at http://online.wsj.com/article/SB10001424052702303978104577364262736412398.html?mod=WSJ_hp_LEFTWhatsNewsCollection (accessed April 24, 2012).

28. "Secret Fed Loans Gave Banks $13 Billion," *Bloomberg Markets Magazine*, November 27, 2011, at http://www.bloomberg.com/news/2011-11-28/secret-fed-loans-undisclosed-to-congress-gave-banks-13-billion-in-income.html (accessed November 29, 2011) and "Fed Once-Secret Loan Crisis Data Compiled by Bloomberg Released to Public," *Bloomberg*, December 23, 2011, at http://mobile.bloomberg.com/news/2011-12-23/fed-s-once-secret-data-compiled-by-bloomberg-released-to-public (accessed January 24, 2012).

29. Quoted in "Regulator to InterBank: Boost Capital—or Else," *Minneapolis/St. Paul Business Journal*, July 13, 2009, at http://www.bizjournals.com/twincities/stories/2009/07/13/story1.html (accessed January 25, 2012).

30. Ibid.

31. See http://www.fhlbdm.com/Docs/Products_Services/MPP/Subprime%20Change%202007%2012%2012%20-%202008%2008.pdf (accessed January 24, 2012).

32. At http://www.fnb-hartford.com/a_history.htm (accessed January 30, 2010).

33. "Not All on the Same Page," *The Economist, July 1*, 2010, at http://www.economist.com/node/16485376 (accessed January 24, 2012).

34. De Jouvenel (1945), p. 174.

35. English (1996), p. 261 and McGrane (1935), p. 71.

36. Reinhart and Rogoff (2009), p. 104.
37. The data are taken (and rearranged) from Hummel (2012a), whose source is the Federal Reserve.
38. Kane (2011).
39. Reinhart, Reinhart, and Rogoff (2012), pp. 20-21 and Reinhart and Rogoff (2011), pp. 27 and 29.
40. CBO (2011b), p. 28.
41. Reinhart and Rogoff (2009), p. 143 and, more generally, Reinhart and Rogoff (2011).
42. Hannoun (2011).
43. "Europe Banks Hungry for Second Helpings," *Financial Times*, February 28, 2012, at http://www.ft.com/intl/cms/s/0/73ba02f4–6204–11e1–807f-00144feabdc0.html#axzz1nXZqinp4 (accessed February 28, 2012).
44. "Banks Borrow €530 From ECB Scheme," *Financial Times*, February 29, 2012, at http://www.ft.com/intl/cms/s/0/52ed18e4–6237–11e1–872e-00144feabdc0.html#axzz1nXZqinp4 (accessed February 29, 2012).
45. "Regulating European Insurers: From Brussels, with Shove," *The Economist*, April 7, 2012, at http://www.economist.com/node/21552224/print (accessed April 10, 2012).
46. Reinhart and Rogoff (2011), p. 41.

Chapter 8 Reducing Expenditures: Mission Impossible?

1. Kliesen and Thornton (2011), p. 1.
2. CBO (2011a).
3. Technical detail: in order not to have a negative amount in the graph, I did not net out the $82 billion of "undistributed offsetting receipts" (mainly composed of the employer share of the federal government pension funds). This introduces about 3 percent of double counting in the total.
4. OMB (2012a), pp. 22 and 97.
5. Riedl (2010), pp. 14–16.
6. De Rugy (2012).
7. According to BLS data from the Current Population Survey, as of December 2010. There may be some double-counting when adding the two figures.
8. This estimate is from Sherk (2010), p. 4.
9. Kling (2012), p. 54.
10. Vedder and Gallaway (1998).
11. Since a newly elected president takes office in January and the previous fiscal year does not end until September 30, he can still influence his predecessor's budget. In a parallel fashion, his last budget can be meddled with by his successor. So the question is whether we should consider the Reagan years as FY 1982 to FY 1989 (that is, calculate his results on the basis of FY 1981) or, instead, take his reign to run from FY 1981 to FY 1988 (and base his results on FY 1980). There is no nonarbitrary answer and, like many analysts, I adopt the first convention. It can be verified that adopting the second does not materially change the results of my analysis.
12. Reagan (1982).
13. Reagan (1985).
14. Reagan (1980).

15. Reagan (1981).
16. "Regan Presents Program to Cut Federal Spending," *Wall Street Journal*, December 6, 1984.
17. OMB (1985), p. 25.
18. "Recent Budget Battles Leave the Basic Tenets of Welfare State Intact," *Wall Street Journal*, October 21, 1985.
19. OMB (2012), p. 193.
20. Ibid., p. 227.
21. Ibid., p. 35.
22. Rahn (2012).
23. De Jouvenel (1952), p. 72.

Chapter 9 Inflating the Debt Away

1. BLS (2012), Table 1.
2. OMB (2012).
3. Thornton (1984).
4. "Just More of the Same," *The Economist*, February 11, 2012, at http://www. economist.com/node/21547248/print (accessed February 20, 2012).
5. Taylor (2012).
6. Hummel (2011a), p. 512.
7. Original data obtained from private correspondence with John Frain, February 21, 2012.
8. More precisely for my readers cognizant of statistical theory, 0.95 is the coefficient of determination.
9. Frain (2004). See also McCandless and Weber (1995) and King (2002), who present similar analyses and graphs. Weber was then an economist in the Research Department of the Federal Reserve Bank of Minneapolis, and McCandless was an associate professor of economics at the Universidad de Andrés in Buenos Aires. Mervyn King was deputy governor, and is now governor, of the Bank of England.
10. McCandless and Weber (1995), p. 3.
11. Keynes (1936), p. 207.
12. Higgs (1997).
13. "Top Banks in EU Rush for Safety," *Wall Street Journal*, February 21, 2012, at http://online.wsj.com/article/SB100014240529702041310045772348425 33868550.html (accessed February 22, 2012).
14. Fed (2005), p. 3.
15. Bullock (1930), p. 266.
16. Reinhart and Rogoff (2009), pp. 176–179.
17. Redish (1993).
18. Reinhart and Rogoff (2009), pp. 126, 186.
19. Ibid., p. 143.
20. CBO (2012), pp. 109–111. See also CBO (2010a).
21. CBO (2010a).
22. CBO (2012).
23. See Hanke (2009) and "Zimbabwe Inflation Rate Soars to 66,000%," *News. scotsman.com*, February 15, 2008, at http://news.scotsman.com/latestnews/ A-loaf-hits—78.3781428.jp (accessed March 20, 2010).

Chapter 10 Contagion: When the Emperor Coughs

1. See for example Edwards (2000).
2. Kaminsky, Reinhart, and Végh (2003).
3. Fisher (1933).
4. See Lemieux (2008a).
5. "Decline and Small," *The Economist*, March 3, 2012, at http://www.economist.com/node/21548923 (accessed March 8, 2012).
6. ECB (2012), p. S-10. See also "The Retreat from Everywhere," *The Economist*, April 21, 2012, at http://www.economist.com/node/21553015 (accessed June 30, 2012).
7. Hummel (2011b), p. 8 and Fed (2012), p. 119.
8. Borensztein and Panizza (2009), p. 713.
9. "Contagion? What Contagion?" *The Economist*, December 3, 2011, at http://www.economist.com/node/21541020 (accessed February 29, 2012).
10. Reinhart and Rogoff (2009), pp. 141–171.
11. Johnson (2012).
12. Sargent and Wallace (1981) and "Good Morning. You're Nobel Laureates," *New York Times*, December 3, 2011, at http://www.nytimes.com/2011/12/04/business/nobel-winners-in-economics-the-reluctant-celebrities.html?pagewanted=all (accessed December 5, 2011).

Chapter 11 The Least Bad of All Possible Worlds

1. Voltaire (1759).
2. Borensztein and Panizza (2009), p. 698.
3. Hummel (2012a), p. 28.
4. See Borensztein and Panizza (2009), pp. 690–693.
5. CBO (2010b), p. 5.
6. Minarik (2012), p. 67.
7. "More Than Half of Greek Youth Unemployed," *Financial Post*, March 8, 2012, at http://business.financialpost.com/2012/03/08/more-than-half-of-greek-youth-unemployed/ (accessed March 8, 2012) and "Spain's Unemployment Jumps, Deepening Crisis," *Wall Street Journal*, April 27, 2012, at http://online.wsj.com/article/SB10001424052702304811304577369253280172124.html?mod=WSJ_hp_LEFTWhatsNewsCollection (accessed April 27, 2012).
8. "Man Kills Himself in Athens Square," *Wall Street Journal*, April 4, 2012, at http://online.wsj.com/article/SB10001424052702303299604577323220453511142.html (accessed April 19, 2012).
9. Borensztein and Panizza (2009), p. 713.
10. Hummel (2012a), p. 28.
11. Data from FRED at the St. Louis Fed at http:// http://research.stlouisfed.org/, a very useful data resource.
12. Jones (2012), p. 42 and Hummel (2012a), pp. 25–26. The government is actually in the process of increasing the maturity of its debt.
13. "Zimplats Happens," *The Economist*, March 17, 2012, at http://www.economist.com/node/21550289 (accessed March 17, 2012).
14. Wallison (2012), p. 75.
15. "China Could Play Key Role in EU Rescue," *Financial Times*, October 27, 2011, at http://www.ft.com/intl/cms/s/0/7505d210–00ba-11e1-8590–00144feabdc0.html (accessed March 9, 2012).

16. See Hummel (2009, 2011b, 2012a, 2012b).
17. English (1996), p. 265.
18. Ibid., pp. 268–270.
19. Hummel (2011b), p. 15.
20. Kling (2012).
21. McGrane (1933), p. 682.
22. Borensztein and Panizza (2009), p. 699.
23. According to data from Argentina's National Budget Office in the Ministry of Economy and Public Finance.
24. See   http://www.heritage.org/index/pdf/2012/countries/argentina.pdf (accessed March 17, 2012). See also "IMF Criticizes Argentina's 'Absence of Progress' on Inflation, GDP Data," *Bloomberg*, February 1, 2012, at http://www.bloomberg.com/news/2012–02–01/imf-regrets-absence-of-progress-on-improving-argentine-inflation-index.html (accessed March 17, 2012); "Argentina Spending More than it Produces; 'Default Situation' Can't Be Discarded," *MercoPress*, February 29, 2012, at http://en.mercopress.com/2012/02/29/argentina-spending-more-than-it-produces-default-situation-can-t-be-discarded (accessed March 17, 2012); and "Don't Lie to Me, Argentina," *The Economist*, February 25, 2012, at http://www.economist.com/node/21548242 (accessed March 8, 2012).
25. Jones (2012).

Chapter 12 Opportunities

1. Voltaire (1759).
2. "Stress Rises on Social Security," *Wall Street Journal*, April 23, 2012, at http://online.wsj.com/article/SB10001424052702303592404577362052094 040414.html?mod=rss_US_News (accessed April 24, 2012).
3. As I am putting the last touch on my manuscript, CBO's (2012) *Long-Term Budget Outlook*, published in June 2012, broadly confirms these forecasts.
4. "Finance Ministry on Tax Evasion Trail," *Athen News*, April 24, 2012, at http://www.athensnews.gr/portal/11/55027# (accessed April 24, 2012).
5. De Tocqueville (1840), Vol. 4.
6. "Swap Offer Is Final: Greek Finance Minister to Bondholders," *CNBC*, March 5, 2012, at http://www.cnbc.com/id/46628729/Swap_Offer_Is_Final_Greek_Finance_Minister_to_Bondholders (accessed June 11, 2012).
7. See Lemieux (2004).
8. De Jouvenel (1945), pp. 282ff.
9. "The Safety-Net Frays," *The Economist,* February 11, 2011, at http://www.economist.com/node/15498231 (accessed March 25, 2012).
10. See   http://fraser.stlouisfed.org/docs/publications/ERP/1954/ERP1954_Appendixes_2.pdf, p. 129 (accessed March 25, 2012).
11. Lemieux (2011a).
12. Keynes (1936), p. 374.
13. Hayek (1978).
14. "Cities See Murder Slide End," *Wall Street Journal*, March 29, 2012, at http://online.wsj.com/article/SB10001424052702303812904577297780157081385 4.html (accessed March 29, 2012).

BIBLIOGRAPHY

Alber, Jens (2010), "What the European and American Welfare States Have in Common and Where They Differ: Facts and Fiction in Comparisons of the European Social Model and the United States," *Journal of European Social Policy* 20:2, pp. 102–125.

Alber, Jens, and Neil Gilbert, Eds. (2010), *United in Diversity? Comparing Social Models in Europe and America* (Oxford and New York: Oxford University Press).

Andersen, Hans Christian (1837), "The Emperor's New Clothes," in *The Complete Andersen*, Translated by Jean Hersholt (New York: The Limited Editions Club, 1949), at http://www.andersen.sdu.dk/vaerk/hersholt/TheEmperorsNewClothes_e.html (accessed January 3, 2012).

Baldwin, Peter (2009), *The Narcissism of Minor Differences: How America and Europe Are Alike, an Essay in Numbers* (Oxford: Oxford University Press).

Barley, Richard (2012), "Bond Myths Are Exposed by Greece," *Wall Street Journal*, February 23, at http://online.wsj.com/article/SB1000142405297020477860457239413367825298.html (accessed February 24, 2012).

Bartlett, Bruce (2012), *The Benefit and the Burden: Tax Reform—Why We Need It and What It Will Take* (New York: Simon & Shuster).

BIS (2011), "The Impact of Sovereign Credit Risk on Bank Funding Conditions," Committee on the Global Financial System, Paper No. 43, July, at http://www.bis.org/publ/cgfs43.pdf (accessed January 19, 2012).

BLS (2010), "Frequently Asked Questions about Hedonic Quality Adjustment in the CPI," July 8, at http://www.bls.gov/cpi/cpihqaqanda.htm (accessed November 5, 2011).

——— (2012), "CPI Detailed Report—December 2011," January, at http://www.bls.gov/cpi/cpid1112.pdf (accessed February 19, 2012).

Bolton, Patrick, and Olivier Jeanne (2010), "Sovereign Default Risk and Bank Fragility in Financial Integrated Economies," Paper prepared for the 2010 IMF Annual Research Conference, March 16, 2011, at http://www.econ2.jhu.edu/People/Jeanne/ARC031611.pdf (accessed January 19, 2011).

Borensztein, Eduardo, and Ugo Panizza (2009), "The Costs of Sovereign Default," *IMF Staff Papers* 56:4, pp. 683–741.

Brennan, Geoffrey, and James M. Buchanan (1980), *The Power to Tax: Analytical Foundations of a Fiscal Constitution* (Cambridge: Cambridge University Press), at http://www.econlib.org/library/Buchanan/buchCv9c0.html (accessed June 26, 2012).

Brown, Gary E. (1989), "Episodes in the Public Debt History of the United States," Working paper No. 540, Department of Economics, MIT, October, at http://dspace.mit.edu/bitstream/handle/1721.1/63551/episodesinpublic00brow.pdf?sequence=1 (accessed January 25, 2012).

Buchanan, James M. (1975), *The Limits of Liberty: Between Anarchy and Leviathan* (Chicago and London: University of Chicago Press), at http://www.econlib.org/library/Buchanan/buchCv7.html (accessed June 26, 2012).

Buchanan, James M., and Richard E. Wagner (1977), *Democracy in Deficit: The Political Legacy of Lord Keynes* (New York: Academic Press), at http://www.econlib.org/library/Buchanan/buchCv8c0.html (accessed November 5, 2011).

Bullock, Charles J. (1930), "Dionysius of Syracuse—Financier," *The Classical Journal* 25:4 (January), pp. 260–276 .

Calomiris, Charles W. (2000), *U.S. Bank Deregulation in Historical Perspective* (Cambridge and New York: Cambridge University Press).

Castles, Francis G., Ed. (2007), *The Disappearing State? Retrenchment Realities in an Age of Globalisation* (Cheltenhan, UK and Northampton, MA: Edward Elgar).

CBO (2010a), "The Budget and Economic Outlook: Fiscal Years 2010 to 2020," January, at http://www.cbo.gov/sites/default/files/cbofiles/ftpdocs/108xx/doc10871/01–26-outlook.pdf (accessed February 22, 2012).

——— (2010b), "Federal Debt and the Risk of a Fiscal Crisis," July 27, at http://www.cbo.gov/sites/default/files/cbofiles/ftpdocs/116xx/doc11659/07-27_debt_fiscalcrisis_brief.pdf (accessed December 25, 2011).

——— (2010c), "The Individual Alternative Minimum Tax," January 15, at http://www.cbo.gov/ftpdocs/108xx/doc10800/01–15-AMT_Brief.pdf (accessed January 2, 2011).

——— (2010d), "The Long-Term Budget Outlook," June (Revised August 2010), at http://www.cbo.gov/ftpdocs/115xx/doc11579/06–30-ltbo.pdf (accessed December 30, 2011).

——— (2011a), "The Budget and Economic Outlook: An Update," August, at http://www.cbo.gov/ftpdocs/123xx/doc12316/08–24-BudgetEconUpdate.pdf (accessed November 5, 2011).

——— (2011b), "CBO's 2011 Long Term Budget Outlook," June, at http://www.cbo.gov/ftpdocs/122xx/doc12212/06–21-Long-Term_Budget_Outlook.pdf (accessed December 25, 2011).

——— (2011c), "Reducing the Deficit: Spending and Revenue Options," March, at http://www.cbo.gov/ftpdocs/120xx/doc12085/03–10-ReducingTheDeficit.pdf (accessed February 2, 2012).

——— (2012), "The Budget and Economic Outlook: Fiscal Years 2012 to 2022," January, at http://www.cbo.gov/sites/default/files/cbofiles/attachments/01–31–2012_Outlook.pdf (accessed June 22, 2012).

Census Bureau (2012), "The 2012 Statistical Abstract," at http://www.census.gov/compendia/statab/2012edition.html (accessed April 27, 2012).

Chassaigne, Marc (1906), *La Lieutenance générale de police* (Genève: Slatkine-Megariotis, 1975).

Cochran, John P. (2012), "A Crisis of Authority: Pierre Lemieux's *Somebody in Charge: A Solution to Recessions,*" *The Independent Review* 16:4 (Spring), pp. 591–598, at http://www.independent.org/publications/tir/article.asp?a=883 (accessed June 23, 2012).

Davis, J. Ronnie (1971), *The New Economics and the Old Economists* (Ames: Iowa State University Press).

De Jasay, Anthony (1996), "Self-Contradictory Contractarianism," in John T. Sanders and Jan Narveson, Eds., *For and Against the State* (Lanham, MD and London: Rowman & Littlefield), pp. 137–169.

De Jouvenel, Bertrand (1945), *On Power: The Natural History of Its Growth* (Indianapolis: Liberty Fund, 1993).

———— (1952), *The Ethics of Redistribution* (Indianapolis: Liberty Press, 1990).

De la Boétie, Estienne (1576), *The Discourse of Voluntary Servitude*, Translated by Harry Kurz, at http://oll.libertyfund.org/index.php?option=com_staticxt&staticfile=-show.php%3Ftitle=2250&Itemid=28 (accessed January 11, 2012).

De Rugy, Veronique (2011), "The Municipal Debt Bubble," *Reason Magazine,* January, at http://reason.com/archives/2010/12/14/the-municipal-debt-bubble (accessed November 2, 2011).

———— (2012) "A Nation of Government Dependents," Mercatus Center, February 6, at http://mercatus.org/publication/nation-government-dependents (accessed February 8, 2012).

De Tocqueville, Alexis (1840), *Democracy in America: Historical-Critical Edition of De la démocratie en Amérique*, Eduardo Nolla, Ed., Translated from the French by James T. Schleifer (Indianapolis: Liberty Fund, 2010), at http://oll.libertyfund.org/index.php?option=com_staticxt&staticfile=show.php?title=2284&Itemid=28 (accessed April 24, 2012).

EBA (2011), "2011 EU-Wide Stress Test Aggregate Report," July 15, at http://stress-test.eba.europa.eu/pdf/EBA_ST_2011_Summary_Report_v6.pdf (accessed January 19, 2012).

ECB (2012), "Monthly Bulletin," January, at http://www.ecb.int/pub/pdf/mobu/mb201201en.pdf (accessed January 19, 2012).

Edwards, Sebastian (2000), "Contagion," Lecture at the University of Nottingham, at http://www.anderson.ucla.edu/faculty/sebastian.edwards/world_economy5.pdf (accessed March 1, 2012).

English, William B. (1996), "Understanding the Costs of Sovereign Default," *American Economic Review* 86:1 (March), pp. 259–275.

Fed (2005), *The Federal Reserve System: Purposes and Functions*, 9th Edition (Washington DC: Board of Governors of the Federal Reserve System), at http://www.federalreserve.gov/pf/pdf/pf_complete.pdf (accessed February 21, 2012).

———— (2011), *Flow of Funds Accounts of the United States: Flows and Outstandings, Third Quarter 2011*, December 8, at http://www.federalreserve.gov/releases/z1/20111208/z1.pdf (accessed March 19, 2012).

———— (2012), *Flow of Funds Accounts of the United States: Flows and Outstandings, Fourth Quarter 2011*, March 8, at http://www.federalreserve.gov/releases/z1/ (accessed April 10, 2012).

Fisher, Irving (1933), "The Debt-Deflation Theory of Great Depressions," *Economica* 1:3, pp. 337–357, at http://fraser.stlouisfed.org/docs/meltzer/fisdeb33.pdf (accessed March 5, 2012).

Frain, John C. (2004), "Inflation and Money Growth: Evidence from a Multi-Country Data-Set," *Economic and Social Review* 35:3 (Winter), pp. 251–266.

Friedman, Thomas L. (2011), "The Clash of Generations," *New York Times,* July 16, at http://www.nytimes.com/2011/07/17/opinion/sunday/17friedman.html (accessed January 10, 2011).

GAO (2010), "Citizen's Guide to the 2010 Financial Report of the United States Government," at http://www.gao.gov/financial/fy2010/10frusg.pdf (accessed November 5, 2011).

———— (2011a), "Citizen's Guide to the 2011 Financial Report of the United States Government," at http://www.gao.gov/financial/fy2011/11frusg.pdf (accessed April 27, 2011).

———— (2011b), "The Federal Government's Long-Term Fiscal Outlook: January 2011 Update," March 18, at http://www.gao.gov/assets/210/204365.pdf (accessed December 26, 2011).

—— (2012), "The Federal Government's Long-Term Fiscal Outlook: Spring 2012 Update," at http://www.gao.gov/assets/590/589835.pdf (accessed April 27, 2012).

Gokhale, Jagadeesh, and Kent Smetters (2003), *Fiscal and Generational Imbalances: New Budget Measures for New Budget Priorities* (Washington DC: AEI Press), at http://www.nber.org/chapters/c0066.pdf (accessed April 6, 2012).

—— (2006), "Fiscal and Generational Imbalances: An Update," in James M. Poterba, Ed., *Tax Policy and the Economy*, vol. 20, (Cambridge, MA: MIT Press and NBER).

Hanke, Steve H. (2009), "R.I.P. Zimbabwe Dollar," Cato Institute, February 9, at http://www.cato.org/zimbabwe (accessed September 11, 2009).

Hannoun, Hervé (2011), "Sovereign Risk in Bank Regulation and Supervision: Where Do We Stand?" BIS, Speech before the Financial Stability Institute High-Level Meeting, Abu Dhabi, October 26, at http://www.bis.org/speeches/sp111026.pdf (accessed June 18, 2012).

Hayek, Friedrich A. (1978), *Denationalisation of Money: The Argument Refined*, 2nd Edition (London: Institute of Economic Affairs).

Higgs, Robert (1987), *Crisis and Leviathan: Critical Episodes in the Growth of American Government* (New York: Oxford University Press).

—— (1997), "Regime Uncertainty: Why the Great Depression Lasted So Long and Why Prosperity Resumed after the War," *The Independent Review* 1:4, pp. 561–590, at http://www.independent.org/pdf/tir/tir_01_4_higgs.pdf (accessed April 13, 2010).

Howard, Christopher (1997), *The Hidden Welfare State: Tax Expenditures and Social Policy in the United States* (Princeton: Princeton University Press).

Hummel, Jeffrey Rogers (2009), "Why Default on U.S. Treasuries is Likely," Library of Economics and Liberty, August 3, at http://www.econlib.org/library/Columns/y2009/Hummeltbills.html (accessed December 27, 2011).

—— (2011a), "Ben Bernanke versus Milton Friedman: The Federal Reserve's Emergence as the U.S. Economy's Central Planner," *The Independent Review* 15:4 (Spring), pp. 485–518, at http://www.independent.org/pdf/tir/tir_15_04_1_hummel.pdf (accessed June 12, 2012).

—— (2011b), "The Likely Consequences of a U.S. Government Default," Working paper, mimeo, November 19.

—— (2012a), "Some Possible Consequences of a U.S. Government Default," *Econ Journal Watch* 9:1 (January), pp. 24–40, at http://econjwatch.org/file_download/527/HummelJan2012.pdf (accessed March 6, 2012).

—— (2012b), "The Upside of Government Default," *American*, February 16, at http://american.com/archive/2012/february/the-upside-of-government-default (accessed February 16, 2012).

Huxley, Aldous (1932), *Brave New World* (Toronto: Vintage Canada, 2007), at http://huxley.net/bnw/1st-edition.html (accessed November 5, 2011).

IMF (2011a), "Global Financial Stability Report: Summary Version," September, at http://www.imf.org/external/pubs/ft/gfsr/2011/02/pdf/text.pdf (accessed January 29, 2012).

—— (2011b), "World Economic Outlook," September, at http://www.imf.org/external/pubs/ft/weo/2011/02/pdf/text.pdf (accessed January 29, 2011).

—— (2011c), "Regional Economic Outlook: Europe, Navigating Stormy Waters," October, at http://www.imf.org/external/pubs/ft/reo/2011/eur/eng/pdf/ereo1011.pdf (accessed November 29, 2011).

Jenkins, Patrick (2010), "Q&A: What is Bank Capital," *Financial Times*, September 13, at http://www.ft.com/intl/cms/s/0/f98164ba-bf65–11df-965a-00144feab49a. html#axzz1nXZqinp4 (accessed February 29, 2012).

Johnson, Steve (2012), "ECB Loans 'Could Harm' Debt Market," *Financial Times*, March 4, at http://www.ft.com/intl/cms/s/0/c4a59556–63b8–11e1–9686– 00144feabdc0.html#axzz1oAZ64pbc (accessed March 5, 2012).

Jones, Garett (2012), "The Bond Market Wins," *Econ Journal Watch* 9:1 (January), pp. 41–50, at http://econjwatch.org/file_download/528/JonesJan2012.pdf (accessed March 11, 2012).

Kaminsky, Graciela L., Carmen M. Reinhart, and Carlos A. Végh (2003), "The Unholy Trinity of Financial Contagion," *Journal of Economic Perspectives* 17:4 (Fall), pp. 51–74.

Kane, Paul V. (2011), "To Save Our Economy, Ditch Taiwan," *New York Times*, November 10, at http://www.nytimes.com/2011/11/11/opinion/to-save-our-economy-ditch-taiwan.html (accessed January 11, 2012).

Keynes, John Maynard (1936), *The General Theory of Employment, Interest and Money* (London: Macmillan, 1967), at http://www.marxists.org/reference/subject/economics/keynes/general-theory/ (accessed April 13, 2010).

Kindleberger, Charles P. (1993), *A Financial History of Western Europe* (New York: Oxford University Press).

King, Mervyn (2002), "No Money, No Inflation—The Role of Money in the Economy," *Bank of England Quarterly*, Summer, at http://www.bankofengland. co.uk/publications/quarterlybulletin/qb020203.pdf (accessed February 16, 2012).

Kliesen, Kevin L., and Daniel L. Thornton (2011), "The Federal Debt: What's the Source of the Increase in Spending?" *Economic Synopses* 21, Federal Reserve Bank of St. Louis, pp. 1–2, at http://research.stlouisfed.org/publications/es/11/ES1121. pdf (accessed February 1, 2012).

Kling, Arnold (2012), "How a Default Might Play Out," *Econ Journal Watch* 9:1 (January), pp. 51–59, at http://econjwatch.org/file_download/529/KlingJan2012. pdf (accessed April 12, 2012).

Kotlikoff, Laurence J. (2004), "Fiscal Policy and the Future of the Euro," *Cato Journal* 24:1–2, pp. 51–55, at http://www.cato.org/pubs/journal/cj24n1–2/cj24n1–2-7.pdf (accessed December 28, 2011).

——— (2006), "Is the United States Bankrupt?" *Federal Reserve Bank of St. Louis Review,* July–August, pp. 235–250, at http://research.stlouisfed.org/publications/ review/06/07/Kotlikoff.pdf (accessed December 28, 2011).

——— (2011), "America's Debt Woe Is Worse than Greece's," *CNN Opinion*, September 20,, at http://www.cnn.com/2011/09/19/opinion/kotlikoff-us-debt-crisis/index.html?hpt=hp_t2 (accessed December 27, 2011).

Kotlikoff, Laurence J., and Scott Burns (2012), *The Clash of Generations* (Cambridge, MA and London: MIT Press).

Lancaster, John (2011), "Once Greece Goes…," *London Review of Books* 33:14 (July 14), at http://www.lrb.co.uk/v33/n14/john-lanchester/once-greece-goes (accessed November 7, 2011).

Lemieux, Pierre (2001), "Parent Licensing," *Laissez Faire City Times* 5:19 (May 7), reproduced in David Boonin and Graham Oddie, *What's Wrong* (New York and Oxford: Oxford University Press, 2010), pp. 327–329.

——— (2003), "Following the Herd," *Regulation* 26:4 (Winter), at http://www.cato. org/pubs/regulation/regv26n4/v26n4–2.pdf (accessed February 9, 2012).

Lemieux, Pierre (2004), "The Public Choice Revolution," *Regulation* 27:3 (Fall), pp. 22–29, at http://www.cato.org/pubs/regulation/regv27n3/v27n3–2.pdf (accessed November 5, 2011).

——— (2008a), *Comprendre l'économie: Ou comment les économists pensent* (Paris: Les Belles Lettres).

——— (2008b), "Public Health Insurance Under a Nonbenevolent State," *Journal of Medicine and Philosophy* 33, pp. 416–426.

——— (2011a), *Somebody in Charge: A Solution to Recessions?* (New York: Palgrave Macmillan).

——— (2011b), "Why Greece Defaulted—and Others Will Follow," *Regulation* 34:4 (Winter), pp. 5–6, at http://www.cato.org/pubs/regulation/regv34n4/v34n4–5.pdf (accessed April 27, 2012).

——— (2012a), "a Welfare State by Any Other Name," *Regulation* 35:1 (Spring), pp. 7–8, at http://www.cato.org/pubs/regulation/regv35n1/v35n1–7.pdf (accessed April 27, 2012).

——— (2012b), "What's Wrong with Europe?" *Regulation* 35:2 (Summer), pp. 4–6, at http://www.cato.org/pubs/regulation/regv35n2/v35n2–7.pdf (accessed June 30, 2012).

Marion, Marcel (1934), in J. G. Van Dillen, Ed., *History of the Principal Public Banks* (London: Frank Cass, 1964), pp. 301–318.

McCallum, Bennett, and Edward Nelson (2010), "Money and Inflation: Some Critical Issues," Finance and Economics Discussion Series 2010–57, Federal Reserve Board, at http://www.federalreserve.gov/pubs/feds/2010/201057/201057pap.pdf (accessed February 16, 1012).

McCandless, George T., and Warren E. Weber (1995), "Some Monetary Facts," *Federal Reserve Bank of Minneapolis Quarterly Review* 19:3 (Summer), pp. 2–11, at http://www.minneapolisfed.org/research/qr/qr1931.pdf (accessed February 15, 2012).

McGrane, Reginald C. (1933), "Some Aspects of American State Debts in the Forties," *American Historical Review* 38:4 (July), pp. 673–686.

——— (1935), *Foreign Bondholders and American State Debts* (New York: MacMillan).

Milne, Richard (2011), "Sarkozy Plan to Prop Up Sovereigns Is Worrying," *Financial Times*, December 14, at http://www.ft.com/intl/cms/s/0/3effdd58–2673–11e1–91cd-00144feabdc0.html#axzz1kPkoji00 (accessed January 27, 2012).

Minarik, Joseph J. (2012), "Courting an Avoidable Financial Crisis," *Econ Journal Watch* 9:1 (January), pp. 60–70, at http://econjwatch.org/file_download/530/MinarikJan2012.pdf (accessed March 12, 2012).

Miron, Jeffrey (2011), "The Fiscal Health of U.S. States," Mercatus Center, Working paper No. 11–33, August, at http://mercatus.org/sites/default/files/publication/Fiscal_Health_of_the_US_States_Miron_WP1133.pdf (accessed October 31, 2011).

Mysak, Joe (2010), "Bond Default Is about Too Much Debt, Too Little Time," *Bloomberg*, July 20, at http://www.bloomberg.com/news/2010–07–21/bond-default-means-too-much-debt-too-little-time-commentary-by-joe-mysak.html (accessed November 27, 2011).

Neiertz, Patrick, and Nicholas Cronk (2012), "Lessons from Voltaire, the Enlightened Economist," *Financial Times*, June 7, at http://www.ft.com/intl/cms/s/0/b7013e44–afd2–11e1-a025–00144feabdc0.html (accessed June 11, 2012).

OECD (2010), *OECD Economic Surveys: Spain 2010* (Paris: OECD).

——— (2011a), *Government at a Glance 2011* (Paris: OECD).

────── (2011b), "Health at a Glance 2011," online database, updated October 28, at http://www.oecd.org/health/healthpoliciesanddata/healthataglance2011.htm (accessed December 15, 2011).

────── (2011c), *OECD Economic Outlook. Preliminary Version* 90 (November) (Paris: OECD).

────── (2011d), *OECD Economic Surveys: Greece 2011* (Paris: OECD).

Olson, Mancur (1971), *The Logic of Collective Action* (Cambridge, MA: Harvard University Press).

OMB (1985), *Budget of the United States Government, Fiscal Year 1986*, February 4, at http://fraser.stlouisfed.org/docs/publications/usbudget/bus_1986.pdf (accessed February 10, 2012).

────── (2011a), *Fiscal Year 2012: Budget of the U.S. Government*, February 14, at http://www.whitehouse.gov/sites/default/files/omb/budget/fy2012/assets/budget.pdf (accessed November 5, 2011).

────── (2011b), *Fiscal Year 2012: Historical Tables – Budget of the U.S. Government*, at http://www.whitehouse.gov/sites/default/files/omb/budget/fy2012/assets/hist.pdf (accessed October 29, 2011).

────── (2012), *Fiscal Year 2013: Budget of the U.S. Government*, February 13, at http://www.whitehouse.gov/sites/default/files/omb/budget/fy2013/assets/budget.pdf (accessed February 13, 2012).

Quignon, Laurent (2010), "Basel III: No Achilles' Spear," *Conjecture*, BNP Paribas, May–June 2011, pp. 3–20, at http://economic-research.bnpparibas.com/applis/www/RechEco.nsf/ConjonctureByDateEN/81391A165B85FB54C12578C0004 2E75A/$File/C1105_06_A1.pdf?OpenElement (accessed February 29, 2012).

Rahn, Richard (2012), "American Income Tax Tyranny," *Washington Times*, April 9, at http://www.washingtontimes.com/news/2012/apr/9/american-income-tax-tyranny/?utm_source=RSS_Feed&utm_medium=RSS (accessed April 12, 2012).

Rawls, John (1971), *A Theory of Justice* (Cambridge, MA: Harvard University Press).

Reagan, Ronald (1980), "Acceptance of Republican Nomination for President at the 1980 Republican National Convention in Detroit, Michigan," July 17, at http://reagan2020.us/speeches/nomination_acceptance_1980.asp (accessed February 10, 2012).

────── (1981), "First Inaugural Address," January 20, at http://reagan2020.us/speeches/First_Inaugural.asp (accessed February 10, 2012).

────── (1982), "First State of the Union Address," January 26, at http://reagan2020.us/speeches/First_State_of_the_Union.asp (accessed February 10, 2012).

────── (1985), "Address before a Joint Session of the Congress on the State of the Union," February 6, at http://reagan2020.us/speeches/state_of_the_union_1985.asp (accessed February 10, 2012).

Redish, Angela (1993), "Anchors Aweigh: The Transition from Commodity Money to Fiat Money in Western Economies," *Canadian Journal of Economics* 26:4 (November), pp. 777–795.

Reinhart, Carmen M. (2010), "This Time Is Different Chartbook: Country Histories on Debt, Default, and Financial Crises," National Bureau of Economic Research, NBER Working Paper 15815, March.

Reinhart, Carmen M., and Kenneth S. Rogoff (2009), *This Time Is Different: Eight Centuries of Financial Folly* (Princeton and Oxford: Princeton University Press).

────── (2011), "A Decade of Debt," National Bureau of Economic Research, NBER Working Paper 16827, February.

Reinhart, Carmen M., Vincent R. Reinhart, and Kenneth S. Rogoff (2012), "Debts Overhangs: Past and Present," National Bureau of Economic Research, NBER Working Paper 18015, April.

Richards, R. D. (1934), "The First Fifty Years of the Bank of England (1694–1744)," in J. G. Van Dillen, Ed., *History of the Principal Public Banks* (London: Frank Cass, 1964), pp. 201–272.

Riedl, Brian M. (2010), *Federal Spending by the Numbers 2010* (Washington DC: Heritage Foundation), at http://www.heritage.org/research/reports/2010/06/federal-spending-by-the-numbers-2010 (accessed April 12, 2012).

Rousseau, Jean-Jacques (1762), *Du Contrat social* (Paris: Garnier-Flammarion, 1966).

Sargent, Thomas, and Neil Wallace (1981), "Some Unpleasant Monetarist Arithmetic," *Quarterly Review* 531 (Fall), Federal Reserve Bank of Minneapolis, pp. 1–17, at http://www.minneapolisfed.org/publications_papers/pub_display.cfm?id=151 (accessed December 5, 2011).

Sherk, James (2010), "Inflated Federal Pay: How Americans Are Overtaxed to Overpay the Civil Service," Heritage Foundation, July 7, at http://thf_media.s3.amazonaws.com/2010/pdf/CDA10–05.pdf (accessed February 8, 2012).

SIGTARP (2011), "Exiting TARP: Repayments by the Largest Financial Institutions," September 29, at http://www.sigtarp.gov/reports/audit/2011/Exiting_TARP_Repayments_by_the_Largest_Financial_Institutions.pdf (accessed January 24, 2012).

Smith, Adam (1762), *Lectures On Jurisprudence*, in R. L. Meek, D. D. Raphael, and P. G. Stein, Eds., vol. V of the Glasgow Edition of the *Works and Correspondence of Adam Smith* (Indianapolis: Liberty Fund, 1982), at http://oll.libertyfund.org/?option=com_staticxt&staticfile=show.php%3Ftitle=196 (accessed January 9, 2011).

Snowdon, Brian, and Howard R. Vane (2005), *Modern Macroeconomics: Its Origins, Development and Current State* (Cheltenham, UK and Northampton, MA: Edward Elgar).

Spooner, Lysander (1870), *No Treason. No. VI. The Constitution of No Authority* (Boston: Lysander Spooner), at http://lysanderspooner.org/node/64 (accessed January 11, 2012).

St. Louis Fed (2011), "Annual Report 2011," at http://www.stlouisfed.org/publications/ar/2011/pdf/2011-annual-report.pdf (accessed June 28, 2012).

Storbeck, Olaf (2011), "EU Banks Hold 194.1bn Euros of Potentially Toxic Bonds," *Economics Intelligence Blog*, at http://economicsintelligence.com/2011/07/15/eu-banks-hold-bn-1941e-of-potentially-toxic-bonds/ (accessed January 18, 2011).

Tanner, Michael (2012), "We're Already Europe," *National Review Online*, February 22, at http://www.nationalreview.com/articles/291628/we-re-already-europe-michael-tanner (accessed April 2, 2012).

Tanzi, Vito, and Ludger Schuknecht (2000), *Public spending in the 20th Century: A Global Perspective* (Cambridge and New York: Cambridge University Press).

Tax Foundation (2009), "Summary of Latest Federal Individual Income Tax Data," *Fiscal Fact* 183 (July), at http://taxfoundation.org (accessed April 8, 2012).

Tax Foundation (2011), "Summary of Latest Federal Individual Income Tax Data," *Fiscal Fact* 285 (October 20), at http://taxfoundation.org/sites/taxfoundation.org/files/docs/ff285.pdf (accessed April 8, 2012).

Taylor, John B. (2010), "The Dodd-Frank Financial Fiasco," *Wall Street Journal*, July 1, at http://online.wsj.com/article/SB10001424052748703426004575338732174405398.html (accessed June 12, 2012).

———— (2012), "Rules for America's Road to Recovery," *Wall Street Journal*, May 31, at http://online.wsj.com/article/SB10001424052702303674004577434774238817 962.html (accessed June 12, 2012).

Tett, Gillian (2012), "Pension Gap Spells Trouble for Muni Bonds," *Financial Times*, February 23, at http://www.ft.com/intl/cms/s/0/20b97eb0–5e38–11e1–85f6– 00144feabdc0.html#axzz1nB3QSKT8 (accessed February 24, 2012).

Thornton, Daniel L. (1984), "Monetizing the Debt," *Federal Reserve Bank of St. Louis Review*, December, pp. 31–43, at http://research.stlouisfed.org/publications/ review/84/12/Monetizing_Dec1984.pdf (accessed February 25, 2012).

UN (2004), *Updates and Amendments to the System of National Accounts, 1993* (New York: United Nations), at http://unstats.un.org/unsd/publication/Seriesf/seriesf_2rev4_ add1e.pdf (accessed April 3, 2012).

Vatter, Harold G. (1979), "Perspective on the Forty-Sixth Anniversary of the U.S. Mixed Economy," *Explorations in Economic History* 16, pp. 297–330.

Vedder, Richard K., and Lowell E. Gallaway (1998), "Budget Surpluses, Deficits and Government Spending," Prepared for the Joint Economic Committee, December, at http://s3.amazonaws.com/zanran_storage/www.house.gov/ContentPages/ 2687506.pdf (accessed April 12, 2012).

Vock, Daniel C. (2009), "Nightmare Scenarios Haunt States," *Stateline*, December 14, at http://www.stateline.org/live/printable/story?contentId=443566 (accessed November 27, 2011).

Voltaire (1759), *Candide* (Genève), English edition at http://www.gutenberg.org/ cache/epub/19942/pg19942.txt (accessed March 12, 2012).

Wallison, Peter (2012), "How and Why a U.S. Sovereign Debt Crisis Could Occur," *Econ Journal Watch* 9:1 (January), pp. 71–77, at http://econjwatch.org/file_ download/531/WallisonJan2012.pdf (accessed March 10, 2012).

INDEX